MEDICAL, MORAL and LEGAL ISSUES in MENTAL HEALTH CARE

6th Annual Taylor Manor Hospital
Scientific Symposium
MEDICAL, MORAL AND LEGAL ISSUES
IN MENTAL HEALTH CARE
Baltimore, Maryland
April 1974

MEDICAL, MORAL and LEGAL ISSUES in MENTAL HEALTH CARE

EDITED BY

Frank J. Ayd, Jr., M.D., FAPA

Director
Professional Education and Research
Taylor Manor Hospital
Ellicott City, Maryland
Editor
International Drug Therapy Newsletter
The Medical-Moral Newsletter

with 12 contributors

The Williams & Wilkins Company
Baltimore

Made in the United States of America

Library of Congress Cataloging in Publication Data
Main entry under title:

Medical, moral, and legal issues in mental health care.

    Papers presented at the 6th annual Taylor Manor Hospital scientific symposium, Baltimore, Apr., 1974.
    1. Psychiatric ethics—Congresses. I. Ayd, Frank J., ed.
II. Taylor Manor Hospital.
[DNLM: 1. Community mental health services—U. S.—Congresses. 2. Ethics, Medical—Congresses. 3. Forensic psychiatry—Congresses. WM30 T244m 1974]
RC455.2.P77M4   362.2   74-11375
ISBN 0-683-00295-3

Composed and printed at the
Waverly Press, Inc.
Mt. Royal and Guilford Aves.
Baltimore, Md. 21202, U.S.A.

Introduction

In the past 25 years phenomenal changes have occurred in psychiatry and in the care of the mentally ill. These changes have been due in part to the advent of the psychoactive drugs, to the evolution of sophisticated research tools and methodologies, and to the emergence of new psychodynamic and behavior-modifying therapies. Public mental hospitals have been transformed from overcrowded, understaffed custodial institutions with limited therapeutic resources to active treatment centers which return the majority of patients to the community after a relatively short stay. General hospitals now provide psychiatric facilities and admit for treatment more patients than at any time in the history of America. Throughout the United States community mental health centers have been constructed. These offer easy access to a variety of hitherto unavailable services, including the prospect of averting hospitalization, for the people in each center's catchment area.

The psychoactive drugs have made it possible for all physicians—not just psychiatrists—to treat the emotionally distressed people whom they see daily in their practices. The effectiveness of these drugs, used alone or in conjunction with other therapies, has lessened substantially the morbidities of most psychiatric illnesses. Some psychopharmaceuticals are being used as prophylactic agents. Lithium and the tricyclic antidepressants, for example, are being administered continuously to thousands of victims of affective illnesses to prevent recurrent episodes that in the past were often responsible for repeated disruptive hospitalizations.

Some psychiatrists have become medical "intranauts" exploring the inner spaces of man to determine the genetic, biochemical, and pathophysiological factors involved in mental illnesses and behavioral aberrations, and to measure the plasma levels of psychoactive drugs and their metabolites. Others are busily engaged in the development and evaluation of new psychopharmaceuticals, and still others are striving to devise predictive biochemical tests that will identify which type of patient will be responsive to which medicine, thereby making psychopharmacotherapy more scientific and precise. Many psychiatrists, particularly those in research, are collaborating with workers in many other scientific disciplines to discover the causes of psychiatric ailments and new treatments for them, as well as ways of preventing them.

Never before in human history have so many people been actively engaged in psychiatric treatment and research and in providing mental health services. Never before has the outlook been better for the psychiatrically ill. There are available for them now a myriad of therapies offering them hope of recovery or rehabilitation reasonably quickly, safely and economically. The future also augurs well for these people as the fruits of ongoing psychiatric research become realities.

Despite these salutary achievements and the favorable impact they have had on the treatment and prognoses of psychiatric patients, psychiatry, its practitioners, psychiatric research, and the delivery of mental health services have been under increasing attack in recent years. Some of the criticisms are justified and constructive; others can only be labeled acrimonious, without substance, and destructive. Some of the justified charges against psychiatry as a whole are overdue outgrowths of the maturing contemporary awareness of human dignity and rights and the demands that they be acknowledged, respected, and not violated; others are the inevitable consequence of the present-day resurgence of interest in the moral and ethical aspects of all human behavior; and others have been generated by the very progress that psychiatry has made.

Wrongs, whether deliberate or inadvertent, can only be rectified when men of good will become aware of them and labor in concert to eliminate them. At the same time human progress of which everyone can be proud is possible only when conscientious, honest, objective men cooperatively share their talents to achieve this objective.

The realization of these truths was the reason for choosing Medical, Moral and Legal Issues in Mental Health Care as the theme of the Sixth Annual Taylor Manor Hospital Psychiatric Symposium. As Symposium Director I was convinced that an uninhibited airing of diverse views on this subject is not only timely but necessary if psychiatry, psychiatric research and the delivery of mental health services are to proceed fruitfully and unhampered by obstacles generated by conclusions from false or partially true premises. Hence, from among many possible candidates, I selected the authorities whose views are recorded herein. Each graciously accepted my invitation to participate in the Symposium and for that I am very grateful. I also am indebted to them for the seriousness and comprehensiveness with which they prepared their lucid distillates of their vast knowledge and experience. Each has made a valuable contribution toward the resolution of a complex human problem: the continued development and the just and adequate delivery of mental health services. Jointly and individually they deserve credit for the contents of this volume. Whatever deficiencies there are in these pages are primarily my responsibility as editor.

All of us who have played a role in the genesis and production of this book fervently hope that it will enlighten, that it will stimulate others to carry this important work further along, and that it will be accepted as a testament that concerned men are striving to ease the plight of the mentally ill and disabled. If these objectives are realized, then we have not labored in vain.

Frank J. Ayd, Jr., M.D.
Director of Professional Education and Research
Taylor Manor Hospital
Ellicott City, Maryland 21043

Contributors

MORTON BIRNBAUM, M.D., LL.B., Executive Director of the Center for Law and Health Care Policy, New York

WILLIAM J. CURRAN, J.D., S.M.HYG., Lee Professor of Legal Medicine, Harvard Medical School and Harvard School of Public Health; Lecturer in Legal Medicine, Harvard Law School, Boston

PARK ELLIOTT DIETZ, The Johns Hopkins University, School of Medicine, Baltimore

ALFRED M. FREEDMAN, M.D., F.A.P.A., President, American Psychiatric Association, and Professor and Chairman of the Department of Psychiatry, New York Medical College, New York

LEO E. HOLLISTER, M.D., Professor of Medicine in Psychiatry, Stanford University Medical School and Medical Investigator, Veterans Administration Hospital, Palo Alto

NICHOLAS N. KITTRIE, S.J.D., Professor of Criminal and Comparative Law and Director, Institute for Studies in Justice and Social Behavior, American University Law School, Washington, D.C.

MAGNUS LAKOVICS, M.D., Upstate Medical Center, State University of New York, Syracuse

A. LEWIS McGARRY, M.D., F.A.P.A., Director of the Division of Legal Medicine, Department of Mental Hygiene, Boston

REV. THOMAS J. O'DONNELL, S.J., Consultant in Medical Ethics to the National Institutes of Health, American Medical Association and U.S. Catholic Conference

JONAS ROBITSCHER, J. D., M.D., F.A.P.A., Henry R. Luce Professor of Law and the Behavioral Sciences, Emory University, Atlanta

JEROME J. SHESTACK, LL.B., Chairman, American Bar Association Commission on the Mentally Disabled

SAMUEL I. SHUMAN, PH.D., S.J.D., Professor of Law and Psychiatry, Wayne State University School of Law and School of Medicine, Detroit

Contents

chapter 1

Ethical Concepts of Consent

THOMAS J. O'DONNELL, S.J.

Louis Harris of the Harris Poll recently remarked on a televised interview (ABC, 12/27/73) that, "Respect for the rights of others has never been higher than it is today." This is indeed an encouraging observation by one whose credibility and career depend on his ability to correctly observe and assess the trends of human reaction in our democracy. How sharply this concern is reflected in the field of medical research is illustrated by the fairly recent publication of "The Institutional Guide to Department of Health, Education and Welfare Policy on Protection of Human Subjects" (1) and subsequent similar directives, as well as the recent rash of seminars and scholarly articles on this subject.

It was, after all, the recognition of the right of the individual to give free and informed consent to actions affecting his person, often called the "the individual's right of self-determination," that gave birth to this nation 300 years ago. Even when this consent is of a vicarious or representative nature (as, for example, it must be in a democracy which is to operate efficiently and still be government with the consent of the governed), the representative who gives consent for another must be adequately informed both as to what he is consenting to and the limits within which his consent is valid.

Indeed the very nature of "consent" implies the added notion of "informed" because consent, in itself, includes the notion of freedom. It is obvious that one who is not free to refuse is neither free to consent. It is equally obvious that adequate freedom presupposes adequate knowledge of that to which one gives consent.

What I would like to make explicit in my exploration of the concepts of consent is that the concepts of "informed" and of "consent" are not always necessarily operationally co-extensive. We sometimes have a way, in our common use of language, of so telescoping a substantive and a modifier as to canonize an unfounded generalization. One example of such telescoping is the semantic fusion, "damyankee." We may be approaching the point where another example will be: "informed consent."

Regarding the general concept of consent in the medical context, Irving Ladimer pointed out that "In all forms of medical endeavor, whether practice or research, the consent *of the patient* [emphasis mine] is legally, if not morally, required." (2) While Ladimer himself, on the same occasion, indicated certain qualifications and distinctions in this regard, my purpose in quoting his statement is to highlight three distinct considerations which are particularly germane to a proper understanding of my subsequent remarks.

First, I believe that the answer to many of the current questions is to be found, not by trying to change the basic premise of consent, but by a more careful delineation and refinement of its appropriate distinctions. Second, as Ladimer indicates, the legal parameters of clinical research may not in all cases be congruent with the moral parameters, and it is only in regard to the latter that I address my remarks today. Third, at least from the moral viewpoint, certain modalities of consent, even though not arising from the patient's consciousness, may quite properly be called "the consent of the patient."

I would like to point out one other important difference between the legal and the moral context. In the moral context there is not only a close correlation between infants and the mentally incompetent, but likewise even the distinction between normal minors and adults cannot be based entirely on the legal fiction made operative by having reached such and such a birthday. While this legal fiction is absolutely necessary for the just application of the civil law, the related moral evaluations frequently must be based on an estimation of the degree of mental competence and responsibility attained by the individual, pretty much irrespective of chronological age.

The most casual perusal of the literature shows that the Nuremburg Medical Trials opened the floodgates of concern regarding clinical research, in the United States and beyond. Indeed this concern about our own research arose not only subsequent to the trials, but even at Nuremburg itself the distinguished witness for the prosecution, Dr. A. C. Ivy, was more than somewhat put upon by the defense attorneys regarding genuine freedom of consent in his own experiments in American prisons. It is likewise clear from the literature that the subsequent writings of that distinguished scholar of human affairs, Eugenio Pacelli, in his role as Pope Pius XII, exercised a worldwide and vital influence on the proper understanding of the ethical limits of research.

In what might be called landmark documents of the Ethics of Clinical

Research, there was a notable advance in the Helsinki Declaration of 1964 over the Nuremburg Code in the clear explicitation of the distinction between clinical investigation in the context of therapeutic treatment and pure clinical research unrelated to a therapeutic regimen of an individual patient. And, it seems to me, since that time there has been a discernible tendency to always insist on the written informed consent of the individual subject in the context of nontherapeutic clinical research, while allowing certain exceptions in the therapeutic situation.

The total implementation of this tendency would obviously preclude any nontherapeutic research on any minor or mentally incompetent person who would be unable to give informed consent.

In addition to this, one fails to find sufficient emphasis on the distinction between merely observational research (which might include minimal inconvenience and possible risks to confidentiality) and active research. Moreover, in view of the fact that pediatric medicine has its own specific characteristics, with some problems that cannot be proved on adult patients, the tendency of some directives would seem to put regulatory agencies in the position of demanding drug-testing while at the same time rendering it impossible.

These considerations alone clearly indicate that consent is an area which still contains some unsolved problems. Indeed a recent article by John Romano (3) reflects his concern with most of the points I have just mentioned and in relation to a research project apparently involving nothing more than observations, questions and suggestions. His project, dealing with children at risk for schizophrenia and their parents, would not seem to go beyond some inconvenience, perhaps psychic discomfort, and the risks of invaded confidentiality, which should be minimal in an appropriately protected context.

It is against this background, then, that we must consider some of the moral modalities of consent. Hopefully these considerations may shed some further light on the dignity of personhood (our own and that of others) in our search for the proper moral parameters of consent. Perhaps they might also help to guide the legal patterns. But we must keep in mind that the fine adjustments of the legal aspects of consent are much more difficult than simply enlightening the ethical concepts. The law seeks to adjust its regulations in a way that will both encourage research and at the same time protect the human dignity of all concerned, in all the varying circumstances of time, place and personnel. Thus the law must sometimes further limit individual liberty in order to preserve that liberty which is proper to the common good.

Returning to the ethical context, let us first note that there is a certain basic validity in the previously mentioned telescoping of the term "informed consent." Consent is, after all, an act of the will. And a will-act is a human act (i.e. the act of a responsible human person) only insofar as its object is known. Or, to put it more simply, personal consent is consent only when one knows what one is consenting to; or only insofar as it is informed consent.

A moment's reflection will show that fully informed consent, whether of the patient in therapy or of the subject in research, is rare in the field of medicine. To be thus fully informed, the patient would have to know all that there is to know about the procedure, and it is evident that not even a sophisticated patient needs to know all that there is to know about even an appendectomy before giving a valid personal consent to the surgery. It would be unrealistic not to acknowledge that most acts of valid, personal and sufficiently informed consent in the medical context are based to a large extent not on direct information as much as on faith in the scientific wisdom, personal integrity and good judgment of the physician. Thus, even in informed consent, the information is largely vicarious.

This of course presents less of a problem in the therapeutic setting. Indeed it is inherent in the idea of medicine as a profession. When I am ill I put myself into the hands of a physician precisely because he has more information (as well as skill) than I either have or can obtain. I want to be able to refuse or to consent to undergoing surgery, and in general I want to be informed as to how extensive it will be, what results can be expected and what complications are likely to arise; but beyond that I best leave things to the judgment of my physician. That, by and large, better be sufficient to verify informed consent, because in most cases that is about as informed as it is going to be able to be.

It is because procedures in the therapeutic context look solely to the good of the individual patient that legitimate limitations of informed consent (in the sense of the fully informed consent of the actual patient) present no great problem. The notion of valid consent is readily extended to the presumed consent of the emergency room, the implied consent of the diagnostic setting and the vicarious consent of the parent or guardian in these and other similar circumstances.

It is in the strictly research context that the real problems arise, when the desired research subjects are infants or are otherwise mentally incompetent. And the question is: how much of what has been described here as presumed consent, implied consent, and/or vicarious consent may be legitimately applied when procedures are contemplated which are not directly in the interest of the patient but in the interest of humanity in general, by way of the advance of medical knowledge.

Here the questions cluster mainly around the concept of vicarious consent as a consent which is given *for* the subject by one who is qualified, either by nature or by law, to give it. Such consent must be, of course, informed consent on the part of the vicarious agent, and it must be sufficiently informed so as to be rightly judged to be a reasonable and responsible consent. And again, as always, the appropriate limitations of "reasonably informed" do not derive as much from the amount of information which is available as from the degree of assimilation which is possible.

And so, in the research context, the precise question is this: when personal consent is unavailable for whatever reason, how much willingness for how much discomfort and risk can be reasonably presumed on the part of the subject, and responsibly interpreted by his vicarious agent, to verify the presumption that the subject certainly would give consent if he could?

This, it seems to me, was the basic question to be answered in evaluating the ethical propriety of the national polio vaccine trials which followed the research of Salk and Sabin, or the Willowbrook hepatitis experiments, to mention two controversial programs with which we are all familiar.

It is not my intention to assess the morality of these two research projects. I would certainly agree with M. H. Pappworth (4) that the morality of a research project is not to be judged on its ultimate success but rather on its initial protocol; but I cannot agree with the reported views of Nielson of San Francisco or Hellegers of Georgetown that doctors cannot ethically do any nonbeneficial experiments on the legally incompetent child or mentally defective person (5).

Indeed it may be that they cannot legally do so, as indicated by Irving Ladimer in a recent Geneva Conference (6) when he pointed out that it is generally held in Anglo-American law that experiments may not be performed on children or incompetents unless for their benefit, even with parental or guardian approval. And while Ladimer perceptively investigates a widening of the concept of "benefit," I believe that it is equally important to more carefully distinguish the possible modalities of "consent."

I would suggest that, from an ethical and moral viewpoint, if the parent or guardian is properly and adequately informed, there are instances in which the valid consent of mentally incompetent (and, by extension, infant) subjects may be properly supplied by the vicarious consent of the parent or guardian. But it is my opinion that, at least in the nontherapeutic research context, such vicarious consent is valid for only—I repeat, *only*—those procedures in which danger is so remote and discomfort is so minimal that a normal adult would be presupposed to give ready consent. Beyond that I believe we cannot go.

REFERENCES

1. The Institutional Guide to Department of Health, Education and Welfare Policy on Protection of Human Subjects. NIH 72-102, Dec. 1, 1971.
2. Ladimer, I. Ethical, Legal and Administrative Aspects of Clinical Research with Children. Ross Conference on Pediatric Research, 1968.
3. Romano, J. Reflections on Informed Consent. *Arch. Gen. Psychiat.* 30: 129–135, 1974.
4. Pappworth, M. H. Letters to the Editor. *Lancet*, June 5, 1971.
5. *Medical World News*, Sept. 28, 1973, p. 40.
6. Ladimer, I. Experimentation on Human Subjects: Clinical Testing of Drugs. Geneva Conference, Nov. 16–17, 1973.

chapter 2

Psychiatry and the Dilemmas of Dual Loyalties

JEROME J. SHESTACK, LL.B.

One of the most difficult tasks for any profession is introspection.

The legal profession has yet to examine the pathology that permitted numerous respectable lawyers high in our government to become so involved in serving the political objectives of a President that they could rationalize the most egregious corruption of the rule of law. The medical profession has yet to examine the phenomena of widespread abuse of Medicare, shoddy treatment and extensive gouging of the government that makes peer review inevitable. Architects have not yet explored the prevalence in their profession of complicity in ugly, cheap, unesthetic construction which has made the face of urban America look like cookie-molds of dreary reinforced concrete that another generation will painfully have to clear away.

So it goes. Introspection is painful, and professions one and all erect elaborate defenses and rationales rather than face the anguish of self-probing.

But one might at least have expected a high degree of introspection from psychiatry; for, after all, introspection is the psychiatrist's stronghold. Nonetheless, like the cobbler's children without shoes or the lawyer who leaves no will, the psychiatric profession has largely ignored a condition within itself which challenges its methodology and which affects the very credibility of the profession.

The condition was long ago highlighted by Matthew when he said, "No man may serve two masters." An English proverb holds that, "No man may serve two masters for that one corrupteth the other." And George Bernard Shaw, in his *Saint Joan*, said simply, "Masters two will not do." Yet today, in numerous institutional settings, psychiatrists act counter to this ancient learning. I refer to the conflict of interest, the dual loyalties that psychiatrists often face when they try to use their skills to serve both the traditional one-to-one doctor-patient relationship and the institutions for which they work.[1]

So long as the psychiatrist acted in the traditional one-to-one relationship, representing only the individual who freely sought his counsel, this problem did not arise. But the psychiatrist's role in modern society is now much broader. Today the psychiatrist is an influential force in powerful institutions of our society: the judicial system, the educational system, the defense establishment, the correctional system and other social institutions. The increased role of the psychiatrist in these institutions raises serious questions as to his conflict of interest or double agent role. Can the psychiatrist be both the agent of his patient and of the institution that employs him? Put in simple terms, who is the psychiatrist supposed to represent?

The very question challenges psychiatric methodology in a variety of institutional settings. Before considering some of these settings, however, it may be useful to describe an archetypal illustration of the problem and the dangers that may flow from it. The example is found in the Soviet Union where psychiatric methodology has become so subservient to institutional goals as to destroy the medical model and to undermine the free practice of psychiatry.

In the Soviet Union today there are hundreds, perhaps thousands, of mentally healthy dissenters, students, writers, artists and intellectuals who have been confined to mental institutions for disagreement with official policy (1). And their confinement is without trial, generally without legal counsel, and without even the small elements of due process that the USSR offers to criminals (2, 3).

These charges are not made casually. They have been substantiated in documents submitted by Vladimir Bukovsky, who sent Western psychiatrists actual copies of reports of psychiatric commissions (4). The charges have also been substantiated by personal accounts of Zhores Medvedev, a renowned psychologist who was forcibly interned in a Soviet mental hospital because extracts from his psychological writings caused the hospital's chief mental officer to have doubts concerning his mental health (5). And British and American psychiatrists who have visited Soviet mental institutions have affirmed that political dissenters are forcibly committed on the basis of psychiatric determinations that would be quite unacceptable in the United States or the United Kingdom (6). Indeed, a group of British psychiatrists concluded that, in six cases which they

---

[1] Anyone writing about this problem, and I in particular, must acknowledge a debt to the pioneer teachings and incisive perceptions of Chief Judge David L. Bazelon of the United States Court of Appeals for the District of Columbia Circuit.

examined, the diagnosis of mental illness seemed to have been "made purely in consequence of actions in which they were exercising fundamental freedom—as set out in the Declaration of Human Rights and guaranteed [*sic*] by the Soviet Constitution." (7)

Other documentation has been supplied by Andrei Sakharov, Valery Chalidze and by other members of the Moscow Human Rights Committee who have addressed appeals on behalf of confined dissidents to the United Nations, to the World Psychiatric Association, and to the International Congress of Psychotherapists (8). In short, informed experts in the human rights field have not the slightest doubt that the Soviet government systematically suppresses mentally healthy dissenters through psychiatric commitments.

It is not my purpose, however, to review that evidence or even to speculate on the reasons why the world psychiatric profession has largely chosen to gloss over such Soviet misuse of psychiatry (9). What is pertinent is why Soviet psychiatrists participate in this process, which seems so ethically and morally reprehensible. One explanation is the ideological one that Soviet psychiatrists have a deep belief in the Soviet system in which the state symbolizes truth and stability. Those who deviate from or dissent from the norms of the state are ipso facto mentally ill. Viewed from such an ideological base, the psychiatrist may not be venal. However, even from that viewpoint, the psychiatrist's acceptance of the state's definition of deviance indicates at least a complicity in the process of controlling social deviance for nontherapeutic purposes.

In fact, however, the ideological explanation of Soviet psychiatric conduct simply does not wash. As Dr. Paul Chodoff has recently pointed out, Soviet psychiatrists are completely dependent on the authorities for employment and advancement (4). Under these conditions few will resist carrying out state policy, especially in a state which deals severely with those who do not conform. Further evidence that Soviet psychiatrists have become the functionaries of the state comes from the fact that the hospitalized dissenters were confined in special hospitals under severe conditions where they were subject to abusive and coercive measures in order to make them recant. This is not therapy in any scientific sense but harsh and punitive treatment (2, 4, 10).

What has happened simply is that the Soviet psychiatrist, faced with the conflict between serving the interest of the state and that of the patient, has resolved the conflict in favor of the state. The Soviet example is, as I mentioned, an extreme example of a resolution of the conflict to the detriment of the patient. But is such abuse confined to the Soviet system? It appears not.

As Judge David Bazelon has cogently pointed out, there is much to be learned from the Soviet example. For such abuse is imminent whenever psychiatrists abandon their role as the patient's ally and use their skills to serve institutional purposes (11). Let us examine how this can occur in our own system. What are some typical institutional settings in which the problem arises?

One is the Army. Consider the case of a soldier who is a troublemaker. He resists routine; he challenges policy; his individualistic conduct appears deviant in an Army setting; he fulfills military responsibility questionably; he functions poorly given the demands of Army routine. His officers send him for a psychiatric examination. If found psychiatrically unfit, he would be discharged, much to the relief of his officers. And the soldier might welcome the discharge too. Except that, later on, the psychiatric discharge might prevent the individual from getting into law school, medical school, government service or even industry. In evaluating this soldier, whose interests does the psychiatrist represent? The Army's? The soldier's? Or that of psychiatric science in the abstract?

Consider next the case of the inmate of the state mental hospital who is examined by a psychiatrist who must recommend whether the inmate should be released. The inmate has been confined for a number of years as a result of a brutal assault upon a young girl. If he is released and commits another such assault, the institution will be blamed, and probably the psychiatrist as well. Assume that the institution is already under attack by a "law and order" legislative committee which believes that the facility releases too many "dangerous" people. Whom does the psychiatrist represent? The patient? The institution? The community? His own career?

Take next the example of the parents who seek to have a retarded child committed to an institution and who seek the recommendation of a psychiatrist. The parents have other children at home; the retarded child causes tensions and is a financial burden. The interests of the parents clearly call for institutionalization. But is that in the best interests of the child, or will a home setting, even with tensions, be better than a state institution?[2] Whom does the psychiatrist represent in this situation? The child? The parents? The family unit?

The sources of conflict are varied and not always readily identifiable. They may come from fear for reputation, considerations of promotion, community pressures, institutional economics and numerous other

---

[2] The nature of the conflict here was posed in the amici brief in *Wyatt v. Stickney*, 325 F.Supp., 781 (M.D. Ala. 1971), as follows: "The parent may be motivated to ask for such institutionalization for a variety of reasons other than the best interests of the child himself, i.e., the interests of other children in the family, mental and physical frustration, economic stress, hostility toward the child stemming from the added pressures of caring for him, and perceived stigma of mental retardation. The retarded child's best interests may well lie in living with his family and in the community, but theirs may not lie in keeping him." (12)

sources.[3] The conflicting interests may be passive and muted, but they can also be active and forceful in competing with the patient. And to compound the problem, the patient is generally not even aware of the competition he faces.

The dilemmas posed by these conflicts or dual loyalties go to the very root of psychiatric methodology. Psychiatry has generally followed the medical model in which the physician acts only as the patient's representative, seeking to alleviate the patient's condition. Traditionally, we trust the psychiatrist who practices within this model to ascertain the difference between a patient whose coping mechanism is adequate and a patient who has difficulty in coping and who could benefit from treatment.

When, however, the psychiatrist is also acting on behalf of the institution, an entirely new set of goals enters the picture—institutional goals. These institutional goals necessarily vary the psychiatrist's posture toward a patient and create in the psychiatrist a role conflict that may alter his judgments. The pressure in favor of institutional goals may be subtle; they may even be disclaimed by the institution; nevertheless, they are there.

In the clear case, the role conflict may cause no difference in result; the institutional goals and the patient's best interests may coincide. And even if they do not, the psychiatric diagnosis may be so clear as to compel only one answer. But the situation is often unclear, and in the unclear situations the role conflict tends to confuse important distinctions in the psychiatric methodology.

One such distinction is that between therapy and social control. Even under the best of circumstances, the line between therapy of the pathologically deviant and control of social deviance for nontherapeutic purposes may be a fine one. But in an institutional setting, such as a prison or mental hospital, the danger is that the psychiatrist will be prone to blur the distinction in order to serve the institution's pressure for social control. In extreme form, that is what happened in the Soviet Union where, under government pressures, social controls dressed in therapeutic guise became dominant.

The role conflict also affects the distinction between therapy and social engineering, that is, the difference between "normalcy" as used in medicine and "normalcy" as used in a nonmedical context. The school psy-

---

[3] Some of the conflicting interests have been pungently described by Judge Bazelon as follows: "At the Napa State Hospital in California a few years ago, the superintendent told me in a public meeting that the staff had 'Sacramento looking over its shoulder' on all internal decisions. I learned that psychiatric opinions are influenced by the public outcry for 'Law and Order' and by personal fears for safety. In some hospitals, shortages of bed space and manpower override medical considerations; in V.A. hospitals, the need to fill empty beds produces the opposite results among voluntary patients. I have even been told that psychiatrists believe they are justified in fudging their testimony on 'dangerousness' if they are convinced that an individual is too sick to know that he needs help." (13)

chiatrist often faces this conflict when, for example, a school seeks to impose white, middle class definitions of normalcy as the standard for psychiatric evaluation.

A third area affected by the role conflict involves the distinction between technical expertise and moral expertise. Even in nonconflict settings, that distinction is often obscure. But under pressure of institutional goals, the psychiatrist is far more likely to identify as "abnormal" that which the mores of his homogeneous establishment group regards as wrong.

Thus, the double agent—dual loyalty—conflict role poses serious dilemmas for the psychiatrist. The conflicts not only undermine the psychiatrist's one-to-one relationship with his patient but they also blur methodological distinctions which should be kept in sharp focus. And when uncovered, the conflict role seriously challenges the underpinnings of trust which the psychiatrist requires to effectively practice his art. In short, the decisional process is flawed.

The need to identify these conflicts has been forcefully stated by Judge Bazelon:

> The more I thought about the hidden agendas behind psychiatric decision making, the more I felt that the conflicts faced by the psychiatrist in the public sector must be acknowledged. Otherwise, they would gnaw away at the roots of the profession's dignity and the public trust. (13)

Thus, in a profession so highly dependent upon trust and credibility, it would seem that self-interest alone should propel the profession to identify, reveal and deal with its conflict settings.

But the problem caused by the psychiatrist's conflict role affects not only the psychiatrist and the integrity of his art. It also affects the patient and, with all deference to psychiatry, this is the most serious aspect. The psychiatrist has enormous power vis-a-vis the patient. The mystique of psychiatry makes it inevitable that the patient will rely heavily on the psychiatrist's judgments. The psychiatrist can take away the patient's freedom, isolate him from society, cause him discomfort, label him in a way which affects his status in society and otherwise affect his life and liberty. When the psychiatrist acts in the one-to-one relationship representing only the patient, such decisional power may be acceptable. But such decisional power is not acceptable when the psychiatrist divides his loyalties. For when the psychiatrist also acts at the request of his employing institution, he may serve institutional goals at variance with the interests of the patient. The dangers for the patient are obviously substantial. And they are compounded because the patient is not even generally aware of his exposure.

Dr. Thomas S. Szasz in his book *Psychiatric Injustice* (14) has come to the conclusion that, in an institutional setting such as a state mental hospital, the psychiatrist is the involuntary patient's adversary at *every point of their encounter*. And certainly enough examples have been accumulated in the reported decisions (15) and elsewhere to make his point persuasive. But we need not go that far. Even if the institutional setting is not adversary to the patient, it is one in which there are differing interests and in which potential conflict may arise. And that may be enough. In the legal profession, a lawyer who finds himself representing clients having differing interests must identify the potential conflict to all concerned and give the clients the opportunity to obtain other counsel (16). If the clients choose to retain his services, the choice must be a deliberate and informed choice made under careful ground rules. Even with full disclosure, the American Bar Association (ABA) Code of Professional Responsibility discourages the dual representation (17).

The patient, unlike the lawyer's client, may not be able to choose, because the conflict is rarely revealed to him. Even if the potential conflict is revealed, the institution may not allow the patient a choice. And even if permitted to choose, the patient may not be sophisticated enough, stable enough or wealthy enough to do so. How then is the patient to be protected, and who is to be the protector?

Enter now the role of the law. Deprivation of a person's liberty or status without due process has long been the law's concern, particularly when the depriving institution is an arm of the state. Here the dangers that may arise from the psychiatrist's role conflict are precisely dangers to human freedom. Hence it can hardly be denied that the role conflict is an appropriate one for the law's intervention.

But the nature of the law's intervention remains to be formulated. In a strict adversary proceeding, the law surrounds a party with a variety of protections such as the right to counsel, the right to cross examine, the right to explore biases, the right to examine documents and the right of review. These rights are particularly important when an adversary such as the state seeks to intrude on individual freedom and liberty.

However, not all of the adversary system safeguards are appropriate to the psychiatric institutional setting. It may be inappropriate, for example, for counsel to be present while an Army psychiatrist examines a soldier. But it may be quite appropriate for a person to have counsel present when the psychiatric interview is for the purpose of determining whether he should be released from a state hospital. And it may be entirely appropriate for the court to appoint both counsel and a psychiatrist to represent a child when parents seek to have the child committed and have hired a psychiatrist to support that desire.

What is needed is a careful identification of each conflict situation and the fashioning of the procedural safeguards appropriate to that situation. I believe that the law is moving in this direction.[4] The progress may be slow here in view of the paucity of knowledge among lawyers and judges of the complexities of psychiatric conflict settings. Still, the law is and will be forging its procedures. And if in that process we err a bit in providing more rather than less safeguards for individual liberty, no apology is needed. Freedom, I submit, has even a higher value base in our tradition than institutional efficiency.

It would be most unfortunate if psychiatry viewed this protectionist role of law toward individual rights as a hostile act toward the psychiatric discipline. It is not. The identification of conflict settings and the working out of solutions to further individual freedom is the law's business. But is it not also the psychiatrist's business? If for no other reason, therefore, psychiatry should welcome the identification of these conflict roles and the development of solutions and techniques to deal with them (18).

Since we have not mastered even the identification stage, it is too early to analyze the nature of these solutions and techniques. Yet even now one can foresee that there will have to be a sharp increase in independent psychiatric services for patients in institutional settings and that the corresponding rise in costs will have to be borne substantially by the community. Such independent services will also provide a de facto peer review for the institutional psychiatrist which, paradoxically, may help free him from the conflicts which engender the need for peer review. And certainly there is the possibility of forging new means to ensure the independence of the institutional professional. The solutions requiring exploration are many; hopefully such exploration will be pursued by both the psychiatric and legal professions.

Indeed, in the process of identifying conflicts and working out the proper safeguards, one would hope that law and psychiatry would regard each other as allies engaged in a common cause. Until very recently, however, neither law nor psychiatry had focused systematically on this problem area of institutional psychiatry. The organized bar remained largely aloof from the entire field of mental health, this area included. And the psychiatric profession seemed almost functionally incapable of self-analysis of this sensitive subject. One attempt by the American Psychiatric Association (APA) to examine the area was aborted when the APA trustees and the committee developing the project found common ground only in mutual suspicion. Happily, this year a new study of the conflict role of the psychi-

---

[4] Lawyers of the Mental Health Law Project, a public interest law project, have instituted a series of landmark test cases which have already materially expanded the frontiers of the law in the mental health field. Cases are listed in Legal Rights of the Mentally Handicapped, Vol. 3, pp. 1457–1512 (PLI 1973).

atrist has been initiated under the forthright leadership of the APA President, Dr. Alfred Freedman. The study will largely deal with identification of the problem settings rather than seek to fashion solutions.[5] Whether the project will continue once it touches the raw nerves of the psychiatric profession remains to be seen. Still, if the project goes forward, it will be a major advance, and it may lead to significant changes in institutional psychiatry.

By fortunate coincidence, 1973 also saw the creation of the ABA's new Commission on the Mentally Disabled. The commission is a 17-person interdisciplinary body of lawyers, jurists, psychiatrists, educators and mental health administrators.[6] Among many areas within its focus is the psychiatric role conflict area. The commission has initiated discussions with the APA and the National Academy of Science in an effort to develop a collaborative mold to deal with the conflict problem. While the APA inquiry appears oriented to identify the conflict settings, the potential of the ABA commission may lie more along the lines of fashioning procedural safeguards to maximize individual rights. Perhaps no better opportunity presents itself for collaboration between the two professions than in this area in which identification of role conflicts and the development of solutions to deal with them touch sensitivities of each profession.

I do not minimize the difficulties of developing collaboration between a *legal* discipline which is deductive, doctrinal, authoritative and practical, and a *psychiatric* discipline which is inductive, empirical, heuristic and theoretical. Yet there is much in common (19). Both law and psychiatry

---

[5] The Research Proposal has been formulated for the APA by the Institute of Society, Ethics and the Life Sciences, Hastings-on-Hudson, N. Y.

[6] The members of the commission, in addition to the author, are: Mildred Mitchell Bateman, M.D., Charleston, W. Va., Director of the West Virginia Department of Mental Health; Chief Judge David L. Bazelon of the U. S. Court of Appeals, Washington, D. C.; Gregory R. Dallarie, Atlanta, Ga., active in the ABA Young Lawyers Section; Hayden H. Donahue, M.D., Norman, Okla., Oklahoma State Commissioner of Mental Health; Gunnar Dybwad, Professor of Human Development, Brandeis University, Waltham, Mass.; Joseph Goldstein, Professor of Law, Science and Social Policy, Yale University Law School, New Haven, Conn.; Charles R. Halpern, attorney, Mental Health Law Project, Center for Law and Social Policy, Washington, D. C.; Nicholas Hobbs, psychologist and provost of Vanderbilt University, Nashville, Tenn.; John H. Lashly, St. Louis, Mo., member of the ABA's House of Delegates; Jonas Robitscher, J. D., M.D., and Henry R. Luce Professor of Law and Behavioral Sciences, Emory University, Atlanta, Ga.; Judge Joseph Schneider, Circuit Court of Cook County, Chicago, Ill.; Saleem A. Shah, Chief, Center for Studies of Crime and Delinquency, National Institute of Mental Health, Rockville, Md.; State Senator McNeill Smith, Greensboro, N. C., immediate past Chairman of the ABA's Section of Individual Rights and Responsibilities; Alan A. Stone, M.D., Professor of Law and Psychiatry, Harvard University, Cambridge, Mass.; John R. Willard, Stamford, Conn., active in the ABA's Young Lawyers Section; and Mrs. J. Skelly Wright, Past President, National Association of Mental Health, Arlington, Va.

focus on human behavior. Both law and psychiatry are concerned with selecting, accumulating and integrating societal norms. Both law and psychiatry seek to comprehend, to predict and to control mankind's attitudes, values and anxieties. In these common interests, there is a sound underpinning for constructive collaboration.

Surely, such collaboration can be therapeutic for each profession and beneficial both for science and for humanity.

REFERENCES

1. A Chronicle of Current Events. *J. Soviet Human Rights Movement*, published in Samizdat (underground publication), Issues 16–21, Moscow, republished in English by Amnesty International Publications, London; *A Chronicle of Human Rights in the USSR*, Issues 1–6, New York: Khronika Press, 1973 and 1974; *Proceedings of the Moscow Human Rights Committee*, New York: International League for the Rights of Man, 1972; *Newsweek*, June 1, 1970, pp. 43–44.
2. Ottenberg, P. Bureaucratic Attitudes as a Psychological Defense. *Psychiatric Opinion* 11: 26, 1974.
3. Chalidze, V. N. On the Rights of Persons Declared Mentally Ill. *Proceedings of the Moscow Human Rights Committee*, Nov. 1970 to Dec. 1971, New York: International League for the Rights of Man, 1972; Chalidze, V. N. Concerning Compulsory Commitment to Psychiatric Hospitals, published in Samizdat, Moscow, May–June 1970.
4. Chodoff, P. Involuntary Hospitalization of Political Dissenters in the Soviet Union. *Psychiatric Opinion* 11: 5, 1974.
5. Medvedev, Z., and R. *A Question of Madness*. New York: Knopf, 1971.
6. Wing, J. K. Aspects of Schizophrenia—Personal Comments on an International Conference, Oct. 18, 1973; Letter of 44 British Psychiatrists to the *Times* (London), Sept. 16, 1971; Rogers, P. R. Psychiatric Hospitalization of Political Dissenters. *Psychiatric Opinion* 11: 20, 1974.
7. Stone, I. F. Betrayal By Psychiatry. *The New York Review*, Feb. 19, 1972, p. 8.
8. Open Letter from Andrei Sakharov and Grigory Podyapolsky to the Secretary General of the United Nations protesting psychiatric hospitalization of Soviet scientists Leonid Plyosch and Vladimir Borisov, June 25, 1973; Statement by the Moscow Human Rights Committee urging international censure by physicians against the repressive use of psychiatry in the USSR and countries of Eastern Europe, July 19, 1973. Copies of these and similar appeals are available at the International League for the Rights of Man, 777 United Nations Plaza, New York, N.Y. 10017.
9. See Stone, ref. 7; compare Lopez-Ibor, J. J. A Spanish Psychiatrist Expresses Doubts. *Psychiatric Opinion* 11: 35, 1974.
10. Esenin-Volpin, A. S. Thoughts on Compulsory Psychiatric Hospitalization in the USSR. New York: International League for the Rights of Man, 1972.
11. Bazelon, D. L. Statement to the President of the American Psychiatric Association, the Board of Trustees of the APA, and to the Members of the Ad Hoc Committee on the Use of Psychiatric Institutions for the Commitment of Political Dissenters, April 30, 1972.
12. See briefs for American Psychological Association, American Orthopsychiatric Association, American Civil Liberties Union, and American Association on Mental Deficiency; see also Murdock, C. W. Civil Rights of the Mentally Retarded: Some Critical Issues. *Notre Dame Lawyer* 48: 133, 139–143, 1972.
13. Bazelon, D. L. The Adversary Process in Psychiatry. Address, Southern California Psychiatric Society, April 21, 1973.
14. Szasz, T. S. *Psychiatric Injustice*. New York: Macmillan, 1965, pp. 56–82.

15. Vann, L. R., and Morganroth, F. The Psychiatrist as Judge: A Second Look at the Competence to Stand Trial. *Univ. Detroit Law J.* 43: 1, 1965; *Leyra v. Denno*, 347 U.S. 556, 1953, is a classic example.
16. American Bar Association Code of Professional Responsibility, Canon 5.
17. ABA Code, Canon 5, EC 5-14–EC 5-24.
18. Bazelon, D. L. Institutional Psychiatry—The Self Inflicted Wound. Address, Conference on Mental Health and the Law, The Catholic University of America, Jan. 19, 1974.
19. For an analogous comparison, see Tapp, L. J. *Psychology and the Law: The Dilemma.* American Bar Foundation pamphlet No. 2, 1969.

chapter 3

Ethical Issues in Short Term and Long Term Psychiatric Research

WILLIAM J. CURRAN, J.D., S.M.HYG.

Psychiatry is a medical-scientific-social field particularly prone to strong swings of fashions and fads (1). The swings have often been in consequence of psychiatry's symbiosis with law. Both are living together in association with man's behavior in society, and both are affected by the social change of man. In another paper (2) I described the past hundred years of legal psychiatry in the United States as passing from a romance with the criminal law to a romance with psychiatry and psychoanalysis, and on to a current era of disenchantment on both sides. My thesis of a few years ago is already somewhat dated as we see evidence of a swing back to the criminal law model in legal psychiatry, with the recent court decisions requiring proof beyond a reasonable doubt in criminal responsibility (3) and the imposition of stricter and stricter procedural standards for compulsory hospitalization (4).

Legal decisions are reflecting a public attitude as well as a professional sense of distrust and outright hostility to many traditional areas of clinical psychiatry. This attitude is now spilling over into the field of psychiatric research. The reason here is the greater legal and ethical attention being given to the objectives and methods of all forms of human experimentation (5).

A case in point is *Kaimowitz v. Dept. of Mental Health* (6), a decision of a three-man circuit court for Wayne County, Detroit, Michigan, in July

This research was supported by a contract (HSM-42-72-160) from the Center for Studies of Schizophrenia, National Institute of Mental Health, Department of Health, Education and Welfare, Rockville, Maryland.

1973. In that case, the court found psychosurgery as an experimental procedure to control aggressive behavior to be inadequately supported scientifically by animal studies and human studies and to involve too great a risk as compared to its benefits to a subject who is involuntarily detained in a mental institution. Based upon testimony from eminent psychiatric witnesses, the court found that involuntarily committed patients could not give fully informed consent because of the very nature and character of their incarceration. The court spoke of the "inherently coercive atmosphere" of the hospital and of the almost complete lack of free movement or free choice of the particular patient during his 17 years of hospitalization. During his commitment, the patient had signed a quite detailed informed consent form, and the procedure and the experiment were approved by a Scientific Review Committee and by a Human Rights Review Committee, the latter headed by a well-known law professor with a strong background in psychiatry, Ralph Slovenko of Wayne State University.

After his release from the institution, however, when it was determined that his commitment was itself illegal and unconstitutional, the patient withdrew his consent to the psychosurgery. The decision to proceed with the surgery was withdrawn, but the court decided to go ahead with the case as a declaratory judgment in order to render a decision expressive of the law regarding similar situations in the future.

Although not a higher court opinion, the decision will have great significance because of the firmness of its findings and the documentation of its position. It clearly requires a scientific review of great rigor and a balancing of risks and benefits to the individual subject of considerable depth and sophistication, particularly when "informed consent" of fully capable, intelligent subjects under no conditions of duress or lack of freedom is not assured.

In the following paragraphs I will refer to some of the major issues in psychiatric research as viewed from an ethical-legal standpoint. The approach will be to move in a basically chronological order as an experimental research design or protocol would be prepared, exploring the critical issues as they would arise in that process if it were required that such an examination be made at these stages. Of course I realize that at present no such rather sequential examination of ethical-legal issues may actually occur. However, the structure which I suggest may offer some model for such an approach.

SCIENTIFIC AND ETHICAL JUSTIFICATION

The threshold question of both scientific and ethical significance is the justification for the selection of the research field itself and the scientific design as an approach to exploring that field. This issue might be set forth in three criteria: (*1*) the significance of the problem, or disease, etc.; (*2*) the relevance of the questions to be asked and the hypotheses to be tested; and (*3*) the scientific quality of the research design of the project.

These threshold issues are largely scientific and ethical rather than legal, but the significance of the problem, such as the prevalence of the disease to be studied, has a bearing on later issues of "benefit" to the subjects and to other patients and society when benefits are measured and balanced against risks to subjects. The landmark exposition of the ethical requirements of justification for human experimentation is found in the so-called Nuremburg Code of 1947 (7). The relevant principles of the Code concerning justification are as follows.

> The experiment should be such as to yield fruitful results for the good of society, unprocurable by other methods or means of study, and not random or unnecessary in nature. (Principle 2)
>
> The experiment should be so designed and based on the results of animal experimentation and a knowledge of the natural history of the disease or other problem under study that the anticipated results will justify the performance of the experiment. (Principle 3)

The above standards are set at an adequacy level, not at a competitive level or as a priority measure which would be applied in judging between or among research proposals for funding based upon additional criteria of merit or relevancy to certain program objectives of a funding agency.

In fact some commentators have put these threshold issues of justification at an even lower level of scientific worth, that of nontriviality, or unnecessary repetition of other accepted, competent research (8). Of course, any such quite low levels would be offset completely if any risks to the subjects were involved. It is realized, however, that research findings should be subject to validation by other researchers through use of the same procedures. However, serious questions are raised ethically concerning the justification for scientifically unnecessary, governmentally required repetition of research exposing subjects and subject-patients to the risks of drug testing of so-called "me-too" drug products when only the trade name is different from accepted and approved compounds.

As to the methods of testing, investigators cannot engage in procedures which are themselves inherently immoral or illegal. These issues were heavily involved in the Nuremburg doctors' trials. For example, researchers cannot ask to test two different types of procedures, both lethal or both leading to serious injuries, in order to determine which is faster, less expensive, or involves less pain to the subject before death or injury. Similar issues have been involved in testing addictive or dangerous drugs or other substances when legal restrictions exist on their use.

The third issue at these early stages concerns the research design itself. A poorly designed project which cannot yield supportable findings in regard to the questions posed is not only devoid of scientific merit, it is unethical if it exposes subjects to any kind of risk or inconvenience. Rutstein has also expressed the view that research designs without controls are unethical when humans are exposed to risk; except perhaps when the disease being treated experimentally has a totally predictable result in all subjects, particularly with regard to fatality (9).

SELECTION OF RESEARCH SUBJECTS

A very serious issue at an early stage in research design is the selection of a study population. The *Kaimowitz* case and the current guidelines of the Department of Health, Education and Welfare raise serious obstacles for psychiatric research (10). The issues are quite complex. They involve questions of the freedom of subjects to give fully informed and uncontrolled consent, questions of exploitation of readily available sources of adequate numbers of subjects and questions of overconcentration of research on particular population groups and communities. Psychiatry and psychiatric research are particularly vulnerable to criticism in these areas because of the fact that much human research in the field does involve institutionalized patients in mental hospitals, institutions for the retarded and correctional facilities. These same groups also tend to include a greater concentration of the poor, the elderly and other racial and social minorities. Great care must be used, according to the HEW guidelines, in securing free, informed consent from such institutionalized persons. Yet the guidelines do not rule out obtaining such consent. The *Kaimowitz* case, however, challenged the entire assumption that any free consent can be obtained for experimentation from committed patients or prisoners or from any person who is in a fully controlled environment. The *Kaimowitz* case also stressed the risks and the low probability of benefit to the subject in the proposed psychosurgery, but the court's language is strong and clear in condemning the atmosphere of a large mental hospital, here Ionia State Hospital, as in any way allowing for the exercise of freedom concerning research, even when there is a claimed direct benefit to the subject. Even less would this court justify engaging patients (or prisoners) in projects when no direct benefit was involved at all, such as the different phases of drug testing for toxicity or even efficacy in merely physiological effects. Would the *Kaimowitz* court approve well-controlled testing of psychotropic drugs for the possible direct benefit of psychiatric patients? What controls would be allowed except other approved, effective medications? Could placebos ever be approved? Could double blind studies ever be approved? All of these are serious issues in view of the *Kaimowitz* case and various proposals for changes in HEW guidelines and in legislation before the U. S. Congress, where special attention is being given to these categories of research subjects.

Psychiatric researchers may well call attention to the fact that most of their work among these populations is not for mere convenience. It is relevant directly to the research itself which is intended to explore the psychiatric diseases which exist in these populations in clearly demonstrable concentration: the psychiatrically ill are found in psychiatric hospitals, the retarded in state schools, the violent and socially deviant and the psychiatrically ill in prisons and other correctional facilities. If access were denied to these populations, much research would be entirely eliminated as it is currently conducted. If only subjects who are not institutionalized were to be studied, the representativeness of the samples would be subject to severe challenge. Other arguments are also made to justify the use of institutionalized, psychiatrically ill patients for psychiatric research. The patients are under closer observation than can be achieved in the community, and variables in diet, activity, etc. can be controlled more efficiently in such an environment.

Even when the above arguments may have merit, and even when they may even convince some of the opposition, they may not justify an exclusive concentration upon institutionalized patients in any research protocol without extensive justification scientifically for such emphasis. Such scientific justification may be very difficult to provide when the study makes any claim to epidemiological significance.

Another group to which continued access may be challenged is children. Like the other groups, children are vulnerable as research subjects because of inability to protect their own welfare and to give their own free, informed consent. There is of course some overlap between children as research subjects and children in state schools for the retarded, in psychiatric hospitals, in child guidance and other community clinics, and in juvenile correctional facilities. The authority of parents to consent on behalf of children in experimental projects is a very murky legal area. Parents of children under 14 or so cannot consent to experimental procedures involving any risk. The reason for noting an age differential here is that above this uneven line of adolescence the children themselves, judged individually, may be found mentally, emotionally and intellectually capable of giving a free, informed consent of their own which could allow some experimental procedures involving some risk which is balanced by the benefit to the child. However, even this exception has support in only a few American legal precedents which can be read either strictly or liberally on these points (11). Parental consent would also be required for these adolescent subjects, of course.

The reduction of majority to 18 in some states will clarify the use of adolescents in research projects in these jurisdictions, and parental consent will not be required. However, when adolescents over 18 but under 21 are still living at home and are supported by their parents, it is probably advisable to continue to involve the parents and to get their consent in experimental situations.

In some psychiatric studies of a long term, prospective nature, children and their families may be observed and tested, and some psychiatric intervention may take place over a period of years (12). Care must be taken in such studies to observe all of the precautions noted above, with the added requirement of changing ethical and legal obligations as the children grow older. When the children reach adolescence, their own informed consent would become essential if they are mentally competent.

OTHER RESEARCH POPULATIONS AND COMMUNITIES

In addition to the issues raised above concerning special patient groups and consent, we must also notice issues of concentration of psychiatric research upon population groups in the community, such as the poor, student groups, racial and ethnic minorities and particular geographic communities. With some of these groups, particularly the poor and students, the questions of vulnerability and reduced freedom to consent may be the same as or very similar to the matters discussed above. With the other groups, however, some different issues are raised. These concern the distortion of the research findings themselves as a result of overconcentration upon convenient, nearby or "interesting" groups or communities. Studies concentrated among such groups often give the public impression that the pathologies found are greater than in other, unstudied groups or populations.

The obligation among researchers is to avoid such overconcentration and to include more representative samples in their studies. For human studies review bodies, the obligation will be to guard against overconcentration, not only in individual projects but in the spread of projects which come before them. The latter type of surveillance is not greatly effective, however, in institutional review committees. The trend may well be toward the establishment of community review committees having authority to examine all types of research in their own geographic areas. There can be problems with these community review groups, of course. It may be difficult to identify and to authorize such groups and to set effective and fair criteria for the exercise of advisory or veto powers by them.

INFORMED CONSENT

In a sequential examination of the ethical and legal problems in psychiatric research, I will next explore informed consent, the issue which many commentators address as the keystone of all methods of protecting the welfare of research subjects. I am not disposed to support this view uncritically. The obtaining of a fully informed consent should not act as a carte blanche, or as a total ethical or legal imprimatur, for all human experimentation. There are things that scientists and physicians and all ethical researchers should not do to people, even with their full and free consent. I do not believe that a *fully* informed consent can be obtained from nonscientifically trained subjects, if by this we mean a complete understanding of the entire project, its objectives, its risks, its benefits, etc. Even the research team may not understand all of these aspects, not only because of self-interest but also because of their own limits of knowledge and experience. We must also recognize that subjects will be influenced by their confidence in the researchers and by their desire to cooperate with researcher-clinicians to whom they feel an obligation. Institutional review committees must examine research protocols in order to protect the welfare of the subjects, even if their free and "informed" consent is assumed to be given. The institutional review committees must, in effect, protect both the researchers and their willing subjects from engaging in projects in which the risks are unnecessarily high and when alternatives and reductions in risk are feasible. In some cases, when adjustments cannot be made or when researchers refuse to make the adjustments, the review committees must disapprove the projects.

Current HEW guidelines require written informed consent signed by the subject except in exceptional situations (13). By experience on a review committee at Harvard University, I have found this to be a practical and workable rule. It is virtually impossible for the review group to be assured that informed consent will be sought and obtained under proper standards of disclosure without a written form signed by each subject. Also, the form should *not* be a universal type of document used in all protocols in the institution. Every research project should be required to "start from scratch" and to write each document of consent freshly for each project. Only then can the researchers be encouraged to go through the difficult mental exercise of putting together the unique aspects of their own project, such as the objectives sought, the drugs to be used, the bodily fluids to be extracted, the benefits to be derived, etc. Some aspects of the current HEW guidelines are very simple to place in a consent form, and some provisions are usually the same in most forms, such as a statement to the effect that the subject can withdraw from the project at any time. These routine matters should not obscure the need for ad hoc preparation in every case, however.

In regard to psychiatric research, many of the particular aspects of obtaining informed consent are discussed above in regard to the special population groups usually involved in such studies. We would here only underline once again the difficulties of the entire subject with committed, institutionalized populations. Perhaps the trend to deinstitutionalization and community mental health programs will lessen the significance of these issues in the future, but precautions must still be taken in obtaining free and full consent from mentally disturbed and mentally troubled subjects of any kind, wherever situated.

We must also take note of the fact that recent court decisions in nonpsychiatric clinical medical situations in the District of Columbia (14) and California (15) have imposed stricter requirements regarding a "duty to inform" patients of all significant risks and benefits of medical procedures. These courts refused to follow the majority view of the American states that the physician can modify what he tells his patient (a sort of therapeutic nondisclosure) if his practice conforms to the normal, accepted standards of other practitioners in his own or a similar community. These recent decisions leave it to the jury to decide whether the patient was entitled to the information withheld in order to make a reasonable judgment about whether to consent.

LONG TERM PROSPECTIVE STUDIES

The ethical issues involved in long term prospective and follow-up studies have received very little exploration in the ethical and legal literature. The current HEW guidelines do not address such studies in any direct way. Public and professional attention has been called to these issues, however, with the release of the *Final Report* on the so-called Tuskegee studies (16). In this research over a period of some four decades, a group of Southern black men were observed in order to learn more about the natural course of the disease of syphilis in a black population. The great public outcry about the study concerned the fact that these subjects were not treated with antibiotics when such treatment became available. In the *Report* this failure to treat was condemned as clearly unethical. However, the entire study was also found ethically and scientifically unjustified from its beginnings as not involving free and informed consent, not having any written protocol, lacking validity and reliability assurances, and having a highly questionable data-base validity. The studies seem to have failed to pass muster in every single area of ethical concern examined in this paper.

There are particular ethical problems involved in long term prospective studies and follow-up studies in psychiatry. In the preceding paragraphs I have alluded to some of these issues in such matters as selection of study populations and the informed consent of children. Essentially the issues concern the very nature of the studies in being carried out over a period of time. Researchers must be conscious of the need to reexamine earlier decisions and obligations in the face of changing conditions. Also, the researchers are inexorably collecting more and more sensitive information on their subjects and their families. This information must be protected against improper use. Its confidentiality must be very closely guarded. Yet there may be times when the project itself or the subjects or a court may demand that the information be released in the interest of the subject or, under some circumstances, for the good of others or the community. Long term psychiatric studies which are primarily observational may also be faced with Tuskegee-like situations when therapeutic intervention is either clearly demanded or is at least professionally warranted. At least as yet, there are no very clear professional or ethical standards for judging issues of intervention in such situations (12).

A last point I would make is that, having begun long term psychiatric studies in which significant results can only be found in years of effort, investigators must constantly resist the temptation to move on to other more easily achieved goals, or to publish too quickly, or to cut short research objectives. The foundations and the government must also persevere in the support of long term studies so that they may be completed. Long term studies are often not very glamorous for funding agencies when "payoffs" are not readily apparent and when support is regularly tied up over years and years, but in many psychiatric areas long term studies are among the best possible research investments that can be made (17). Withdrawal of funds without adequate justification should be viewed as a very serious ethical breach of the long-standing commitments to the researchers involved and to their subjects.

TROUBLED REFLECTIONS AND HEALTHY CONCLUSIONS

In referring in the title of this paper to troubling trends in regard to ethical and legal controls on psychiatric research, I was not merely attempting to characterize the specific types of new restrictions on psychiatric studies. In fact, I must make it clear that I regard many of these restrictions as quite proper and well justified.

My own troubled concern is with the frequently emotional, anti-intellectual hostility being expressed in some of the efforts to control all research, but particularly psychiatric and behaviorally oriented research, in all types of settings from hospitals, to prisons, to schools, to the community. There is a frenetic quality here which frankly frightens me, even though there is much merit in the objectives being sought.

What is our healthy conclusion to all this? I believe that it must lie in the acceptance on the part of the psychiatric research community of justified restrictions on research efforts and techniques in the interest of the protection of the individual. It must also be to recognize that the public reaction is a reflection of concern for the unknown, for the abuse of a technical perfection which we know is still far beyond our grasp. The public response is also a public conscience, a public superego. It need not reflect perfect reality to be a realistic fear. We do not have either the power that these forces believe we have or the technical prowess which they see us as trying to exert, but we do have far more power than the poorest and most powerless of our own patients. We cannot use our imperfect technology too quietly, too secretly, to avoid its public accountability. We must be willing to come out in the open and to justify our research in the light of the bright new day.

REFERENCES

1. Tourney, G. A History of Therapeutic Fashions in Psychiatry, 1800–1966. *Am. J. Psychiatry* 784–796, 1967.
2. Curran, W. J. Community Mental Health and the Commitment Laws: A Radical New Approach Is Needed. *Am. J. Public Health* 57: 1565–1570, 1967.
3. *In re Balley*, 482 F.2d 648 (D.C. Cir. 1973); *Lessard v. Schmidt*, 349 F. Supp. 1078 (E.D. Wisc. 1972).
4. *Jackson v. Indiana*, 406 U.S. 715 (1972).
5. Symposium, Ethical Aspects of Experimentation with Human Subjects. *Daedalus* (*J. Am. Acad. Arts Sci.*) 98: 219–595, 1969.
6. Michigan Circuit Court for Wayne County, Civil 73-19434-AW. *U. S. Law Week* 42: 2063, July 1973.
7. *United States v. Brandt et al.*, Nuremberg Military Tribunal, Medical Case, vol. 2, pp. 181–183, 1974.
8. Beecher, H. K. Experimentation in Man, *J.A.M.A.* 169: 461–478, 1959.
9. Rutstein, D. D. The Ethical Design of Human Experiments. *Daedalus* 98: 523–542, 1969.
10. Institutional Guide to Department HEW Policy on Protection of Human Subjects. DHEW Publications (NIH) 72-102, Dec. 1, 1971.
11. Curran, W. J., and Beecher, H. J. Experimentation in Man. *J.A.M.A.* 210: 77–84, 1969.
12. Garmezy, N. Vulnerability Research and The Issue of Primary Prevention. *Am. J. Orthopsychiatry* 41: 101–116, 1971.
13. HEW Institutional Guide, p. 13.
14. *Canterbury v. Spence*, 464 F. 2nd 772 (D.C. Cir. 1972).
15. *Cobbs v. Grant*, 104 Ca. Rptr. 505 (1972).
16. Final Report of the Tuskegee Syphilis Study Ad Hoc Advisory Panel. HEW 1973.
17. Mosher, L., Gunderson, J., and Bucksbaum, S. *Special Report: Schizophrenia.* Center for Studies of Schizophrenia, 1972.

chapter 4

The Use of Psychiatric Patients as Experimental Subjects

LEO E. HOLLISTER, M.D.

The introduction into psychiatry of biomedical methods of treatment and research has been a major advance during the past two decades. Paradoxically, just as these methods bore fruit, they were abandoned. Freudian psychodynamics promised a unitary hypothesis for the cause and treatment of all emotional ills. Yet the only two psychoses to be eliminated so far in the 20th century, those associated with paresis and pellagra, yielded to biomedical approaches. Although no major psychiatric disorder has been eliminated during the past two decades, much has been accomplished. We have specific pharmacological treatments for schizophrenia, endogenous depression and manic-depressive disorder, and increasing evidence suggests that these disorders are genetically determined. We have testable hypotheses about the biochemical mechanisms which permit their development.

Such progress has required the participation of psychiatric patients in clinical experiments. Usually clinical experiments were tried early rather than late for, in most instances, suitable animal models for these disorders were not available. A repetitious theme in the history of new pharmacological treatments in psychiatry has been that the major impetus for their development evolved from clinical experience. More human experimentation, rather than less, is needed if we are to discover new treatments or gain new insights into the nature of psychiatric disorders. Yet at this most auspicious moment, increasing constraints are being placed on experimentation with psychiatric patients.

EMERGENCE OF THE PRESENT CONSTRAINTS ON EXPERIMENTATION

In any democratic form of government, an abrasive interface always exists between the rights of individuals and the rights of society. The trend in the United States since the 1950s has been to strengthen rights of individuals. These changes were effected by court decisions, and many having to do with civil rights were long overdue. Some changes followed efforts of specific minority or special interest groups, such as the Women's Liberation Movement, other liberation movements and consumer organizations. One may argue, as some in prominent public position have, that the pendulum has swung too far and that the law currently protects the criminal more than his victims. But the pressure to extend the rights of individuals shows no perceptible sign of decreasing.

Psychiatric patients, while not as widely publicized as other groups, have also gained increased individual rights. Involuntary commitment, formerly almost routine, has now become so difficult that it is only employed in the most obviously threatening circumstances. The uncertainty of psychiatric diagnosis has been exploited on the one hand to argue that emotional illnesses are only in the eye of the beholder, and on the other hand to justify the release into the community of patients who quickly and palpably demonstrate their psychopathology. The doctrine of self-incrimination has been extended to psychiatric patients: they must be warned that what they say may be used against them in a commitment proceeding. Civil suits have been successfully argued that current standards of hospital care for some mental patients are so poor as to be inhumane. No longer are mental patients legal orphans. The American Bar Association has a special Commission on the Mentally Disabled to assure that these patients obtain the same constitutional rights and protections as other citizens.

No one would argue that mentally ill or disabled patients should not have such rights. We do not mourn the passing of the days of the ducking stool, the spinning treatment, physical restraints and, even more recently, the casual colectomies or lobotomies. Many horrible treatments have been inflicted on the mentally ill, far more from ignorance than from malice. What does concern us is that the zeal to protect patients against such misadventures may also protect them against those advances in treatment which might truly give them full status as citizens. We may be in danger of protecting our patients to the extent that, while nothing bad may happen to them as the result of experimentation, nothing good will happen either.

SPECIAL PROBLEMS OF INFORMED CONSENT

The notion of informed consent is not at all new but is a tradition of ancient Greek medicine. Consent of the patient was implicit in his entering a relationship of mutual respect with his physician. The Hippocratic oath specifies the physician's duty to do what he thinks is for the benefit of his patient; no charge to do good for society as a whole ever entered the contract. Implied consent, therefore, has always been based on the notion that only the patient's interests were involved. Experimentation has the obviously broader goal of yielding information of value not only to a specific patient but to many similar patients.

The recent demand for informed consent for experimental procedures derived from the movement toward increased individual rights. The individual, rather than his physician, should control whether or not he becomes an experimental subject. To make such a determination, he requires a thorough and frank disclosure of the facts, probabilities and opinions which a reasonable man might be expected to consider. From this premise, a set of criteria for informed consent has gradually evolved. First, the subject should understand why he had been selected for participation in a study. Second, he must be aware of its experimental nature, that it seeks to benefit others than himself. Third, he must be made aware, as best one can, of the potential risks of the experiment. Fourth, he should be made aware of alternative treatments. Finally, he should have the right to refuse to participate without prejudice, or to withdraw from the study once it is commenced.

It is not my purpose to belabor further the minutiae of informed consent. Its definition, the proper implementation of techniques for obtaining it, and even whether or not completely informed consent is possible have elicited volumes of words. What is most germane to our present discussion is that the psychiatric patient is not as able as the unimpaired patient to comprehend the information offered or to make a valid decision. Informed consent by the psychiatric patient, at least in any acceptable sense, is at best partial and often is impossible.

An alternative to having the psychiatric patient make the decision would be to delegate this responsibility to someone else: a relative, a guardian, legal counsel, or institutional review committees. The exact mechanisms by which such delegation of responsibility will be done are still being considered. One can be certain that some procedures will be adopted. Whether these procedures will be so cumbersome as to stultify research in psychiatric patients is less certain.

THE PSYCHIATRIC EXPERIMENTER

We have been far more precise in developing criteria for satisfactory informed consent than for what constitutes a satisfactory psychiatric researcher. That he should have scientific expertise in his special area of interest is a foregone conclusion. One would hope that scientific expertise would also be associated with impeccable intellectual honesty, although this is not always the case. He should have had experience with patients and an ability to establish rapport with them. His identification with his patients should not be so close that he will be overly timid in his research, never really ever standing a chance of developing useful new information. On the other hand, his zeal for scientific accolade should not push him to do experiments so bold as to be either dangerous or uncomfortable for his patients. His experiments should be efficient, in the sense of delivering the most useful data for the least cost and risk. He should see his experiments to conclusion, sharing knowledge with his colleagues. One can think of other criteria than these, but they provide some general qualities which are desirable.

No matter how well the experimenter fulfills the above criteria, the essential attribute is a well-developed sense of what is appropriate to do to patients. One might propose a kind of Golden Rule for experimenters: "Do unto patients what you would have done to yourself (or your family)." Obviously, one can't enter oneself as a subject for all one's experiments. But it does help, whenever possible, to participate to some extent. Over the years, I have taken small doses (often I thought they were too large) of most psychotherapeutic drugs. The information gained has seldom been useful and, in the case of antipsychotic or antidepressant drugs, might have been misleading. Still, any reservation on my part to take a drug which I proposed to give a patient would question the propriety of using that drug.

Finally, the ideal experimenter should be willing to improve his ethical concepts consonant with changes in society. All of us who have been in this field for any length of time have done experiments in the past that we would not do at present. Three years ago I was visiting an esteemed colleague, now retired. In the course of our conversation, I mentioned a most interesting and valuable study that he had done 10 years earlier, administering heroin blindly to normal individuals. His first comment was, "You know, I could not do that experiment today, largely as a result of my own efforts." He was right; he had become the ethical conscience of the medical community sooner than anyone else. So we must all be willing to change as the situation may demand.

TYPES OF EXPERIMENTS IN PSYCHIATRIC PATIENTS

A number of different types of experiments are done with psychiatric patients. The most common, fortunately, is the therapeutic experiment. We may want to know whether or not a new drug is effective in some disorder, or whether drug A differs from drug B in some special therapeutic action. Such experiments are the most easy to justify. The patient will usually be treated with an active drug, although a placebo control may sometimes be required. The risk he takes is that the new drug may not necessarily be as effective or safe as others currently available. In early studies, he may even take the risk that he might not be treated adequately, as often the optimal doses are not known. Because the drug is new, he may be the dubious beneficiary of more frequent laboratory or clinical monitoring than would be the case were the drug one in common use. In developing informed consent forms for such experiments, listing the potential disadvantages and all the alternative treatments, one can't help wondering whether anyone who assented to such an experiment might not be crazy. Fortunately, some patients and their families still do consent, both because of the remote possibility that the new treatment may be a major advance or because they really want to help society.

Another type of study involves investigations into the etiological bases of a disorder. Such studies offer the individual patient little except considerable inconvenience. No such experiment yet has been definitive, and even if it were, it is not at all certain that a new therapeutic advance would immediately follow which might benefit the individual patient. Studies of this type are increasingly important as the development of new drugs slows, but the use of old drugs as tools for exploring etiology increases. One such study a number of years ago involved the determination of the disappearance rate of a biogenic amine in cerebrospinal fluid following the intervention of a drug. To obtain a well-fit curve, each patient was subjected to eight spinal taps over a 24-hour period. Such a study is more than I would be personally willing to undertake. For several years, I have been sitting on two protocols pertinent to the role of dopamine in schizophrenia, but I have been loath to undertake them as our expectation in each case is that patients will be made worse. This type of study, important from the scientific point of view and yet questionable enough to raise serious ethical qualms, demands the attentions of all of us to reconcile these conflicting forces.

A third type of study might pertain to the elucidation of a side effect of a drug. Early on, some clinicians maintained that jaundice associated with chlorpromazine treatment represented the simple coincidence of viral hepatitis in someone exposed to the drug. I decided to scotch that notion once and for all by using challenge tests of drug in patients who had previously had jaundice and had now recovered. We did the challenge tests under carefully controlled circumstances, and I am happy to say that the point was established that the reaction was allergic, with no harm done to patients. Yet it is not a study that I should now do.

We may soon be able to consider possible chemoprophylaxis of psychiatric disorders. The demonstration that lithium prevents recurrent manic-depressive disorder, and that possibly either lithium or tricyclic antidepressants may prevent recurrent episodes of depression, raises the question of preventive treatment in patients considered to be at risk, even though the diagnosis may not be firm. Should some chemical marker be found for determining the person genetically at risk for developing schizophrenia, one might propose early and prolonged treatment with antipsychotic drugs. While one can scarcely argue against any truly preventive treatment, the situation with psychiatric disorders is not the same as giving immunizations against bacterial or viral diseases. Ethical guidelines for these situations are still not at all clear.

Finally, hospitalized psychiatric patients have been used in the past for studying nonpsychiatric conditions. Two major studies, one in Los Angeles and the other in Finland, have used large populations of hospitalized psychiatric patients to establish the relationship between diet, serum lipid levels and myocardial infarctions. It has been possible to show that, by appropriate dietary restriction, one can reduce the number of myocardial infarctions. Coronary heart disease is a major public health problem. Opportunities are rare indeed to study large groups of persons over long periods of time under situations in which diet, exercise, smoking, blood pressure levels and other risk factors can either be manipulated or known. Yet currently proposed regulations would restrict the study of psychiatric patients to the investigation of whichever psychiatric disability they had. Here is another area in which proper ethical guidelines need to be determined.

SPECIAL PROBLEMS CREATED BY EXPERIMENTAL DESIGNS

Experimental designs may create situations which temporarily subvert the best interests of individual patients. The use of a placebo control creates such problems. When we first undertook controlled trials of antipsychotic drugs, using placebo controls, I adopted two principles to mitigate any potential disservice to individual patients. The first principle was that no study would be any longer in duration than the minimal period adequate to demonstrate a clear effect or lack of effect of the treatment under consideration. In this way, no patient would be exposed to a potentially ineffective treatment longer than required. The second principle was that any patient who received a placebo medication (determined after his final evaluations were made) would be offered an opportunity to be treated with the active drug. In this way, no patient still requiring more treatment would not have access to one potentially effective. When the illness is one for which one can demonstrate little placebo effect or tendency toward spontaneous remission, such as schizophrenia, the subsequent use of active drug is usually obligatory. When spontaneous remission or placebo effect may occur, as in depression or anxiety, subsequent treatment with active drug may not always be required.

Sometimes the point of a study is to determine whether or not a patient formerly on drugs can have his dose discontinued or reduced with impunity. The end point in such studies is relapse. We have used the earliest signs of relapse as an indication of failure, dropping the patient from the study at that point and retreating him immediately. While no evidence indicates that patients who relapse when drugs are discontinued do not subsequently respond when they are restarted, one is hesitant to test this point by inducing prolonged or severe relapse. I have never liked studies which attempt to return patients to an essentially untreated state by withholding medication so they can become the subjects of a trial with a new drug.

When one is dealing with an investigational new drug, it is always appropriate to warn the patient that his access to the drug will be limited to the period of the study. Some new drugs may be highly effective for selected patients, so that the patient may wish to continue treatment. As it is probable that another drug might be found which would approach the efficacy of the new drug, one need only specify that, upon completion of the clinical trial, treatment will be resumed with the most appropriate drug as determined by clinical experience. Failure to alert patients to this change in procedure may lead to misunderstandings.

Usually an experimental design calls for some specified length of treatment, such as 4 to 6 weeks for newly admitted schizophrenic patients, or 3 to 4 weeks for newly admitted depressed patients. What does one do if the patient is ready to leave the hospital prior to completion of the arbitrarily determined treatment period? In my opinion, there has never been any question. It is never justifiable to keep a patient hospitalized any longer than necessary just to complete experimental protocol. One simply makes a rating as the patient departs and the data need not be lost. This problem occurs with increasing frequency as patients have the right to leave whenever they choose, and often before they are as much in remission as the professional staff would desire.

Most of this discussion has been concerned with experiments using drug therapy, but the same considerations apply to the introduction of other types of therapeutic maneuvers, whether surgical or psychological. The public outcry against surgical approaches to treating mental disorders has all but eliminated such procedures, even though so far as one can tell recent experiments were done sparingly, carefully and in well-controlled situations. Psychological treatments have had an easier time, although even these will be closely scrutinized in the future. A year or two ago, I heard that on one of the wards of our hospital a consultant was using a technique in which the patient was subjected to tickling by a group of "co-therapists." The rationale for this treatment sounded rather flimsy, so I sent a memorandum to the chief of the psychology service suggesting that such treatment be subjected to a review similar to that which might be applied to an investigational new drug. He agreed, and that was the last heard of this "therapy" in our hospital. Within a month, a newspaper article revealed that a large judgment had been awarded against the same therapist evolving from his similar treatment of another patient at another hospital. No one wants to stifle innovative approaches to treatment, but it is essential for legal as well as ethical reasons that they be carefully reviewed.

PROBLEMS FOR RESEARCH CREATED BY THE CURRENT ZEITGEIST

If we assume that research in psychiatric patients has been of enormous value in improving their management, and abundant evidence is available to support this conclusion, how may we continue to make progress and still observe the current ethical principles? So far as one can tell, the current furor about research in humans has resulted from the exposure of experimental studies conducted among poor blacks in the South three or four decades ago not using present ethical guidelines, or trivial studies in prisoners in poorly run prisons, or questionable procedures employed by various entrepreneurs who make a living principally from testing drugs. Little evidence is at hand to suggest that research done in psychiatric patients has been a major source of the present concerns. We stand in a position in which, to prevent a few bad guys from operating, we may put all the good guys out of business.

Already some serious threats to psychiatric research have occurred. In several states, arbitrary edicts of commissioners of mental health have abruptly curtailed or eliminated any type of research in psychiatric patients. These rules, motivated mainly by fear of political pressures, have effectively eliminated hospitals and research institutes with an excellent past record of contribution to psychiatric research from any future efforts. As has always been the case, it is far easier for bureaucrats to say no than to say yes.

Even where research continues with psychiatric patients, some of the new ground rules create real problems in evaluating results. The stricter requirements for obtaining informed consent have increased the number of refusals to participate in new studies. As mentioned earlier, when one is forced to make the strongest case possible against accepting a proposed new treatment, those who accept these conditions may represent a skewed sample. No one has yet done a study to determine the prevalence of refusals of experimental protocols and whether those who refuse differ from those who accept. The whole basis for doing any experimental study is that the results may be extrapolated from a small sample to a relatively large population of patients. To the extent that the sample may not represent the total population of patients, the generalizability of results becomes limited.

Even when patients assent to enter an experiment, it is by no means certain that they will produce useable data. Although we have never deterred a patient from being discharged when his condition warranted it, simply to complete the duration of a study, at present patients leave on their own recognizance when they have had relatively little exposure to the new treatment and are far from well. This new freedom for patients increases the drop-out and incomplete data rates in experimental studies. As these rates increase, the remaining complete data are weakened.

Faced with difficulties both in getting research started or with completing it in a meaningful manner, the psychiatric researcher today is entering a state of demoralization. Research with psychiatric patients has never been easy, for scientific research has never been a strong influence in psychiatry. The sad plight of psychiatry in comparison with other medical specialties has been most commonly ascribed to the hesitancy to adopt the scientific method to a field thought to be so abstruse as to make this impossible. Work during the past two decades has shown that the scientific approach is not only feasible in psychiatry but has produced more progress than at any other period. Yet one cannot help wondering whether the latent anti-intellectualism that has pervaded most of the history of psychiatry is not about to become again overt, reflecting the current anti-intellectualism so evident in other walks of life. It would be a pity indeed if, just as the light has begun to shine, psychiatry should once again enter the Dark Ages.

CONCLUSIONS

The basic conflict between the rights of individuals and the rights of society has entered the psychiatric domain. Psychiatric patients should and do have the same rights as individuals, no less in degree but different in execution, as those enjoyed by other citizens. They have a right to be treated in the best possible fashion so as to restore them to a full participation as citizens. To achieve the latter right it will be necessary that research in psychiatric patients continue. The progress of the past two decades has only begun to scratch the surface of what might ultimately be done. In this endeavor, the rights of psychiatric patients and those of society coincide. It would be a pity if some modus vivendi could not be found that would permit scientific progress in psychiatry to continue, while still respecting the rights of those patients who must help us find the way

chapter 5

The Redefinition of Psychiatric Treatment

ALFRED M. FREEDMAN, M.D.

Think of yourself in a movie house in the 1930s, and let me describe the scenario to you. Eight-year-old Susie, blue eyes, long blonde curls, the darling of the community, is suffering from a dread disease and is going blind. The only way to cure her and restore full sight is to have an operation that must be performed by a great surgeon in the big city. This will cost $2,500, or 1,000 pounds, depending on which movie you are seeing. Of course, this is far beyond the means of Susie's family. However, there is a beautiful wild horse that only responds to Susie. After many adventures, Susie is able to persuade the horse to be ridden by a jockey and, of course, the horse wins the County Fair race or the big race at Epsom Downs. The prize is the $2,500 or the 1,000 pounds. Susie is operated on successfully, and everyone lives happily ever after.

Today not even the most simple-minded TV producer would consider that scenario. The notion that the lack of medical care for Susie was her personal misfortune that could only be obviated by a supernatural stroke of good fortune was quite acceptable 40 or 50 years ago. Now one could anticipate protests, sit-ins or demonstrations if Susie were denied her operation. Thus the situation has been redefined from a misfortune to an injustice.

The redefinition of lack of adequate health care from a misfortune to an injustice is indicative of a major social movement. Indicators of the strength of this trend are the numerous class actions with regard to "right to treatment." Members of Congress and other political leaders make this issue a major issue in their campaigns, and the consumer groups press for proposed new legislation. This redefinition has historical antecedents.

Turner (1) points out that "any major social movement depends upon and promotes some normative revision. In case of movements having the greatest significance for social change, this normative innovation takes the form of a new sense in what is *just* and what is *unjust* in society." Turner differentiates between concepts of a problem as being either a misfortune or a state of injustice.

Historically, major social changes have occurred when a misfortune has been redefined as an injustice, and large sections of the population have demanded correction. Poverty was a misfortune to the leaders of revolutionary movements in the 19th century. To be denied the material needs of life was redefined as an injustice, with resultant revolutions in the 19th century, the organization of labor unions and, as a later manifestation, the New Deal here in the United States.

It is now evident that Turner's hypothesis can be updated to include adequate health care as a subject of normative revision. The implications of this redefinition are vast for the nation, as well as for those of us who are health providers. It is this redefinition that fuels the "right to treatment" movement.

It would be a serious error to assume that the demands made are the creations of crackpots and malcontents. The truth of this notion can be illustrated by an examination of the role of one powerful movement, that which seeks consumer participation in the delivery of health services. Its latent power derives from the redefinition of lack of health care as an injustice. In mental health, particularly, this potential constituency is very broad. The most obvious members are those who are receiving treatment, as either outpatients or inpatients in a hospital or at some other facility. However, those who make demands and desire a voice in decision-making with regard to services include relatives and friends of patients, potential users of mental health services and concerned citizens. In a sense, we end up with the entire population as consumer advocates.

The increasing role of consumer or citizen participation is manifest now in legal and quasi-legal requirements. Thus, in various federal and state health planning programs, it is a requirement that more than 50% of various boards be made up of real consumers. Federal guidelines require a consumer contribution to community mental health centers. In many areas it is required that hospital boards have community boards of consumers. Many of these start as advisory boards but end up as active participants in decision-making.

Most articulate as defenders of the consumer, or as consumer advocates, have been certain critics of mental health care in general and of the psychiatric profession in particular. These critics, with varying mixtures of penetrating facts and gross distortions, have become identified as the voice of the consumer, as if they really speak for patients or families of patients.

What is most significant here is the absence of a constituency or voice for psychiatry in this public area. I believe that it is the isolation of the psychiatric profession, as well as of other professions in the mental health field, that must give us pause. One can agree with many of the points made by the critics, take others under advisement, and try to correct deficiencies or errors. A defense by denial is always weak. Affirmative action is the preferable means for making a convincing case. The appropriate response is not one of apology; rather, it should be self-criticism and scrutiny, and it should include the development (with consumers) of a program to cope with the enormous mental health problems in this country.

What are some of the other implications of this redefinition, apart from the rise of consumerism? Decision-making in regard to planning and implementation will have to be shared. Where will the line be drawn? Many who are committed to the "doctor knows best" school feel that there is unusual intrusion into treatment programs by mental patients and their families as "defenders." Adherents of this school scoff at statements such as those produced by the Mental Patients Liberation Project (MPLP) in their Bill of Rights, but when one compares the MPLP Bill of Rights (2) with the American Hospital Association (AHA) Bill of Rights (3), one realizes that the two documents are more alike than different. This can be seen in comparing a few items from each.

From the MPLP:

"3. You have the right to the integrity of your own mind and the integrity of your own body.

"4. Treatment and medication can be administered only with your consent and, in the event you give your consent, you have the right to demand to know all relevant information regarding said treatment and/or medication."

From the AHA: the patient has the right:

"2. . . . to obtain from his physician complete current information concerning his diagnosis, treatment and prognosis, in terms the patient can be reasonably expected to understand.

"3. . . . to receive from his physician information necessary to give informed consent prior to the start of a procedure and/or treatment.

"4. . . . to refuse treatment to the extent permitted by law, and to be informed of the medical consequences of his action."

Again from the MPLP:

"13. You have the right to refuse to be a guinea pig for experimental drugs and treatment and to refuse to be used as learning material for students. You have the right to demand reimbursement if you are so used."

Likewise from the AHA: the patient has the right:

"9. . . . to be advised if the hospital proposes to engage in or perform human experimentation affecting his care or treatment."

Whatever the strengths and weaknesses of these declarations, the beginning of an overriding concern for patients is now clearly expressed. And with this expression, if not with every detail, the psychiatric profession has a duty to identify. If the psychiatric profession cannot explain to, educate and join the consumers, we may face the widespread conviction that mental health is too important to be left in the hands of psychiatrists. The profession may then find that it has minimal or no input in decision-making or in the establishment of priorities in mental health. That power will then reside with those outside the mental health profession.

This is a period characterized by attitudes of antiprofessionalism, antiintellectualism, anti-science, and antipsychiatry. There has been a precipitous decline of confidence in those who previously enjoyed the highest esteem with the public. Respect for physicians in general, psychiatrists and Supreme Court Justices has declined very markedly in public opinion polls comparing the late 1960s with the early 1970s.

Such doubts of the mental health professionals by the public give rise to close scrutiny by the mass media and critics of psychiatry. A sequence of events involving the 275,000 patients in state hospitals is illustrative of this situation.

In spite of the important developments of the past decade, including impressive psychopharmacological developments and the halving of the state hospital population, many class actions in the courts, TV exposés, and muckraking articles in newspapers and magazines have focused on this group of patients. The usual response from the profession has been to blame inadequate funding, manpower difficulties and the fact that medical staffs are composed largely of graduates of foreign medical schools who have difficulty with the English language.

Is there a ready solution? One might decide that many patients in state hospitals could be treated as well or better at home or in neighborhood facilities. This possibility has been established in several studies, and some voices have therefore proposed massive discharges. Is this a solution or does it create new problems?

After it was decided that many of those confined in state hospitals, particularly those in the geriatric age group, do not need hospitalization, there appeared to be little consideration of the consequences of discharge. As a consequence we have witnessed a barrage of newspaper exposés as well as articles in psychiatric journals regarding the unfortunate sequelae of a decision to embark upon a program for cutting down the patient census without preparation for the consequences. Reich (4), for example, points out that in New York City too many of the dischargees have no family to return to, and that psychiatric units in general hospitals refuse to admit them as inpatients. Thus the care of the chronically ill falls to an already beleaguered, much criticized city welfare system.

In New York City, discharged patients are placed in whatever settings are available. The aged are referred to nursing homes where they receive little psychiatric care and no real therapy. Is it therapeutic to send an ambulatory, mentally ill person to an environment shared with the severely physically ill and dying, who are largely bed patients? Of the 5,000 or more proprietary-home beds, half are occupied by the chronically mentally ill. These proprietary homes in the main are unsuccessful motels and older hotels that supply room and board, but little else. There are no day programs, little recreation, and no one even to check on the physical well-being of the occupants. These people, many of whom have been in state institutions for fifteen years or more, rarely leave the building. They sit and stare into space and regress as if in the back wards. (4)

This situation has been highly publicized in the local press and other media. The *New York Times* ran a series of articles. More recently, Long Beach, Long Island passed an ordinance prohibiting the placement of patients discharged from state hospitals in hotels and motels in that city because of alleged misconduct and behavior destructive to the community. Similar events are occurring in other large metropolitan areas across the country.

We professionals are between Scylla and Charybdis. One can and must properly object to keeping patients in the back wards of state hospitals where they receive no treatment. In fact, the courts have ruled such confinement illegal. But to move them into the sort of facility described above is not a change for the better. The condition of inmates at public hospitals might look better, but this is really a distinction without a difference. However, to conclude that it is better to keep patients in state hospitals would be an egregious error.

There would be no excuse for the cruelties perpetrated on discharged patients if appropriate community facilities had been developed before their discharge. Langsley (5) described the development of community programs in Sacramento County, California, to the point where the need for state hospital services was almost eliminated. In a period of 9 months, only one patient was sent to a state hospital. Similar results have been reported elsewhere.

The lesson is clear: *The consequences of any action involving people must be anticipated and plans must be made to cope with them before action is taken.*

The state hospital population is just one illustration of the many unsolved problems in the mental health field. Thus we are faced with conflict and ambiguity, with strong countervailing trends, with frantic activity in some quarters and with total passivity in others. To try to make some sense in this confusing scene, we need a catalytic force to formulate and implement policy, to give it direction and impetus and to pinpoint obstructions to the development of rational mental health programs, whether the obstacles are within the field or outside it.

I have previously called for the establishment of a new approach or school in psychiatry: "Critical psychiatry" (6). Let me review some of the basic notions of critical psychiatry. In this school we will be particularly concerned with the needs and demands of society upon psychiatry and the behavioral sciences and, conversely, with the impact of new developments in psychiatry and the behavioral sciences on society. Critical psychiatry will be as unsparing of those within the field who are selfish, self-preoccupied, lethargic or different, as it will be of those in positions of power who would deny, cut back, withhold or divert necessary funding, not only for mental health services, training and research, but also for the ancillary support that is necessary to provide a reasonable existence for the citizens of this country.

The word "critical" is being used in two senses: first, as applied to an analysis that transcends ordinary study in its depth, exploration of ramifications, and placement of the immediate problem in the context of relevant social and scientific issues; and second, in the sense of crisis. Critical psychiatry will seek to restore to the mental health field a sense and place of leadership. Too often change or pressure for change has come only from outside, from journalists, investigators, civil liberties lawyers, court decisions or the mass media. It is time to stop granting a monopoly of indignation to others. Critical psychiatry will seek to restore some part of the leadership to those of us who are in the field of mental health.

In the synthesis of scientific knowledge with humanitarian considerations, critical psychiatry will use reason, scientific information, argument and political tactics to arouse public concern on matters of human welfare. Critical psychiatry will attempt to look at the present state of the field and to anticipate dangers or conflicts before battle lines are drawn. In this way, problems can be studied early enough to develop working solutions that might obviate resort to adversary confrontation. Only in the development of joint projects working toward common goals is there any social hope. Critical psychiatry must be action-oriented, with primary concern not for the profession but for our patients and for society as a whole.

What is the relationship of critical psychiatry to the major issues facing the field? On previous occasions I have tried to formulate these issues in parsimonious categories.

The *validity* of the field is the first issue. While I am persuaded that there are identifiable mental illnesses, the public needs reasoned statements about the existence and scientific basis of mental illness. Statements about our ability to diagnose and to differentiate are also necessary. How effective are treatment methods, and in what situations, and for what disturbances? What can be said about diagnosis? Prognosis? And behavior following the end of treatment?

Second, there is the matter of *equity*. Does the delivery system provide care for all who need it equally? Are our mental health facilities distributed evenly? How appropriate is the distribution of providers of mental health care compared with the numbers of those who are in need? Is most of the energy, the man-hours of people in our field, devoted to those who most need it?

Third, we must face the critical question of the *legitimacy* of our field. In recent years we have witnessed a spate of criticism, opposition and even virulent attacks upon the facilities and personnel of the mental health care system. These criticisms have come from within our field as well as from without. The critics include consumer advocates, former patients and lawyers, and they have been uncompromising in their stance. Targets for attack have included both voluntary and involuntary hospitalization, commitment procedures, conflicts of interest on the part of those engaged in providing services, the right to treatment, the extent of confidentiality and privilege and the use of mental patients for experimentation.

Lastly, we must come to some agreement about the *appropriate roles* of those engaged in the mental health care system. We have the job of organizing in one coordinated system all those who are engaged in providing care. Our task is to treat those who are troubled and in distress. We can achieve success in this endeavor only if we stress "connection and membership, rather than distance and superiority" (7).

Let me illustrate actions that can be taken in accordance with the principles of critical psychiatry relevant to the state hospital situation that I described earlier. While the right to treatment cases such as the original *Wyatt v. Stickney* case in Alabama were very important steps, they had their limitations. Their thrust was confined to inpatients and, apart from appealing the case, the response was to empty the hospital without providing alternative facilities for patients. Recognizing this loophole, for the first time in its history the American Psychiatric Association (APA) became a plaintiff in a right to treatment suit against the federal government and St. Elizabeth's Hospital in Washington, D.C. In this case the concept of the right to treatment is extended to include a whole panoply of services, not only inpatient services but also outpatient services. If successful, this case will establish the principle that there is a continuity of responsibility on the part of the federal government, and subsequently local governments, for the care of those who are mentally ill.

Another example of the kind of action which can be taken arose in response to an ordinance passed by the city of Long Beach, Long Island, which would prohibit persons requiring continuous medical, psychiatric or nursing care from residing in that city's hotels and boarding houses. The APA has joined two other organizations as plaintiff in a class action suit challenging the constitutionality of the ordinance. The other plaintiffs are the New York Civil Liberties Union and the Mental Health Law Project.

These are examples of immediate actions in response to situations or procedures which are detrimental to the best interests of patients needing psychiatric care. In such instances the psychiatric profession is truly acting as a patient-advocate.

Critical psychiatry may seem to provide a new role for the psychiatrist, but I believe that it is a call for a return to the traditional role as a physician. The psychiatrist is the heir to much that is best in medicine. In this day of "organ specialists" and a steady march toward computerized medicine, it is the psychiatrist who still practices in full awareness of the person who surrounds a lesion—his or her life, the family, the job, the society to which he or she is related.

In an eloquent address entitled, "The Best and the Brightest—The Missing Dimension in Medical Education" (8), Dr. George Engel expresses sharp dismay at the failure in the curriculum of our medical schools to equip the physician with the psychological knowledge and skills necessary for his task. By overlooking the human element in medicine, thousands of "current medical school graduates taught by the best and brightest of today's medical educators may be . . . flawed in their preparation for their future professional responsibilities. This is the missing dimension, the bog of modern medical education."

It is passing strange that so little attention is paid to the well-known fact that more than half the visits to physicians' offices are not because of physical illness but are due to emotional upsets. More than half the patients may be consulting a doctor who is not best equipped to manage their particular problems.

Yet psychiatrists seem apologetic in regard to their role. The opportunity to synthesize biological and psychosocial factors puts the psychiatrist on the road to the complex model of illness toward which all medicine must move. Psychiatrists also appear to be embarrassed by involvement in social issues; it is unphysician-like behavior, it is political. But all medicine is becoming increasingly political. The development of national health insurance, peer review, regulations in regard to research and drug abuse programs, to mention but a few items, indicates the steady intrusion of politics into day-to-day medical practice. Physicians must be involved in problems caused by the environment of their patients—in social issues.

One of the founders of modern medicine, the celebrated pathologist Rudoph Virchow, stated over a century ago, "Physicians are the natural attorneys of the poor and social problems fall to a large extent within their jurisdiction." (9) That is a real medical model!

Will the redefinition of health, the increased public participation in health decisions, the joining with consumers, the sensitivity to demands from the public, mean the downgrading if not the demise of physicians? On the contrary. By participating in accessible, available and comprehensive programs of undoubted excellence, the psychiatrists will receive wide, affirmative recognition.

It is particularly noteworthy to read an editorial by Dr. Frank Riessman in the *Journal of Social Policy*, of which he is editor, entitled "When It Comes to the Poor—Suddenly Doctors Are Not the Answer" (10). Dr. Riessman was a pioneer in the development of paramedical training programs, and his contributions in this area are well known. He states:

"In recent years we have been told the poor don't need psychiatry and case work, don't want family planning assistance, and would find higher education irrelevant. In a recent editorial we pointed out the dangers of this attitude with respect to higher education, the resulting tendency to cheapen and vocationalize that product when the poor can no longer be discouraged from insisting on a part of it.

"Now that the poor are demanding expanded health services and Medicare costs a lot of money, we are faced with a new and very interesting position that downgrades the value of medical care.

"A *New York Times* article reports expert after expert arguing that the most significant way to improve health care is not through more medical services: rather, it is through changing the environment, upgrading janitorial services in the slums in the belief that 'Man for man, a good building superintendent can do more for the health of most East Harlem residents than a doctor.' "

Dr. Riessman decries the argument that we can do just as well with fewer doctors, and he emphasizes the need for the skills of physicians and psychiatrists. While he certainly agrees that cultural, psychological, environmental and sociological factors are decisive in the improvement of the health of the people, he also points out that:

"Blaming the environment and society successfully avoids the problem by expanding it. It's a magnificent displacement. If it is a question of all the environment, if all society needs to be changed, then the problem becomes so big that it is impossible to deal with it in the specific arena in which the adequacy and quality of services are in question. Interestingly enough, we in the middle class who have all the services—medical care, higher education, psychotherapy—are not giving them up too rapidly. . . .

"Currently, in response to the demands of the poor for more service, we are hearing arguments for large-scale provision of services on a much cheaper basis. So, in higher education we get an escalation of external degree programs and work-study programs in which students do not have to be on campus. Health care is to be provided at far less cost by paramedics, rather than by doctors. Mental health aides can dispense mental health services on a less expensive basis. Legal services are to be provided by neighborhood people and lawyers in training.

"My point is not that good service cannot be provided in this manner, but that the less expensive way of doing things seems to be found only when it comes to the needs of the poor. The question is then, What should be done about old services for the poor and the need for better ones for everyone?"

Dr. Riessman makes several other important points, but one more I would like to quote.

"If a service like medical care needs to be combined with preventive approaches and other social environmental changes, combine it, but don't substitute the larger approach for the smaller one."

Over the past decade, Dr. Riessman's thinking has been in advance of the field in general and I think that here he is anticipating the growing awareness on the part of the public that the poor may be stuck with poorer services.

There is need for the broad skills of a psychiatrist in mental health services. Many changes are going to take place as a consequence of the redefinition of psychiatric treatment. It has been pointed out by several observers that the old hierarchical order in which groups are placed as if standing on a ladder will give way to a mosaic in which groups coexist and interact on a horizontal plane, and in which all are relatively equal. I think that this will be true in the whole health field.

However, one must keep in mind certain fundamental historical and political aspects of the United States (11). In addition to our pluralism, pragmatism and veneration of change, there is a tendency to change by accretion. New forms are added "on top" while the old are preserved "below." Thus as new forms emerge with the redefinition of psychiatric treatment, it is incumbent upon professionals to join together with all other groups concerned in the delivery of mental health services—particularly the consumers. In this creative action, new delivery systems can be developed that will be superior and more effective because of combined input from the various groups. Conversely, by not joining, by not anticipating new systems, professionals may find themselves bound down by an unsatisfactory system—unsatisfactory because of their failure to participate in its creation.

REFERENCES

1. Turner, R. H. The Theme of Contemporary Social Movements. *Br. J. Sociol.* 20: 390, 1969.
2. Wyckert, J. Mental Patients Get a Rights Bill. *Miami Herald*, Feb. 8, 1973, p. 22.
3. American Hospital Association. Statement on a Patient's Bill of Rights, Jan. 8, 1973.
4. Reich. Care of the Chronically Mentally Ill: A National Disgrace. *Am. J. Psychiatry* 130: 1973.
5. Langsley. California Hospitals. Letter in *Psychiatr. News* 8: Aug. 1, 1973, p. 2.
6. Freedman, A. M. Critical Psychiatry: A New and Necessary School. *Hosp. Community Psychiatry*, 24: Dec. 1973.
7. Schaar, J. The Case for Patriotism. *American Review: Number Seventeen*, T. Solotaroff, editor. New York: Bantam Books, 1973, pp. 59–99.
8. Engel, G. The Best and the Brightest—The Missing Dimension in Medical Education. *Pharos* Oct.: 129, 1973.
9. Eisenberg, L. The Future of Psychiatry. *Lancet* no. 7842, Dec. 15, 1973, p. 1371.
10. Riessman, F. When It Comes to the Poor—Suddenly Doctors Are Not the Answer. *J. Soc. Policy* 2, 3: 3, 4, 1971.
11. Freedman, A. M. Historical and Political Roots of the Community Mental Health Centers Act. *Am. J. Orthopsychiatry*, 37: no. 3, April 1967.

chapter **6**

The Emotional, Medical and Legal Reasons for the Special Concern About Psychosurgery

S. I. SHUMAN, PH.D., S.J.D.

The current debate about psychosurgery (PS) is characterized more by irrational extremist views than by any effort to understand the dimensions of the problem. Perhaps this is why the director of the National Institute of Mental Health (NIMH), when he appeared as the first witness before Senator Kennedy's Subcommittee (1) at the session concerning PS, began by saying: I welcome this opportunity to discuss with you, in what I hope is a balanced and rational manner, an issue which has served as a lightning rod for highly emotional responses on both sides of the issue: Should psychosurgery be encouraged or even permitted as a technique to bring about desired therapeutic changes in a patient's behavior." (2) It would not be unfair to say that the extremist views have gone from polar position to polar position with only the smallest concern for the possible alternatives which avoid the unfortunate consequences of either extreme. Dr. Peter Breggin and his allies take the view that all psychosurgical interventions are suspect, if not outright wrong. By way of introduction to his testimony before the Kennedy Subcommittee (to be contrasted with that of Dr. Bertram Brown, quoted above), Dr. Breggin said:

> The theory and practice of behavioral modification is really at the root of psychosurgery, and whether or not Skinner himself supports psychosurgery, his mechanistic, anti-individual, antispiritual view, which I call totalitarian, is what gives justification to the mutilation of the brain and the mind, in the interest of controlling the individual.
>
> Jose Delgado . . . is the chief apologist for psychosurgery politically, and his totalitarian views are very similar to Skinner's.

48

He ridicules the basic American values: Love of the individual, love of liberty, personal responsibility, and the spiritual nature of men.

These men, Skinner and Delgado, the psychosurgeons here today, represent the greatest future threat that we are going to face for our traditional American values, as promoted in the Declaration of Independence and the Bill of Rights. This totalitarianism asks for social control, including social control of the individual, at the expense of life, liberty, and the pursuit of happiness. It determines Jefferson's self-evident truths.

These men, I believe, are doing nothing more than giving us a new form of totalitarianism "in medical and ethical language."

The reliance on professional ethics and medical control over these issues leaves the physicians in charge of the situation. It creates for themselves an elitist power over human mind and spirit. If America ever falls to totalitarianism, the dictator will be a behavioral scientist and the secret police will be armed with lobotomy and psychosurgery. (3)

Not uncharacteristically, many clinicians, relying upon anecdotal successes, urge the very opposite: the doctor, in his unimpeded judgment, should decide what is best for each individual patient, regardless of the kind of intervention which is contemplated. In his testimony before the Kennedy Subcommittee, Dr. O. J. Andy, a neurosurgeon from the University of Mississippi, urged that: "The ethics involved in the treatment of behavioral disorders is no different than the ethics involved in the treatment of all medical problems. The medical problem concerning behavior may have a more direct impact upon society than other medical problems such as cardiac or kidney dysfunction. . . . However, if treatment is desired, it is neither the moral nor the legal responsibility of society to decide what type of treatment should be administered. The ethics for the diagnosis and treatment of behavioral illness should remain in the hands of the treating physicians. . . ." (4)[1] It seems to me that both extremes lead to unattractive consequences, and if we are to avoid these consequences it is necessary to understand that the problem with which we are concerned is not a matter of only or both law or medicine; it is a political problem as well. We are moving into a time when almost all medicine will be regarded as having political dimensions, and I refer not merely to the delivery of health care but also to the specific interventions which doctors recommend, be it prescription of an aspirin or a surgical intervention on the brain.

Little imagination is required to appreciate that, although psycho-

---

[1] Dr. Andy did concede that the patient and his relatives do have a role. He said: "The ethics for the diagnosis and treatment of the behavioral illness should remain in the hands of the treating physicians who are qualified to treat the illness, and the patient, the relatives and designated friends who are vitally interested in the patient's illness and well being."

surgery is at this moment in the forefront of biomedical ethics, it will not be long before much of medicine is subjected to comparable consideration and attack. Surely this will be true for all forms of psychiatric intervention. Even if one does not go all the way with Dr. Thomas Szasz (5), it is easy to appreciate why psychotherapy will be a natural target for bioethical concern once we recognize, as we must, that psychotherapeutic interventions are at least as significant in terms of personality modification and behavior control as are surgical interventions on the brain. In addition, one need but read lightly in the literature of psychiatry to recognize the significance of psychopharmacological interventions and the capacity which is presently available for behavior modification and control by the use of psychotropic drugs. As stated in the 1973 Department of Health, Education and Welfare (HEW) publication which the NIMH prepared, *Psychosurgery: Perspective on a Current Issue*, "Although psychosurgery is a powerful means of changing behavior, the ethical problems posed by the modification of behavior with drugs or psychotherapy are probably of greater import because these means of control are available to a much wider range of potential 'abusers' than are the techniques of psychosurgery." (6) Indeed, I am startled by the fact that psychosurgery is regarded as the prime target by many of the contemporary "reformers." If all the neurosurgeons in the country were laid end to end and worked 24 hours a day, the number of surgical procedures which they could "inflict upon their victims" is minuscule compared to the number of behavior modification victims who could be reached by drug-dispensing doctors.[2] I leave aside here the even more serious problem about behavior modification drugs dispensed by physicians untrained in psychiatry and also leave aside the still more serious problem of such drugs prescribed for young children, even by so-called child psychiatrists, let alone the problem about such drugs when prescribed by pediatricians.

---

[2] Senator Kennedy questioned Dr. Heath of Tulane about his work with implanted electrodes and asked him, ". . . How are we to know that [this technique is] always going to be used constructively, positively?"

Dr. Heath: For one thing, about a million dollars worth of equipment is required for our studies, as well as a large number of highly skilled personnel.
Sen. Kennedy: What about in five years or so? Is it that complex from an engineering viewpoint?
Dr. Heath: I think it is probably too complex. I do not think you will have to worry about too many being done. By these technics, we can work with one or two patients a year at the most. I cannot conceive of it being done off the cuff simply and quickly. I hope we can come up with less complex procedures in the future.
Sen. Kennedy: Should we not be concerned about mass application?
Dr. Heath: I do not see any cause for concern of mass application of such technics. I think drugs do have marked effects and they are readily available. I think they will continue to be a problem unless their use can be effectively controlled. (7)

Thus we see that the current attack upon psychosurgery is but the smallest tip of a large iceberg, since the infliction of a psychosurgical procedure is a rarity compared to the daily assault upon integrity and personality which can and does occur in so many other ways.[3] From hardly unavoidable exposure to blaring radios, from non-news newspapers and from virtually inevitable exposure to television, we are constantly subjected to behavior modification techniques which are often more subtle, more insidious, more dangerous, less readily controllable and more obnoxious than the psychosurgical procedures carried out by even marginally competent, reasonably sincere doctors. We would have to construct the image of a money-hungry surgeon inflicting a procedure on a brain merely for mercenary reasons in order to come near the kind of danger which confronts us through compulsory public education which is characteristically irresponsible in the precise sense of "irresponsible" relevant to the arguments about regulating PS: "irresponsible" as meaning no public accountability. For radio, television, the press and for communication media in general, including compulsory education, there are virtually no

---

[3] Dr. Willard Gaylin, President of the Hastings Institute, in his appearance before the Kennedy Subcommittee, began this way:

"I think behavior control is an enormously serious problem that has not been attended to adequately; that it needs a kind of regulation that is not at present available, that some of these are legislative, and some of these are not legislative; some of them are already indicated and designed and some have still to be researched.

"About three years ago the Hastings Institute began to be concerned about the prospects of behavioral control technology. It was seen as roughly analogous to the situation of ecology before that term was invented. In those days technologists were concerned about urban crowding, marine biologists were concerned about the rivers and waterways, etc. yet there was not an awareness that these isolated people were dealing with similar problems.

"Behavior control is seen by many of us in the field as a problem arising in a similarly disparate way. Psychosurgeons are beginning to do more meticulous and detailed operations for purposes of behavior modification. There are new drugs becoming much more refined than the old ups and downs we used to have, and there is the increasing impact of television (with an estimate of 4 year olds watching 40 to 60 hours per week). Total institutions are shaping people; the nature of the response to Dr. Skinner's book with its "recommendation for mass social engineering" indicated the seriousness of the problem.

"So we undertook a kind of research, beginning with what we thought was the simplest and narrowest form of behavior control—psychosurgery. I still feel psychosurgery is probably attended to much more than is warranted in terms of its real threat to manipulation of the population as compared with some of the other things. . . .

"It seems unlikely, if there were some plot to take over the country by a totalitarian, to use some of the ideas suggested today, that psychosurgery would be the method of choice. I doubt that they would find the most efficient technique for mass control would be planting electrodes on a population of 200 million, or psychosurgery, when they have access to a limited national television, and to schools with compulsory education, to psychological inputs and to drugs, all of which afford a more convenient, cheaper, economic mass method of manipulation." (8)

institutional mechanisms for any kind of public accountability. Nor is there any such accountability for medicine in general, let alone for such potentially more serious psychologically invasive "medical" therapies as psychotherapy, chemotherapy, electrical stimulation of the brain (ESB), etc.

Despite the fact that the "public accountability" issue involves many icebergs and even many more serious ones than PS, we shall today focus upon the tip of just this one particular iceberg. In doing so, we ask first, "What is it about PS which makes it such an emotionally hot issue?" It may well be the case that surgery for the correction of a hernia has higher mortality and morbidity rates than does any current stereotoxic PS intervention. Why then are we not at least equally hot about hernia surgery?

THE BRAIN IS SPECIAL

Although the metaphor seems to confuse proctology and neurology, at least part of the reason for the intense concern with PS is based upon the belief that "the seat of the soul is the brain." As is often the case in trying to translate feelings into words, it is difficult to be precise about just what is intended. Nonetheless it is just such feelings which do play an important role in the attack upon PS, especially with Dr. Breggin, who does seem to have some view about the "essence" of what is human existing in the brain. To use his own language: ". . . What goes on in your mind is a very different thing from what goes on in your kidney or your heart. Blood passes through your heart and circulates in a rather limited fashion. I believe your eternal spirit passes through your brain and lives there for a while and then goes on. Tampering here in the brain is considerably different than tampering with the heart or the lungs. It must impair the expression of your spiritual self." (9) Just why our "spiritual self" is more nearly a function of brain tissue than say, of heart, eye or hand tissue, is hard to understand unless we do recognize, as I think we should, that "brain" in these contexts functions as an intellectual construct for something closer in meaning to character or personality than as a label for those 2 pounds of tissue found inside the skull. Writing in the *Saturday Review/World*, in an exceptionally well-balanced presentation, Dr. Richard Restak, a neurologist, said: ". . . The brain is the essence of what we refer to as personality. . . ." (10) Understood this special way, the "sanctity of the brain" theory begins to make some sense, and we better understand what may be meant by those who defend such views.

In the course of a discussion about PS under the auspices of the Hastings Institute, the director of the Institute, Dr. Willard Gaylin, a psychiatrist, said this about why PS is special: "To a psychiatrist at least, the fact that [psychosurgery] could produce this much passion, this much vitriol, suggests that it seems substantively different. We may come to the conclusion that there is indeed a substantive difference between entering the brain and manipulating it artificially as distinguished from manipulating it with ideas." (11) Dr. Perry London, a professor of psychology and psychiatry, added this: "But there is something about this new technology that is different from most of the issues of public versus private interests which have preoccupied men in the past. Unlike compulsory education, unlike vaccination, unlike the traditional domain of conflict between the state and the individual, the arena of discourse here is the executive apparatus of the individual." (11) In this same discussion, Prof. Robert Neville, a philosopher much concerned with behavioral science added this:

> The brain, I think, should be conceived as a special environment for the person. Behavior-control techniques, specially these, seem to me to be altering the environment to make possible certain personal actions or certain personal continuities, careers, certain highly prized human emotions and the like. By conceiving of the brain as an environment that inhibits or fosters these human activities, we can conceive the techniques relative to the freedom and values of the person. The question has been raised of the privacy of the brain in the wider environment. There are lots of ways of defining privacy but it seems to me that in the social context, privacy is something that people demand for certain spheres of their life, and that society grants. Individuals and society may not always agree. Sometimes we would not like to have our brain be private, if, in fact, we can be freer, better, or cured of disease by intrusion.
>
> I'm quite confused myself about the particular values used for defining what ought to be recognized as the private sphere. But it seems to me that the techniques we're discussing now raise two important practical questions. Modifying the brain, since it's the most intimate environment for our humanly prized emotions and thought, is likely to have more pervasive effects than modifying certain other kinds of environment. (12)

Dr. Herbert G. Vaughan, Jr., a professor of neurology, added this: "My experience as a neurologist is that people do consider the brain to be one of the areas in which the possibility of a surgical or physical procedure is most feared. Is there, within each of us, perhaps inborn, some fear that requires us to protect ourselves against encroachment upon the brain?" (13)

In a terse dozen words, Dr. Jose Delgado, professor of neurophysiology and author of the well-known book *The Physical Control of the Mind*, restored the issue: "The inviolability of the brain is only a social construct, like nudity." (13)

No matter how presented, and even if there is something arresting about the "seat of the soul" theory, the problem remains of trying to formulate with language just what is meant. Is there some advance in clarity or understanding when instead of speaking about the sanctity of the mind we speak instead about "the spiritual self" (Breggin), "a substantive difference" (Gaylin), "the executive apparatus" (London), "a special environment" (Neville), "the privacy of the brain" (Neville) or about "inborn" fears of "encroachment upon the brain" (Vaughan)?

Did Senator Kennedy learn anything as to what is special about the brain from Dr. Bertram Brown's answer? Referring to "thought control, a la *1984* or *Clockwork Orange*," the Senator asked the Director of the NIMH, "Is there any validity to those fears?" Dr. Brown answered: "I think there is great validity in the sense that there is something special indeed about the brain. There is something very special about experimenting on the brain. And the anxiety of course is very deep in terms of the control of feelings, thought and behavior. There is validity in the depth of concern with taking cognizance of the need of troubled people to receive help, of the need for us to develop more knowledge in order to treat these people; and in order to treat people with these difficulties, we must deal with that valid set of anxieties." (14)

By recourse to varying metaphors and with varying degrees of "poetic" language we see brilliant men struggling to use language to give public life to a *feeling* they wish to share. I do not wish to be misunderstood to be saying that such exercises in communication are somehow wrong—whatever "wrong" might mean in such contexts. On the contrary, I want rather to suggest that precisely because of the need to deal publicly and not privately with this matter of PS, we should better content ourselves with recognizing that, even if there is some deeper layer of experience (incapable of expression by ordinary language) which supports the inviolability of the brain thesis, it is as Delgado said: only a social construct. I would prefer to say, the thesis is the expression of an attitude which deserves recognition and possibly even protection, despite the fact that there is no "scientific" basis for the attitude and despite the fact that it is incapable of clear articulation in ordinary, nonpoetic, nonmetaphorical language.

The conclusion which I draw regarding the inviolability thesis is based upon the following principle: Even if unjustified, widely shared moral feelings deserve at least as much respect and protection as can be accorded them without compromising equally important feelings, whether or not the latter are more justified. Applying this principle to the PS issue implies that there should be at least such public accountability as will suffice to avoid the "horror stories"—needless brain surgery, surgery performed on young or otherwise incompetent persons unprotected by adequate legal institutions, and experimental human brain surgery initiated prematurely or otherwise scientifically unjustified. In addition, the principle suggests that there should be not just this minimum accountability element, but that institutional mechanisms should maximize public accountability whenever it can be done without compromising other important considerations, even if they are morally or scientifically more justifiable than the inviolability thesis. Applying this principle to the inviolability thesis would warrant the creation and imposition of as much accountability machinery as can be developed consistent with those "other important considerations." As regards PS these other considerations would include some which are moral (e.g. try to minimize human suffering), some which are scientific (e.g. try to conquer the last great medical frontier—the functioning of the brain) and some which are both (e.g. try not to discourage the search for new knowledge).

In short, even if the inviolability thesis is incapable of scientific formulation or justification, it deserves at least as much recognition as is regularly accorded other "social constructs." To use Delgado's example, we do protect community attitudes about nudity, and it is surely not irrational to believe that widely shared community sentiments about the "seat of the soul" deserve no less. Just as there is neither logical nor scientific connection which moves from tissue to body to nudity, so too are there no such connections in the movement from brain tissue to mind to soul. But in neither case should the absence of logical or scientific connection imply that the "social construct"—the attitude—*therefore* be regarded as unworthy of legal protection.

PSYCHOSURGERY IS IRREVERSIBLE

The second major reason for the intense moral and social concern about PS is based upon somwhat more scientific grounds. But here too there are serious difficulties in trying carefully to formulate just what is involved. The thesis here is that PS is irreversible. In the course of the Hastings discussion mentioned above where the participants were trying to discover what is special about PS, the point about irreversibility was made by Dr. E. A. Bering, Jr., from the National Institute of Neurological Diseases and Stroke (NINDS). He said: "A very important point that has not been brought out is the difference between a surgical procedure on the brain and electrical stimulation of the brain. By stimulating the brain with electricity one can start and stop certain activities. The procedure is essentially reversible but a surgical lesion destroys part of the brain and is an irreversible, permanent anatomical change. If you don't like the result you're stuck with it and it can only be changed by making the lesion larger or another somewhere else." (15) In the Detroit PS case the plaintiff's primary "technical" witness, Dr. Ayub Ommaya from NINDS, also stressed that PS is irreversible, as did Dr. Breggin when he testified. In the *Saturday Review* article already mentioned, the argument is made this way: "An important distinguishing feature of any psychosurgical procedure is irreversibility. Once the brain tissue is altered, it can never be the same again. Since the brain is the essence of what we refer to as personality, it follows that psychosurgery irrevocably alters personality." (16)

Although the irreversibility thesis may be based upon more scientific considerations than the inviolability thesis, it also suffers from lack of clear and careful formulation. The hypothesis upon which the irreversibility thesis rests is what may be referred to as the integrated brain function theory. However, without exploring that theory, it may be instructive to notice how loose, and therefore misleading, are the above formulations by Drs. Bering and Restak—and I wish to emphasize that neither of these doctors were engaged in the kind of emotional, extremist attack upon PS which has characterized much of the public literature.

Dr. Bering suggests that (unlike PS) ESB *is* reversible because the electrical stimulation can be stopped, whereas a surgical lesion destroys "part of the brain" and is therefore a "permanent anatomical change." Similarly, Dr. Bertram S. Brown testifying before the Kennedy Subcommittee said: "There are some who would also criticize, with some reason, the changing of behavior by stimulating the brain through implanted electrodes, even though this is a less drastic treatment because it does not cause irreversible damage to the brain." (17) While I shall not try to marshal the technical evidence here, I do believe there are sound scientific reasons for questioning: (a) whether electrical stimulation alone can cause "permanent anatomical change," and (b) whether destruction of brain tissue is necessarily either (*1*) a permanent or (*2*) an anatomical change. There is reason to believe that electrical stimulation of a certain intensity and/or of a certain duration, or of a lesser intensity but with a certain frequency, may cause as much permanent anatomical change as a surgical lesion. There is also reason to question the concept of permanent anatomical change, since it may well be that in the above contexts it is either trivially true or false. It is trivially true in the sense that, by definition, any tissue destruction is tissue destruction and therefore, if "permanent anatomical change" means only tissue destruction, then cutting one's fingernails is also a "permanent anatomical change." If this is all that is meant by the irreversibility thesis, then surely every surgical intervention and probably every chemical intervention and possibly every psychotherapeutic intervention, is equally a permanent anatomical change.

It is not urged here that the irreversibility thesis *need* be thus trivialized, but rather I am trying to suggest that the usual formulation of the thesis, or rather the lack of formulation, does not provide much in the way of clarification. In Dr. Restak's generally excellent *Saturday Review* article we see again how the statement of the thesis avoids the real problems. He writes that a PS procedure is irreversible because (*1*) altered brain tissue can never be the same, and (*2*) since the brain is the essence of personality, (*3*) an altered brain necessarily produces an irrevocably altered personality. Despite having the appearance of a perfect syllogism, there are reasons for questioning both the content of the minor premise and conclusion, as well as the logic of the argument. As we saw above, (*1*) is either trivially true or subject to considerable doubt. There is reason to believe that even if what is altered is therefore altered irreversibly, altering some brain tissue does not therefore necessarily imply that brain function is (a) altered, (b) altered irrevocably, or (c) altered permanently. It is entirely plausible (i.e. there is scientific evidence to support the belief) that the destruction of some brain tissue (a) does not alter brain function, that (b) some alterations in function which do occur are reversible and (c) that some alterations are not permanent. In addition, most important, and indeed absolutely cardinal for the development of a rational analysis about the PS issue, is the need to recognize that even if step *1* in the irreversibility argument was correct and even if we grant some plausibility to the major premise, step *2*, despite all the reasons discussed above in connection with the several different formulations of the inviolability thesis, step *3* would still *not* be the logically necessary conclusion. Again using Dr. Restak's argument as the model, what I am urging is that even if his (*1*) was true and even if we give some creditability and scientific meaning to (*2*), it would still not be the case (except in the trivial, definitional sense) that irrevocably altered brain tissue necessarily produces irrevocably altered personality. Again, without canvassing the available, elaborate scientific evidence, I would advance just three reasons in support of my argument. It has yet to be demonstrated that: (a) the loss of some brain tissue *necessarily* produces personality change, or (b) that the brain is incapable of replacing lost tissue without change in personality, or (c) in view of the fact that for at least some functions we may have "two brains," even if some tissue is lost and not replaced, irrevocable loss of tissue necessarily produces an irrevocably altered personality.

It should be clearly noticed here, that in one important sense, the entire irreversibility argument is irrelevant to the core question, should PS be regulated and, if so, how? Although there are some surgical procedures which are reversible and some in which there may be a choice between a procedure which is reversible and one which is not (e.g. some kinds of sterilization), probably almost all surgical procedures are undertaken in the hope that the results will be irreversible. Indeed, one measure of the attractiveness of a procedure may be the probability that the consequences of the intervention will be permanent and not reversible. In other words, the far more important question about a surgical intervention, PS or otherwise, is not just the matter of its permanence, but rather the question of its consequences. Even if a PS intervention did always and necessarily result in a permanent alteration of personality, that seems to me to miss the real question. If the change is undesirable or even very likely to be undesirable for social, political, moral or anatomical reasons, it ought not be produced even if reversible; whereas if the change is desirable, irreversibility is a virtue. In other words, if the change is undesirable, reversibility will not make the change desirable. The core question is not reversibility, but desirability of the change. If personality changes resulting from PS are very likely to be bad, or even likely to be undesirable, then such interventions are surely objectionable and hardly less so if reversible. Or, to put the matter affirmatively: only after there is adequate scientific reason to believe that the change will surely or at least probably be desirable and permanent or at least permanent enough to warrant the discomfort, risk, etc., should the intervention be considered as a potentially proper treatment modality.

SOME SO-CALLED MEDICAL REASONS FOR CONCERN ABOUT PSYCHOSURGERY

In what follows I shall try to show what are some of the nonmedical aspects of the so-called medical questions about PS. This is done so that we may better understand why lawyers and judges are often unwilling to have only doctors decide these questions.

There are at least the following 10 major "medical" reasons why socially conscious and conscientious people are especially nervous about the clinical practice of PS. (1) The integrated brain function theory; (2) the "medical" meaning of causal connection; (3) the evidence of organicity; (4) the accuracy of the lesion; (5) the identification of a syndrome which warrants a *medical* intervention; (6) the inadequacy of testing instruments for ascertaining the specific effects of a PS intervention; (7) the possibility that no intersubjectively communicable testing mechanism could be constructed for uncovering all of the important consequences of a PS intervention; (8) the possibilities for adverse side effects; (9) the possible unknowability of long range effects, genetic or otherwise; and (10) the meager scientifically acceptable literature about general human brain function and the virtual absence of any such literature as to the effects thereon of a specific lesion in the brain. If these 10 problems were not enough we could add even more subtle matters such as (11) the connection between epileptic and para-epileptic phenomena[4]; (12) the medical treat-

---

[4] Testifying before the Kennedy Subcommittee, Dr. Brown said:

"The surgical treatment of epilepsy, while in one sense a form of psychosurgery

ment of overt conduct even in the absence of medical evidence of abnormality; (*13*) the relevance of psychiatric evaluation in determining the appropriateness of a nonpsychotherapeutic intervention; (*14*) the relative efficacy of alternative treatment modalities in constructing a hierarchy of treatment choices.

Clearly, it is important that each of these issues be carefully dealt with if a rational strategy is to be developed for dealing with the PS question. However, I shall not attempt to do so here but instead will only try to show why the analysis of these seemingly "medical" questions generates important legal and philosophical concerns.

In order better to appreciate what is here at stake, it may be helpful if instead of proceeding abstractly we deal with a case situation. The case we will consider is closely modeled upon the one which was involved in the Detroit PS litigation. In that case John Doe (as he is identified throughout the proceedings) was the first person identified (largely on the basis of chart review) as a subject who might be a suitable candidate for the research project. The project (as it concerned John Doe) was directed

---

since behavioral symptoms are altered, should be excluded from this discussion when the disease can be clearly diagnosed and there is convincing evidence that epilepsy is caused by organic pathology in the brain.

"Some investigators have suggested that certain episodic behavioral manifestations may appear as a symptom of epilepsy. The ethical aspects of work in this borderline area are obviously troublesome, and I will return to this subject later." (18)

The NIMH report about PS contains a similar suggestion:

"The surgical treatment of epilepsy, while in one sense a form of psychosurgery since behavioral symptoms are altered, should be excluded from this discussion when the disease can be clearly diagnosed and there is convincing evidence that epilepsy is caused by organic pathology in the brain. Of course any other neurosurgical treatment to repair or remove damaged brain tissue, or to remove tumors, is not psychosurgery." (19)

Even Dr. Breggin would permit brain surgery for the treatment of epilepsy.

Sen. Kennedy: Epilepsy?
Dr. Breggin: That would not be psychosurgery. The definition of psychosurgery is to destroy normal brain tissue to control the emotions or behavior or, a diseased tissue when the disease has nothing to do with behavior of the man is trying to control.
For example, some of Dr. Andy's patients may be brain damaged, but that is not what makes them violent. It is just a good excuse to mutilate further: damage, damage, damage, until you get the calming effect.
So if you are operating on epilepsy, you are not talking about psychosurgery. (20)

What is interesting about this unanimity of view is that it would be very difficult to differentiate on the basis of available scientific hard data just what is surgically treatable epilepsy as contrasted to some cases of para-epileptic phenomena. In addition, it would also be difficult to lay down just what is the clinical syndrome of epilepsy which justifies a surgical intervention. But apparently some 2,000 temporal lobectomies (retroactively) bestow "scientific" credibility upon the existence of the requisite syndrome.

towards the evaluation of the subject as candidate for an amygdalotomy, and if deemed advisable such a procedure was to be carried out.

John Doe had a childhood history which included successive foster home placements, possibly because he was "unmanageable." There was also a possibility that he had had measles encephalitis. As a teenager he had exhibited evidence of some unusual aggressivity, largely connected with sexuality. At about age 17 he allegedly attacked a girl with a mallet in order to rape her, and this led to his commitment to a state hospital for psychiatric evaluation. While there he apparently asked a student nurse to take him downstairs and allegedly strangled her with his tie and then had intercourse with the dead body. He was committed to an institution for the criminally insane pursuant to the "criminal sexual psychopath" statute. In the course of the Detroit PS trial, the statute was declared unconstitutional, and John Doe was released into society. He had already been confined for about 17 years and, although there had been minor episodes of aggression, either because of the character of his confinement or for other reasons, he did not have a significant history of uncontrollable aggression while confined. Apparently on several occasions during those years of confinement he had been alone with women.

After his selection as a participant in the research project, John Doe was transferred from the state hospital for the criminally insane to the research institution and was there subjected to very extensive psychological and biological testing as well as neurological evaluation. In addition he was under virtually constant observation by a trained professional staff. While there were no significant biological findings, the psychological testing did strongly support the belief that he lacked the ability to control his aggressivity, and his ward behavior indicated that there was sexual pathology, as did the psychiatric evaluation. Throughout his confinement, both before coming to the research clinic and while there, the patient complained of physical illness and inability to continue to function. Apparently this was precipitated by severe frustration or by some other emotionally disturbing experience. The surface electroencephalograph (EEG) was inconclusive, as it so often is, and the decision was made to proceed to depth EEG study of the subject.

Was the decision to initiate depth EEG studies justified?

In the Detroit case, plaintiffs supported by their technical (medical) witnesses argued that it was not, because: (1) depth EEG studies are, if not entirely worthless, of dubious evidentiary significance; (2) the high rate of morbidity, if not also mortality, connected with depth EEG work mitigated against such studies, especially if they would anyway be inconclusive; (3) even if the depth recordings did support or even strongly suggest organicity in the tissue of the amygdala, that would not support a decision to proceed to a lesion; (*4*) since the patient had no such history of epileptic seizure as would warrant a lesion on the brain, the lesion on the amygdala would be unwarranted even if there was evidence of organicity there, since it had not been proven that the patient did suffer from any medical syndrome (since uncontrollable aggressivity, it was argued, is not such a syndrome); (*5*) even if uncontrollable aggressivity were identified as a medical syndrome, it had not been proven that a lesion on the amygdala would be therapeutic; (*6*) even if such a lesion might be therapeutic, it had not been proven that the cure would not be worse than the disorder (the adverse side effects argument); and finally (*7*), it was also argued that since surgery, let alone brain surgery, ought in general be the treatment modality of desperation and not of choice, it had to be proven that less intrusive therapies had been tried and failed, or would fail if tried.

Can anyone fail to see that each of these arguments raises issues which are not only or even primarily scientific, but rather that each of these arguments exudes philosophical, moral, legal, social and political concerns? Clearly, questions are generated about the meaning of causation, about what is evidence, about what constitutes good evidence and good enough evidence, about brain function theory and the isolatability of function, about criteria for the identification of a medical disorder, about whether every disorder is therefore a medical disorder, about what it means to say that something is a medical disorder, about how to ascertain whether electrochemical change is improvement, about how to weigh electrochemical improvement against biological improvement, about how to decide whether biological improvement is a socially or politically attractive gain, about the allocation of scarce resources, etc.

Let me illustrate one aspect of the above by an anecdote from the Detroit trial. The plaintiffs called no witness qualified in neurology or in EEG. The only witness called by the plaintiffs who had any kind of scientific background even remotely related to PS was a neurosurgeon from the NINDS whose speciality is cerebrovascular disease and head injuries. He testified that there was no causal connection between a lesion in the amygdala and the control of aggressivity. He took this view largely because of his belief about the integrated brain theory and despite the reports in the medical literature of some 500 amygdalotomies or amygdalectomies. It had been this literature which had largely influenced the decision to undertake this project since the reported cases do suggest a connection between the amygdala and aggression. In my cross examination of this witness, I wanted to try and discover what he meant, as a medical scientist, by causation. What follows is taken from the trial transcript.

Q. ... Is there some special sense of causal connection applicable in medical research?

A. No, it's exactly the same. It's the same as is used in physics, chemistry, science.

Q. ... If you place a depth electrode and you stimulate the electrode, and each time you do so the subject twitches in a certain place, would you say there's a causal connection?

A. There may be.

Q. What would be the evidence which would lead you to believe there is not a causal connection ... ?

A. I think, as I described earlier, you'd have to show it in a significant number of observations, and you would have to show it in a significant set of observations, such that in a given group of patients, the same electrode in the same place, confirmed by pathological evidence, really did the same thing. Only then can you really accept a hypothesis as a fact, as a law, as a theory.

Q. In other words, a causal connection is not something which is determined by a litmus paper test, there's a body of evidence which has to be accumulated. Is that your view?

A. A syndrome is established at various levels.

Q. No, no, I'm not asking—I'm asking you about a causal connection.

A. A causal connection is established at various levels.

Q. Right. In other words, the level at which you establish it and how you establish it depends on the purpose for which you're going to use that causal connection?

A. Correct.

Q. And so that your theory, then, is that there is no connection between electrical abnormality and aggressive behavior for what purpose?

A. For defining a syndrome in patients. In other words, there is no data showing there are, say, 20 patients who invariably do this episodically violent behavior and who have this bad an EEG. This is not available. If you have that evidence, I'd like to know it.

Q. ... If, after a surgical procedure has been performed on the brain, the patient is better, does that show there is a causal connection between the surgical procedure and the condition which was sought to be alleviated by that procedure?

A. Not necessarily. (21)

At another time, in connection with his direct testimony, the witness was questioned by one of the judges. The following is also taken from the trial trancript.

Judge Gilmore: ... You say no syndrome has been defined for neurosurgery to affect behavior. Now, are you speaking of the experiment in Michigan or are you speaking generally? Would you elaborate on that just a little bit?

The Witness: Yes. It has been proposed that such a syndrome exists. In other words, the hypothesis has been advanced that there exists—and this is in all— I am talking generally now—that there exists a group of patients who are— have electrical abnormality in their brain and are subject to episodic bursts of violence. This is an idea that has been floating around for many, many years. There are patients in whom this association is found.

What has not been defined is that this is a causal relationship, that there is such a causal relationship between the electrical abnormality measured—or between the physical abnormality and the resulting aggression, the aggression being an episodic causal invariable consequence of that abnormality.

What has only been shown is an association, not a causal relationship. And until you show or have evidence for causal relationship, there is no syndrome in the clinical sense.

The Court: How do you show causal relationship in a situation like that?

The Witness: Well, it depends upon the category. . . .(22)

What we see here is a competent medical scientist, who I believe was conscientious even if wrong, struggling to make sense to scientifically untrained judges of conceptual material which is not scientific. Whether he did much worse than Aristotle, Kant or Hume in trying to explain causation is arguable. Indeed, I was asked after this particular court session whether I had intended to conduct a cross examination or a seminar in philosophy! The conceptual constructions upon which the doctor relied in trying to deal with the questions were at least these: (*1*) causal connection, (*2*) hypothesis, (*3*) law, (*4*) theory, (*5*) levels of causal connection, (*6*) purpose, (*7*) association, (*8*) syndrome, (*9*) relation between purpose and causation, and (*10*) relation between syndrome and association or causal connection. Would anyone wish to argue that the elucidation of all, some or even any of these conceptual constructions was only or primarily a matter of medical science?

THE ROLE OF THE MEDICAL EXPERT WHEN THE JUDGES PRACTICE MEDICINE

The argument that none of these matters is only a matter of medical knowledge would be much reinforced if we were to examine the way in which the defendants and their witnesses responded to each of the above seven arguments raised by the plaintiffs. However, in the hope that there is no need to make more convincing what is already clear, we proceed to consider an exceedingly important "lesson" learned from the Detroit case about the judicial management of medicine. By referring to the judicial management of medicine I do not mean to suggest that any court involvement with the practice of medicine amounts to management, or even that judicial management would necessarily be bad. Rather the point here is that one reason why the Detroit PS case did attract so much international attention is because we had one of the very rare cases in which the courts were asked to undertake the management of virtually a whole field of medicine. This is to be contrasted with the usual kind of judicial intervention when an individual patient seeks redress from an individual doctor or institution for an alleged specific wrong. But the important lesson referred to relates not to the unusual character of the judicial intervention, but rather to the role of the technical, scientific, medical witnesses when judges are asked to practice medicine. It is just that the misuse of the medical witness is particularly easy to see in the Detroit PS case because of the unusual role the court was asked to play. From a limited legal perspective the court had as its primary concern the question of whether an involuntarily committed mental patient or his guardian could, under certain circumstances, consent to a PS intervention. However, in order to decide this question it was deemed necessary to consider the "status" of PS, and it is in this area, and not that of consent, where we are able to perceive how a judicial proceeding can be expected to function as the institutional mechanism for "evaluating" the current status of a medical procedure.

As to the utility of depth EEG studies, the defendants called as their principal technical witness the president of the American EEG society, a doctor with very wide experience, board-certified in EEG, etc. They also offered testimony by one of the most distinguished neurosurgeons, a doctor who had recently retired from his important academic position, a man with an international reputation. In addition, one of the named defendants, also board-certified in EEG, testified on this subject; his expertise in this field was conceded and unquestioned. The single plaintiff's witness (who stated in court that he was not an expert in EEG and not board-qualified in EEG) testified that depth EEG was largely useless and also had a rather high mortality and morbidity rate. He conceded on cross examination that the published literature did not support his estimates as to mortality or morbidity rates, and his statements were flatly contradicted by the other medical experts. He based his statements upon work done at NINDS which, he stated, was as yet unpublished. Although while still under oath he agreed to furnish the court with material in support of his statements, to date none has been furnished. Interestingly, in testifying about the adverse effects of PS, Dr. Breggin also stated that his testimony was not supported by the published literature and, like the other plaintiff witness, he too said that he was relying upon his own unpublished "investigations." Like the other plaintiff witness, while under oath he also agreed to furnish the court with material in support of his views. Again, as with the other witness, none has yet been received.

What we see in regard to these two plaintiff witnesses is one of the most important lessons to emerge from the Detroit PS case. Competent, and I believe sincere, lawyers interested in suppressing some experimental or innovative medical approach are not likely to have too much trouble in finding "experts" with a sufficient paper record to make their views admissible, regardless of how those views are supported or indeed contradicted by the primary criterion for determining what is scientifically acceptable as of a certain time: namely the published scientific literature of the world. Indeed, the effectiveness of Dr. Breggin's advocacy is in large part due to the fact that it is not scientific. Although in his testimony before the Kennedy Subcommittee he referred to his "research papers in the Congressional Records" (23), he did not characterize them that way on cross examination in court. Rather, his "research papers" were there described by him as publications not designed to reach the scientific community. Instead, he said he was trying to present materials for a popular audience. Indeed, no one familiar with his contributions to the Congressional Record, or elsewhere, will have any difficulty in seeing why his distorted, prejudicial review of the PS literature has not appeared and would not be printed in any scientific journal.

It is very important that I not be misunderstood here. I am *not* here criticizing Dr. Breggin for resorting to Madison Avenue techniques in order to attain a goal which he sees as political (as contrasted to medical). Dr. Breggin in his testimony before the Kennedy Subcommittee (quoted above) made it clear that he sees the problem as a political one. In his closing statement he added: "I believe it is time to give up study. I do not think it is a medical issue. . . ." (24)

In saying that I am not critical of Dr. Breggin's use of Madison Avenue methods to attain a political goal, do not think either that I am praising him for having done so or that I am uncritical of the role he performed either in the Detroit case or with Congress. Whether the end justifies the means in politics, if ever, and if so, when—that is a matter beyond my immediate concern in this paper. Consequently I leave aside here the question about the propriety of a doctor using sales strategy for reaching political goals. However, I am here very much concerned about the medical expert's role and function *qua* medical expert, and hence I am very critical of Dr. Breggin's role in court (and also critical, but less so, of his role before the Kennedy Subcommittee).

I have been commenting about Dr. Breggin because his case is particularly egregious, but what is here urged is no way limited to him or his involvement in the current PS controversy. Rather, the problem is the larger one of separating the medical scientist role from the other roles that doctors play, for example, the role of a concerned and conscientious citizen. Clearly there are cases in which it would be difficult or useless to make a distinction: for example, a doctor sitting on a commision to decide whether a new hospital was warranted in a particular community. But just as there are easy cases in which role differentiations are not worth making or are useless if made, there are also cases at the other polar extreme in which the failure to make and keep different roles separated can only be destructive of important social, political and scientific interests. I think that the medical scientist who gains access as an expert to the institutionalized judicial decision-making process has a professional and political obligation to perform as a scientist and not as a political huckster. If a medical scientist comes into a decision-making institution and says that depth EEG work has a high degree of morbidity or that PS has very severe adverse side effects, the decision-maker should not be required to depend upon the wiles or guiles of opposing counsel to show that in this instance the scientist appears in the politician's clothes. Among medical scientists, psychiatrists have been particularly guilty of playing the double agent role and thus have lent unnecessary additional support to Szasz's attack upon public policy-oriented psychiatry. Of course, no one profession has a monopoly on this double agent strategy, and perhaps lawyers are even more frequent offenders than other professionals because of their willingness to characterize any problem as legal and thus to create the impression that political or social concerns are less relevant. One need not be a Marxist to appreciate that the very contrary is the case, and that legal solutions to a problem either suppress or accommodate specific social and political values: i.e. the legal solution is probably never neutral.

To the contrary, I do believe that there are instances when, even if the medical solution to a problem is also not value neutral, one need still distinguish between the medical scientist and the political fascist who happens also to be a medical scientist. The scientist will contribute to the decision-making process only his expertise if it is on that basis that he enters the process; the fascist will enter the process by creating reasonable expectations in the minds of the decision-makers that he will perform as a scientist, but then instead he performs as a political decision-maker. The scientist, especially when part of an institutional mechanism as specifically structured as a court, will not perform as though his scientific and other roles were necessarily fungible. Of course I am not suggesting that a scientist ceases to be a father or citizen while peering into his microscope. Rather I am suggesting that, despite the need to recognize that attitudes and beliefs affect if not determine perception, it is still possible and sometimes necessary to recognize that the wearing of a white laboratory coat is not a relevant criterion for determining what role the wearer is playing.

Deliberately and even "accidentally" packaging politics and social values as medical science is particularly objectionable because there is virtually no effective way to protect the political decision-maker from the deception. This is particularly true of the institutionalized judicial decision process because the adversary character of the process tends to polarize positions which are then tenaciously defended as if though they were the private property of the witness. In addition, even when the relevant process is legislative and not judicial, the medical fascist is particularly objectionable and difficult to deal with because those medical scientists who are not willing to be politicians about their science characteristically and almost universally will not come forward and participate *even as scientists* in the decisional process. As a result the decision-maker suffers from a double blindness: first, he receives the relevant scientific material as it is deliberately filtered through a political screen and then he is left ignorant as to that material when it is not so filtered.

Although in my opinion there were medical witnesses in the Detroit case who were deliberately evasive and who were willing, indeed anxious, to utilize their medical "status" as a vehicle for advancing political or social values, I do not wish to be misunderstood to have said that, for example, Dr. Breggin deliberately lied under oath. Rather, in my judgment, he failed to perform as a medical expert ought to have performed, and he suffered this failure largely because he did not see that the roles of medical scientist and citizen-politician are not fungible even if they are not always or ever entirely separable.

It may be no excuse to admit that I have knowingly belabored the argument about the role of the medical expert in a judicial proceeding, and of course there is a rich literature on the subject. There is this difference, however. Probably none of this rich literature and almost none of the concern about doctors in court has dealt with the problem in the context of a case in which the judges were to sit as a medical review committee passing on the scientific status of an entire field of medicine. The subject was therefore labored in this context in order to suggest what I hope is now the question in your mind: If there is need to subject PS as a field to regulation, what should "regulation" mean, and is there some better way to achieve such regulation than by the use of the judicial process? As this is not the primary focus of this chapter, I shall only touch upon this question in connection with the last subject we shall here consider: that is, some of the legal reasons for the special concern about PS.

THE "LEGAL" REASONS FOR THE SPECIAL CONCERN ABOUT PSYCHOSURGERY

Although I refer to these as the legal reasons for the special concern about PS, it is clear that, as with the "medical" reasons, there is much that is philosophical. There are at least three important legal-philosophical reasons for the special concern about PS: (*1*) informed consent; (*2*) regulation of patient and procedure selection; and (*3*), social control of new knowledge. Each of these deserves full and careful treatment, and on each there is a good deal of literature. However, here I will develop each of these reasons only enough to show why the regulation of PS has been such an explosive issue.

Informed Consent

In my post-trial brief in the Detroit case, about 70 pages were devoted to the informed consent problem. It was argued that, if informed consent requires that there be competence, knowledge and voluntariness, then almost never is there likely to be any really informed consent, and this will be true regardless of whether (a) the patient is voluntarily hospitalized or committed, (b) the proposed procedure involves brain surgery or foot surgery, (c) the procedure is experimental or well established, or (d), the procedure is innovative or conventional. The court disagreed. In the opinion, the judges write: "We do not agree that a *truly* informed consent cannot be given for a *regular* surgical procedure by a patient, institutionalized or not. . . . But we do hold that informed consent cannot be given by an involuntarily detained mental patient for *experimental psychosurgery* . . ." (my italics) (25). The primary reason advanced by the court for their conclusion is this: "Involuntarily confined mental patients live in an inherently coercive institutional environment. Indirect and subtle psychological coercion has profound effect upon the patient population. Involuntarily confined patients cannot reason as equals with the doctors and administrators over whether they should undergo psychosurgery. They are not able to voluntarily give informed consent because of the inherent inequality in their position." (26) The court had earlier in the opinion advanced the following argument as to competence: "Although an involuntarily detained mental patient may have a sufficient I.Q. to intellectually comprehend his circumstances . . . the very nature of his incarceration diminishes the capacity to consent to psychosurgery. He is particularly vulnerable as a result of his mental condition, the deprivation stemming from involuntary confinement, and the effects of the phenomenon of 'institutionalization.' . . . Institutionalization tends to strip the individual of the support which permit [*sic*] him to maintain his sense of self-worth and the value of his own physical and mental integrity. An involuntarily confined mental patient clearly has diminished capacity for making [*sic*] a decision about irreversible experimental psychosurgery." (27)

Now the question is this: How can one agree, as I do, with virtually everything the court has said about the relation between institutionalization and informed consent, yet strongly reject, as I do, their conclusion? In large part the answer is connected with the italicized adjectives "truly," "regular" and "experimental" in the above quotation from the court in which they state their conclusion.

What possible explanation could there be for believing that a committed patient who enjoys sufficient competence and equality of "bargaining power" to give "truly" informed consent for such complex but non-experimental surgery as a portal-caval shunt for cirrhosis, an internal mammary artery myocardial implant or even an ileostomy for ulcerative colitis suddenly loses that competence and equality because the procedure is experimental PS? Is there *necessarily*, i.e. logically by definition or empirically, some such greater intrinsic complexity or subtlety about any and every experimental PS procedure as compared to any "regular" surgical procedure? The court's answer to this key question is a clear non-sequitur. What they appear to say is that, because as a matter of law the involuntarily committed patient cannot consent to experimental PS, therefore he lacks the requisite capacity. But of course the patient lacks that capacity only after this decision. Therefore, translated into plain English, what the court has said is that these patients lack capacity as a matter of law because the court holds, as a matter of law, that they lack capacity. Since the court was specifically asked to decide the question of whether an involuntarily committed patient can give legally adequate consent for experimental PS, I do not wish to create the impression that the court was wrong for deciding the question. Rather what is wrong is that courts are supposed not only to decide questions but to do so in a particular way: namely by the use of rules, principles and reasons. If all we wanted was a "decision," we could save much effort and money by rolling dice. Unfortunately, in this important case the court did not furnish any reasons for their conclusion. To have done so would have required that the court show why, not as a matter of law but as a matter of fact, any procedures denominated experimental PS are necessarily so much more complex or obscure that a patient sufficiently competent and endowed with equality of bargaining power to understand any "regular" surgical procedure suddenly loses both. In other words, the court should have shown how the nature of the contemplated procedure affects the equality of bargaining power or the patient's competence. To tell us only that the procedure does so as a matter of law is to teach us only that, if the conclusion is put into the premise, it should come as no surprise if it comes out in the conclusion.

The court's method of decision by definition or non-sequitur is illustrated in two further aspects of the opinion as it concerned the consent question. Some 13 involuntarily committed patients from the institution where John Doe had been kept, after reading some newspaper accounts of the pending trial, on their own initiative wrote a letter stating that they did not want to be considered as subjects for the research project. It was suggested that this militated against the argument that institutionalized patients are necessarily so coerced by their environment that they will give consent for any medical procedure. The court apparently thought that it was responding to the argument when they said: "The fact that thirteen patients unilaterally wrote a letter saying they did not want to be subjects of psychosurgery is irrelevant to the question of whether they can consent to that which they are legally precluded from doing." (28) One need not be a Ph.D. in mathematical logic to wince at this substitute for an argument. The court is quite right in saying that the letter is irrelevant if the patients could anyway—as a matter of law—not consent. However, again, the question which the court was supposed to be deciding in this case is precisely whether, as a matter of law, there could be consent. Presuming the answer to the question, in putting the question, hardly seems like a model for rational, principled decision-making.

Exactly the same technique for avoiding the question is used by the court in connection with the very important problem as to whether, and if so, how, a legal guardian could give informed consent for an involuntarily committed patient. Clearly this is a question of the greatest significance and, since this was a specific part of the question put to the court, one would have hoped that the court would at least analyze the matter. Instead, this is how they dispose of the entire subject: "The guardian or parent cannot do that which the patient, absent a guardian, would be legally unable to do." (29) Apart from the fact that this is probably wrong as a matter of law (e.g. could not a guardian effectively execute a contract regarding the management or disposition of a patient's assets, even though the patient "would be legally unable to do so"?), the statement is even more objectionable for the reason already mentioned. Here again the court is deciding by definition or non-sequitur since the very precise question which the court is supposed to decide in this case is whether the patient (or the guardian) could consent. To say that because we will hold, as a matter of law, that the patient cannot consent, therefore the patient cannot consent, is bad enough, but to say that because we will so hold, therefore the guardian cannot consent, clearly is to have left the substantive question untouched.

On the relevant substantive question (Can a guardian consent if the patient cannot?) this is the entire discussion of the court which precedes their conclusion (quoted above): "Equally great problems are found when the involuntarily detained mental patient is incompetent, and consent is sought from a guardian or parent. Although guardian or parental consent may be legally adequate when arising out of traditional circumstances, it is legally ineffective in the psychosurgery situation. The guardian or parent cannot do that which the patient, absent a guardian, would be legally unable to do." (29) The "equally great" refers largely to the notion that: "Institutionalization tends to strip the individual of the support which permit [sic] him to maintain his sense of self-worth and the value of his own physical and mental integrity. An involuntarily confined mental patient clearly has diminished capacity for making [sic] a decision about irreversible experimental psychosurgery." (29) As pointed out above, the conclusion of the court vis-a-vis guardians is logically irrelevant. In addition, it should be clear that it is empirically irrelevant. Granting the truth of all that is said in the last quotation from the opinion (about institutionalization), what is the significance of those factors as regards consent by a guardian? Is it presumed that the guardian has also been institutionalized? Or, on the contrary, does not the question about guardians presume that a guardian will be chosen who does not suffer the disadvantages of his ward? In addition, could not a guardian be chosen who would not only be of equal bargaining power to the doctors, but even superior to them? In the alternative, could it not be required that independent scientific experts be furnished to the guardian so that any gap in bargaining power between him and the doctors is diminished, if not eliminated? Obviously there are many crucial questions which the court never even considered. Yet they did decide that a guardian may not do what the patient cannot do!

We may now better understand how one could agree with virtually everything the court said about the relation between institutionalization (especially when involuntary) and informed consent and yet vigorously reject, as I do, the conclusion that an involuntarily committed patient or the guardian, as a matter of law, cannot give legally adequate consent for a procedure which is denominated as experimental PS. Apart from the fact that the decision of the court is logically defective and apart from the fact that the court clearly failed to take account of important empirical realities, the conclusion of the court about informed consent is objectionable because the court did not even give consistent weight to the realities which it did consider. Had the court done so, we might have had a useful opinion about how to proceed when, for any surgical or medical procedure, a doctor wants to comply with the legal standards relevant to consent obtained from an involuntarily committed patient.

Although the above analysis of the consent issue has been largely legalistic, it is easy to perceive that large social and political problems are lurking just below that legal veneer with which we so often plaster over troublesome matters. Regarding the real social problems about experimental PS, experimental surgery or experimental medicine, have we been helped at all by the informed consent analysis of the Detroit court? It is quite clear that we have not been helped, and this is so because this court was unwilling to confront the difficult, real, social problems. Among these are concerns about what to do with committed patients for whom society is willing to commit enough resources to keep them confined but not enough to do whatever may make them well. And related to this difficult sociopolitical problem is the connected concern about institutional management when scarce resources are deliberately (by legislative decision) withheld from the institution which must nonetheless function. Then there is the further political problem about the so-called basic civil rights of committed mental patients. Does the court's decision about informed consent suppress or protect those rights?

Regulating Patient and Procedure Selection

Although the court's analysis of the civil rights issue was undertaken in support of their conclusion about informed consent, the thrust of their argument relates more to what has been referred to above as the second of the major legal reasons for the special concern about PS. By labeling this reason "regulation of patient and procedure selection," I intend to suggest that among the legitimate reasons which have precipitated the controversy about PS are concerns about who will be regarded as a suitable candidate for some specific surgical intervention. Will anyone qualify for any procedure, if he can afford it? Should no one qualify, regardless of ability to pay? Should entire classes of persons be declared unqualified, as either a matter of law (e.g. those involuntarily committed) or as a matter of social policy which is not primarily legal (e.g. those who are poor, or poor and black)? As you may know, one of the scare pieces in the popular media is an article in *Ebony* suggesting that PS is a new white man's tool for "taming" black people.[5] (30) Here again, even if there is absolutely no evidence whatsoever to support such a view, there may nonetheless be good policy reasons for disqualifying all black people from any PS. Of course, the question will still need to be answered of whether disqualifying black people or those involuntarily committed best serves even their sociopolitical interests, let alone their medical interests. But assuming that political or social interests are better protected by such wholesale group disqualifications, there is the further question of how is it to be decided, and by whom, whether the protected sociopolitical interest is worth whatever may be the loss in biological or psychological health.

Apart from these difficult enough questions, I am troubled even more by the fear that, in declaring entire classes of persons ineligible for any "experimental PS" out of a concern for their civil liberties, we may be asking already unfortunate enough people to suffer still further in order to advance the civil liberties of those who are doing the protecting. Let me illustrate by rearranging slightly the facts involved in the John Doe case which was before the Detroit court. Given all the facts related earlier from the John Doe case history but supposing that he was not committed under

---

[5] The article carries the caption, "New Threat to Blacks" and has the subtitle, "Controversial Operations Are Coming Back as Violence Curbs." On page 68 of the article there is a half-page picture of a black psychiatrist, Dr. Alvin Poussaint, Associate Prof. of Psychiatry, Harvard University Medical School, and he is there quoted as saying: "These brain studies are racist. They say that black people are so animal and savage that whites have to carve on their brains to make them human beings. . . ."

a statute which was declared unconstitutional, what would be the present social-political-legal-biological-psychological position of John Doe? Instead of being free in the community as he is because he was being detained pursuant to an unconstitutional statute, he would be back in a facility for the criminally insane where during each day he would be free to tell himself and the world, "See, the ever vigilant courts in this great land have guaranteed that I can continue to spend the rest of my natural life in confinement safe in the comforting knowledge that no one took advantage of my (legally manufactured) incompetence to consent." Somehow I cannot help feeling that the already long suffering John Does of our society are not getting very much in exchange for those of their civil rights which would supposedly be compromised were they or their guardians, under appropriate circumstances, permitted to give legally adequate consent even for experimental PS. Indeed, when I see cases even worse than those of the lost John Does, in which the person is not only lost and confined but perhaps also self-mutilating or otherwise tormented, I wonder what conceivable social or civil right which they possess would not be worth compromising, even if that were necessary, in order to have just the dim chance of some amelioration of their biological or psychological condition. Even the quite properly cautious NIMH in its 1973 report, *Psychosurgery: Perspective on a Current Issue*, recognizes the need to consider even a lobotomy (and remember the court in Detroit "condemned" all PS—it was not talking about lobotomy): "Faced with the choice of leaving a patient raving in the back ward of a mental hospital, soiling himself with his own feces, and attacking other patients and staff, or performing a lobotomy with a reasonably good chance of improving his condition so he can be moved to a ward with better conditions, many reasonable people would make the latter choice. Although in many cases lobotomized patients who were able to be discharged from the hospital functioned at a lower intellectual level than prior to the onset of their mental illness, this was better than the realistic and grim prospect of spending the rest of their lives in the hospital." (31)

Who then are the real beneficiaries, if any, of the decision that neither involuntarily committed persons nor their guardians can consent to experimental PS? Can it even be maintained that those who continue in confinement and/or torment somehow have their lot improved, or is this another nice case in which the class of persons least able legally to protect themselves (the impoverished, committed, mentally incompetent) are again used to advance interests of those who are so much better off? Even if there are legitimate fears about the possibilities of behavior control by surgery, whose fears are assuaged by the "no consent" doctrine: those of people who do have access to law and lawyers? We surely have reason enough these days to be anxious about the protection of our civil rights, but I wonder about what has happened to our sense of justice if we are willing to permit those who already are asked to survive on the crumbs of life to pay for our "right" to sit at the banquet tables of life.

It would be naive to suppose that those who support the "no-consent" doctrine are unaware of the consequences of that doctrine for the John Does. Rather, what they might argue is that the entire area of involuntary commitment must be reexamined and perhaps even abolished. Indeed, I share the belief that with very narrow exceptions incarceration because of social deviance should be abolished (32). Thus, those who favor the no-consent doctrine will likely also give strong support to the belief that a committed person has a right to treatment, and that means to treatment which is reasonably calculated to improve or cure. In addition, many who favor these positions, as I do, would also argue, as I would, that even if the committed patient has a right to treatment, it does not follow that the state has a right to impose some or any treatment. Yet it is precisely because I do believe that committed persons have a right (1) to treatment, and (2) to effective treatment, as well as (3) to refuse some or any treatment, I find the no-consent doctrine morally, socially and legally objectionable. We may refer to these three rights as the basic civil rights of the committed mentally ill. It is just because I do believe that committed people deserve to have their options for salvation maximized that I find it wrong to close off from them that which some scientifically untrained judges happen to believe is medically unimpressive. Indeed, I share with the court the belief that we should maximize the conditions under which a committed person (voluntary or not) may consent for *any* surgical or even any "nonroutine" medical intervention. In my view this requires more stringent conditions than those which now obtain regarding such consent. However, from these convictions it follows only that scrupulously careful concern should be exercised by the doctors and equally careful vigilance by the courts to ensure that in each case, and for every nonroutine intervention, the proper consent procedures are followed. The no-consent doctrine is inherently contrary to the intellectual and moral basis for the basic civil rights package of the mentally ill because it disenfranchises and further dehumanizes these people. By holding, as a matter of law, that under no circumstances can these people consent, the court in effect has further ostracized the involuntarily committed person from the rest of society. The philosophy behind the basic civil rights package is just the contrary: it is to ensure that the committed are not further alienated, forgotten or effectively removed from the community by treating them differently from the rest of society when their legitimate interests can be protected without treating them differently. Holding that the involuntarily committed, as a matter of law, are so different from the rest of society and therefore cannot consent or even have a guardian do so is absolutely antithetical to the best interests of these persons and clearly inconsistent with the moral and political reasons which have led to the development of their basic civil rights package.

Social Control of New Knowledge

Although I include this problem among those which are primarily legal, as with all the other important reasons for the special concern about PS, whether medical, legal or political, there are always important general philosophical and moral considerations which cannot be ignored. This is particularly clear in connection with this problem, and it helps explain why this is one of the most difficult issues with which to deal.

There is an ancient tradition according to which social and political stability is regarded as sufficiently important in the hierarchy of values to justify suppression of new knowledge, let alone prevent its acquisition. Bruno and Galileo could probably tell us quite a good deal about the need to choose between stability and new knowledge. But even despite their unavailability we can have a pretty good idea of what they might say by listening to Berthold Brecht in his *Galileo* and Eric Bentley in his *The Recantation of Galileo Galilei*. No one of my generation, or even those younger, can possibly be unaware of the stability versus knowledge controversies which have surrounded the development of atomic energy, genetic engineering, behavior control techniques, etc. In view of the vast literature and the general familiarity with this matter, and since I have no flash of wisdom with which to eliminate the problem or diminish the real fears which many do have about the *1984* consequences of new scientific knowledge, it might suffice if this essay is closed after calling to your attention a couple of points about these controversies as they relate specifically to PS.

Perhaps because I have not yet learned how to avoid the disadvantages of my training as a lawyer, when confronted with a question in applied morality or politics, I tend to ask not what would be best, but rather: What legally effective institutional models are available for constructing a mechanism which will avoid the worst? Thus you will notice that I regard the issue here not as to whether new knowledge should be suppressed, but rather, how can it be controlled. This approach, in my judgment, is both philosophically more defensible and, as regards PS, probably also inevitable. I shall not here try to support my belief that anyone who argues for the suppression of knowledge, under any circumstances and as for any kind of knowledge, should have to carry the burden of "proof beyond a reasonable doubt." [6] But it may be helpful if we consider why control rather than suppression is inevitably the question as regards new medical knowledge and PS.

If international espionage were not such a science, and had the relation between Roosevelt and Stalin been different at a certain crucial time in history (some say, had Roosevelt not been so naive) it is conceivable that the virtual American knowledge monopoly on atomic energy could have continued for some substantial length of time. But could any similar monopoly survive for new knowledge in medical science? On the contrary, one of the features which characterizes so much of the development of medical knowledge is its international character. In his 1971 book entitled *Bioethics* (33) Potter cautions that ". . . Once we have made the decision to open Pandora's Box of Knowledge, we can never put back its contents . . .," to which I am adding that, as least as regards medical knowledge, the decision to keep the box closed can never be made effectively on a national level. Even if it were deemed better to suppress new medical knowledge because of its Orwellian potential, it probably cannot be done, and it surely cannot be done on a national basis. Neither Narabayashi nor Sano in Japan, Hassler in West Germany, Balasubramaniam in India, Bailey in Australia, Crow in England, Baker in Canada, Chitanandh in Thailand, nor Delgado in Spain, to name only a few, will be deterred, let alone prevented, by the decision in the Detroit case or even by Congressional legislation from continuing with their work on experimental brain surgery. Unless Congress were also prepared to ban their publications from the United States and to prohibit American doctors from attending conferences abroad or reading prohibited foreign medical journals, American doctors will still acquire the "dangerous" new knowledge and still be able to tell desperate enough patient Mr. X that in England or Japan so-and-so has treated cases like his with some apparent success.

I have sketched this caricature of knowledge suppression in medicine to support the belief that the real problem is not whether potentially dangerous new knowledge should be suppressed. On the contrary, and especially as regards new knowledge in medicine, the task should always be at least twofold: first, to encourage the development of as much new knowledge as possible so as to ensure that we will not make mistakes out of ignorance, and second, to institutionalize such restraints upon the use of the new knowledge as would seem to be warranted by its potential for

---

[6] "Scientific inquiry has been the chief instrumentality in bringing men from barbarism to civilization, from darkness to light, while it has incurred, at every step, determined opposition from the powers of ignorance, misunderstanding and jealousy." Quoted by De Bakey, "Medical Research and the Golden Rule" *JAMA* 203: 574 (Feb. 19, 1968) from a paper delivered by Visscher in 1966 at a symposium in Baltimore on Science, Society and the Public's Health: Ethical Issues.

harm.[7] The lawyer's job is most likely to concern the second task, and as regards PS it seems to me that the following are among the most important concerns which should guide the search for a regulating mechanism that will protect the legitimate interests of society.

1. Avoid ad hoc, unsystematic, case-by-case intervention (as would be the situation if regulation were left to the courts).

2. Avoid regulation by a decision-making mechanism which does not have built into it some effective way for preventing the treatment of scientific and sociopolitical concerns as fungible. Or, at least avoid a mechanism which cannot minimize the adverse effects thereof. (Again, suggesting that the courts are not the mechanism of choice.[8])

3. Avoid institutionalizing regulations in a way which will permit so much discretion at local levels that the appropriate scientific and political standards can be effectively eroded by provincial control.

4. While avoiding provincialism in the articulation of standards, encourage local initiative in developing criteria for the (local) application of the standards.

---

[7] "We must somehow evolve a system of technology assessment whereby the state of knowledge can be assessed and its readiness for application can be addressed within the context of relevant social, human, and ethical issues. Such a system would assure the timely application of relevant technology and help prevent the premature use of those techniques not thoroughly explored for their human and social implications.

"We believe that the answer to the dangerous use of knowledge is the creation of new knowledge, combined with a sensitive, rational, and humanitarian perspective on the applications of that knowledge. It is also important to broaden the training of scientists and practitioners to include such ethical issues and the humanities." (34)

[8] It is by no means obvious that the legislative inquiry is necessarily less "prosecutorial" than is cross examination in court. For example, Senator Kennedy, in questioning an essentially sympathetic scientific witness, tried to push him beyond what he could say as a scientist, in order to acquire a "fact" which might help the Senator in his legislative capacity.

Dr. Brown: If one could pinpoint accurately the precise locus of the center in the brain that stimulates the abnormal behavior or the tract through which it is disseminated and then remove or destroy only that portion of the brain, the patient could be relieved of his pathology over which he had no control and be returned to the community as a functioning, responsible member of society.

Sen. Kennedy: Can you do that accurately?

Dr. Brown: That is the basic issue—

Sen. Kennedy: Well, that is your conclusion?

Dr. Brown: In many situations, it can. In the majority of situations, the very nature of the research is to determine if there is such a locus; and this is the dilemma we are faced with. It is not yet clear in a majority of instances that this can be accurately done for all cases.

Sen. Kennedy: Well, your testimony is that in a majority of cases, it cannot be?

Dr. Brown: In the majority of cases where you have abnormal behavior without obvious brain pathology, you cannot accurately locate the brain locus responsible. (35)

5. Discourage any further PS intervention by private clinicians until national policy has been developed.[9]

6. Facilitate the development of such national policy by commissioning the leading specialists to review the existing world literature and on the basis of such review recommend such immediate further study as would produce the kind of data bank which could be relied upon for guiding decisions as to what, if any, further work should be permitted or encouraged. In effect, this is what S.J. Resolution 86 (93d Congress, 1st Session) would seek to accomplish. The resolution was introduced on March 29, 1973 by Senators Beall, Buckley and Dominick.

7. Provide for an ongoing scientific national review mechanism to ensure that the relevant data bank is kept current.

8. As distinguished from the kinds of behavioral research permitted to institutions with the proper equipment and personnel, maintain a current list of the kinds of PS interventions which private clinicians may recommend or use and under what circumstances.

9. In fixing such a list, the decision-making instrumentality should be structured so as to ensure that social, political and moral factors are openly and deliberately considered and that the approved list consciously reflects decisions which take account of these considerations as well as the scientific data. In effect, that is part of what S. 2072 aims at. This legislation was introduced in the Senate on June 26, 1973 by Senators Kennedy, Javits, Hathaway, Hughes, Pell and Randolph. This is not the place to discuss this particular bill, although I do have major reservations about it.

10. Finally, the HEW and other federal guidelines for medical research

---

[9] Sen. Kennedy: Let me ask you this: If a private doctor wants to practice psychosurgery is there any way that you can prohibit it?

Dr. Brown: No. We only have direct control over those clinical and experimental procedures that are done under our research grant funds.

Sen. Kennedy: Do you know of every case, or every place where psychosurgery is performed in the country today?

Dr. Brown: No; I do not. I would guess that somewhere from several hundred to perhaps a few thousand are performed. We do not have an overview or purview of all the clinical practice that is now taking place.

Sen. Kennedy: So these procedures are taking place in the numbers that you have mentioned and you have no way of knowing whether those are under the very carefully controlled conditions that you have outlined as being absolutely minimal at best?

Dr. Brown: That is correct. We have no direct knowledge. (36)

Later in his testimony Dr. Gaylin said:

"There is a great need for greater regulation of surgical procedures. We should demand distinctions between therapeutic and experimental. Distinctions and clearly stated definitions.

"We should know the kind of operations done, by whom, and for what purposes. The confusion demonstrated today about the number of cases of psychosurgery does not, I think, represent duplicity, but simple ignorance. It is time for a registry of surgical procedures performed." (37)

need to be reexamined with a view toward strengthening the effectiveness of scientific review committee functions in order to avoid back-scratching problems, and to encourage the development of some degree of systematic continuity in the relevance of the criteria relied upon for decisions. In addition, the function of the human rights committees needs to be further developed in order to ensure that legitimate social and political considerations are not passed over in the name of science. This is one of the most difficult and serious problems, and at many medical research institutions and at even more hospitals, the malfunction, misfunction or nonfunction of human rights committees is one of the strongest reasons for suppressing PS. However, as regards PS and particularly now with the newest techniques for a stereotaxic lesion, which make "office" PS a real possibility,[10] it is essential that the clinical practice of PS be subjected to effective human rights review.

By way of conclusion let me summarize the argument advanced in this essay.

1. The reasons for the special concern about PS, even when they appear to be primarily medical, scientific or legal, characteristically involve important moral, social and political concerns.

2. Even if these latter concerns are not capable of clear articulation and even if they are not "scientifically" verifiable or even confirmable, it does not mean that they should be ignored.

3. When moral or social concerns are widely shared, and even if they are not as justifiable as other relevant concerns, they should be protected whenever this can be done without unduly compromising other important considerations.

4. Because of the keenly felt concern about medical behavior modification procedures, they should be subjected to a regime of regulations which will ensure that no important human or social values are sacrificed because of some individual doctor's perception of the situation.

5. The need for national standards and the need to prevent unnecessary obfuscation generated by treating scientific or medical data as fungible with social concerns militate against the use of the courts as the institutional decision mechanism.

6. The articulation of national standards should be accomplished by first developing the data which emerge from the relevant scientific literature of the world and then feeding these data into a decisional mechanism which can also openly and deliberately evaluate the relative significance of concerns other than and in addition to those which emerge from the scientific data.

---

[10] "At least one West Coast neurosurgeon . . . has taken to performing psychosurgery on children as an office procedure." (38)

7. Scientific peer review and human rights committees should function to ensure that the legitimate purposes of those committees are secured, and the domain, particularly of the human rights committees, needs to be expanded.

REFERENCES

1. Hearings before the Subcommittee on Health of the Committee on Labor and Public Welfare; Quality of Health Care—Human Experimentation, 1973, Part 2.
2. Hearings, 338.
3. Hearings, 358.
4. Hearings, 351–352.
5. Szasz, T. S. *The Myth of Mental Illness.* New York: Hoeber-Harper, 1961; *Law, Liberty and Psychiatry.* New York: Macmillan, 1963.
6. *Psychosurgery: Perspective on a Current Issue,* Dept. of Health, Education and Welfare Publications, No. (HSM) 73-9119, 1973, p. 9.
7. Hearings, 368.
8. Hearings, 373–374.
9. Hearings, 358.
10. Restak, R. The Promise and Peril of Psychosurgery. *Saturday Review/World* 54, Sept. 25, 1973.
11. Physical Manipulation of the Brain. The Hastings Center Report, Special Suppl. 9, Mar. 1973.
12. Hastings Report, 10–11.
13. Hastings Report, 11.
14. Hearings, 342.
15. Hastings Report, 9.
16. Restak, 54.
17. Hearings, 342.
18. Hearings, 335.
19. *Psychosurgery,* HEW, 1.
20. Hearings, 359.
21. *Kaimowitz v. Dept. of Mental Health,* Wayne County Circuit Court, unreported, July 10, 1973. Trial Transcript at A47–A49/28.
22. *Kaimowitz v. Dept. of Mental Health,* 31–32/29.
23. Hearings, 359.
24. Hearings, 362
25. *Kaimowitz v. Dept. of Mental Health,* 21.
26. *Kaimowitz v. Dept. of Mental Health,* 29.
27. *Kaimowitz v. Dept. of Mental Health,* 25–26.
28. *Kaimowitz v. Dept. of Mental Health,* 30.
29. *Kaimowitz v. Dept. of Mental Health,* 26.
30. Mason, D. "Brain Surgery to Control Behavior," *Ebony* 28: 62, Feb. 1973.
31. *Psychosurgery,* 2.
32. Shuman, S. I. Responsibility and Punishment: Why Criminal Law. *Am. J. Jurisprudence* 15: 25, 1970; Shuman, S. I. The Placebo Cure For Criminality, *Wayne Law Rev.* 19: 847, 1973.
33. Potter, V. R. *Bioethics: Bridge to the Future.* Englewood Cliffs: Prentice-Hall, 1971.
34. *Psychosurgery,* HEW, 10–11.
35. Hearings, 339.
36. Hearings, 343.
37. Hearings, 375.
38. Restak, 57.

chapter 7

The Flowering and Decline of the Therapeutic State?

NICHOLAS N. KITTRIE, S.J.D.

Deviant behavior is human behavior. What is deemed deviant in a given social organization is a product of that society's ideology and labeling processes. These define also the forms and institutions of the societal response to deviance.

It is inherent in the very existence of the state, and every other social organization whether more or less complex, that certain rules of conduct are required of its members. Anthropologists examining the complexity and rationality of the labeling process have designated these rules taboos, customs, laws. Lawyers, reacting to the severity of the infractions, have classified them under a variety of other and different nomenclatures: felonies, misdemeanors, petty crimes, civil offenses.

These bodies of rules define the outer limits of acceptable social conduct and mark as outsiders those who deviate from the established standards. Outsiders, or deviants, are exposed to stigmatization, social disciplining and control through diverse sanctions. A survey of the historical emergence of these sanctions will constitute our major undertaking at this time.

Significantly, what is described in modern days as the system of criminal law is but one body of rules and sanctions applied to those who deviate from social norms. Criminal law is primarily a system of state sanctions, relying in the main upon negative reinforcement. Yet the state and its penal sanctions have been only one stage in the development of societal controls. In our survey of social responses to deviance we will be more comprehensive and will go considerably beyond the confines of criminal justice.

It is beyond the scope of the present assignment to prod deeply into the societal forces and interactions responsible for the labeling or definition of deviance. Some will argue that there are certain common, minimal and therefore natural law standards (derived from godly manifestations, or from man's most basic psychological needs, or from society's most fundamental organizational requirements) which are reflected in the codes of all societies. Others will urge that deviance is culturally or economically bound. The philosophers of the Age of Reason, on the other hand, have pleaded the cause of the voluntary social contract as the social arbiter. While some have thus viewed the definition of deviance as determined by "natural," cultural or economic factors, others have viewed it as a product of free social negotiation and consensus.

Although modern social scientists continue struggling with the nature of the deviance-making process, neither the traditional nor the newer religions have been much troubled by this issue. In ancient Judaism and Christianity, as in most fundamental religions, the definition of deviance was accepted as decreed by divine natural law. For the modern Marxian determinist, deviance is similarly dictated by the needs of the exploiting classes for control over those subdued by them or, conversely, by the proletariat's need for self-protection. For the more eclectic tastes there remains an unstructured and relativistic conception of labeling through the social contract, which views deviance as a result of the interaction of diverse and often conflicting social forces which constantly define and redefine it.

Seeking to concentrate on the history of the social responses to deviant behavior, one nevertheless cannot divorce himself of these threshold questions concerning the labeling process. Clearly, if one could discern the dynamics of labeling, one would gain important insights into the employment of particular sanction systems in response to specified prohibited conducts. But one must realize, however, that the undercurrents of the labeling process, which defines deviance, are difficult to identify. This is so even with modern legislation, and much more so in the case of ancient taboos and customs. A study of social responses to deviance appears much simpler. For this can be derived from the empirical observation and analysis of programs instituted for the sanctioning of deviance. Accordingly, it will be the sanctioning institutions rather than the labeling process that will here gain our attention.

IDEOLOGY AND SOCIAL RESPONSE TO DEVIANCE

It is a major premise of this presentation that societal response to deviance is dependent upon the ideological conception of deviance by a given society at a given time. How you conceive or conceptualize deviance determines how you treat it.

That social responses to deviance have undergone dramatic changes over the course of human history might be widely acknowledged. What these changes have been, and what their major impact upon offender, offended and society has been, is less known. The public probably has even lesser awareness of the general direction of current trends and their future flow. This presentation will therefore undertake to survey the major historical, ideological and consequently programmatic changes in the societal response to deviance and crime.

Not only our Western societies reflect fundamental changes in their response to deviance. Similar trends have been documented in much less complex societies outside the realms of Western culture. Dr. Guillermo Calderon Narvaez has conducted intensive research into the handling of alcoholism amongst the pre-Columbian Aztecs. His report reads as an elaborate anecdote. Yet it contains the major kernels of the message intended by this chapter.

Having become concerned with the excessive use of alcohol, the Aztecs sought to curtail its use through resort to public pressure, or to what is described by social scientists as sanctioning through shame. Accordingly, those charged with alcoholic abuse had their heads shaven as a social stigma. As time went on and this sanction failed to produce all desired results, more severe punishments were introduced. The habitual offender became subject to increasingly harsher penalties, culminating finally in capital punishment.

But with time this drastic sanction gave in to new approaches. Concluding that excessive drinking was more a result of personal weakness and boredom than of evil intentions, the Aztecs overhauled their response to drunkenness by liberalizing the punishment and by decreeing that alcoholics be exposed to compulsory sports and games as motivating and rehabilitative tools.

With the passage of time even this reform was replaced with a new social program which tolerated alcoholic consumption, as long as it was limited to the older and nonproductive citizens. Immediately before the arrival of the white conquistadors, those members of the Aztec society who had met their life's work expectancy were thus permitted to spend the remainder of their days in alcoholic leisure.

We will describe the progression, somewhat paralleling the Aztec example, of the social response to deviance in Western society from the ancient revenge model to the current rehabilitation or medical model. The intermediate stages will be detailed in the process. Once the earmarks as well as the implications of the various past stages have been described and assessed, we will look into the directions and options for the future.

THE CRIMINALS: CHARTING FIVE THOUSAND YEARS

To isolate the major strands in society's response to deviance and their ideological underpinnings could be a gigantic task if one sought to document the developments in accurate chronological and geographic detail. What will be attempted instead is a more stylized and schematic picture, cutting across confining times and places. Yet in essence this approach should permit a valid critical assessment of most past and present developments.

The key for this schematic approach rests first upon the identification of the social entity or interest viewed as being disturbed by the deviant act. It relies next upon the definition of the central personality which the resultant sanction seeks to assuage or satisfy. Finally, it seeks to classify the resultant sanctioning tools.

Using this simplified formula for analysis, Chart 1 summarizes mankind's progress to date.

Chart 1 fails to reflect accurately the progression of the social response to deviance in all societies or even in any given society. The chronological schedule fails similarly by suggesting a clean shift or switch at a given time from one single social ideology and emphasis to another. None of these failings, however, should deter the reader from acknowledging the existence of the diverse reported responses and from seeking, through understanding them better, a realistic assessment of the contributions of each to social tranquility and justice.

Reflecting upon the first stage in the historical development, one notes that the rational needs of neither the victim nor the offender are central to the doing of justice. The response to deviance was much shrouded in the mythology of offended deities and in the primitive urge to punish, viewed as a means of restoring divine order. Punishment was decreed by the gods, not people. Its measurement depended upon how offensive the deviant act was to established taboos, not upon how effective punishment was in de-

Time	Offended social interest	Entity to be satisfied	Sanctions
3000–500 B.C.	Divine order	Deity	Revenge
500 B.C.–1000 A.D.	Victim's proprietary interest	Victim and his family	Compensation
1000–1800 A.D.	King's peace	State	Punishment as deterrence (negative reinforcement)
1800 A.D.–?	Well-being and health of community	Offender	Treatment or cure

Chart 1

terring similar behavior or in making the victim whole. Finally, the enforcement of the divine order did not need to be delegated to the priests or other divine officials. Through revenge, laymen and especially the victim's kin were equally capable of restoring the disturbed order.

The second stage in the social response elevated the victim to the central stage of societal consideration. It was his and his kin's loss and well-being that were of major consideration. The utilization of compensation and "blood money" as payment even for the loss of life were typical. Indeed, the offender became liable for the rehabilitation of the victim. And it was upon the latter's rehabilitation that the offender was allowed to return to society. The compensation schemes in the Old Testament (Exodus 22: 12–37) are typical of this stage. They contain elaborate formulas for assessing the victim's loss (five oxen for the stolen ox and four sheep for the stolen sheep), and they call for the offender's payment—or work in bondage in lieu thereof—until the damage was rectified.

It was not until the 12th century that the third stage of social response came about in English justice. Prior to that time no criminal law system was in existence. Blood fueds by the victim's kin remained a major means for correcting wrongs, and a complex body of rules was developed in order to measure and to give proper expression to the avenging principles. Equally dominant until the time was the reliance upon "weir-geld," or blood money, as a substitute for physical violence in the case of lesser or unintentional offenses. Only with the emergence of the king's power, and the consolidation of his authority over the previously fragmented feudal realms, was the royal writ instituted in the sovereign's courts, and the criminal process was introduced by permitting the citizen to purchase royal sanctions.

By turning his claim over to the state for enforcement, the victim slowly became less important, until finally he was reduced to being the forgotten man of the system of justice. No longer was the rectification of the victim's losses the major concern of society. The state, acting as the agent for the total population, was less concerned with the victim's loss than with the future protection of society. The newly selected sanctions were therefore designed to offer such protection by excluding the offender through transportation, by incapacitating him through mayhem or capital punishment, and by seeking through these severe sanctions to deter all others similarly inclined.

The peak of the third stage was reached in the late 18th or the early 19th century with the emergence of classic criminology and its leaders: Cesare di Beccaria and Jeremy Bentham. The classicists were believers in free will. They were also hedonistic in orientation. They argued that men choose between the anticipated pleasures of criminal acts and the pains imposed by society upon such behavior. Thus, a fitting and certain schedule of penalties would effectively serve to limit temptations. "Pleasure and pain," held Beccaria, "are the only springs of actions in beings endowed with sensibility." It followed logically therefore that punishment should be "not less in any case than what is sufficient to outweigh . . . the profit of the offense." In the final analysis, the only consideration of the state in its response to deviance was to be the adequacy of the sanction to ensure the state's future safety.

After the middle of the 19th century new deterministic philosophies, advancing the cause of either heredity or environment as controlling factors in shaping human behavior, finally produced the abandonment of classic penology. Rejecting the classic period's reliance upon free will and hedonism, criminologists in the fourth stage put forth the ideology of deviance as an aberration and the offender as a captive of deterministic forces. The deviant required not so much punishment as retrieval and cure. With the deviant pictured more as ill than evil, the social sanctions likewise had to undergo a transformation. Deterrence lost its primacy, for how could one expect to deter through sanctions those who lack the requisite sensibility and self-control?

No longer were severe penalties viewed as necessary or effective. The sanctions, it was now argued, should not be proportionate to the offenses but should be responsive to the offenders. In other words, the punishment should fit the criminal and not the crime. The modern penitentiary and reformatory were then advanced as places in which the offender could be rehabilitated, reeducated, reoriented and reconstituted. His value system was to be reformed through religious and ethical training. His earning skills were to be increased through vocational training, and his mental health was to be improved through psychological and other counseling.

While this illness and treatment ideology has marginally affected the criminal justice system itself, it has had its major and most dramatic impact upon a subsidiary and independent system of social sanctions, which I describe as the "parens patriae" or therapeutic system. To this system (encompassing primarily the mentally ill, juvenile delinquents, alcoholics and drug addicts) I devoted my recent book, *The Right To Be Different: Deviance and Enforced Therapy*.

THE MENTALLY ILL: FROM EXCLUSION TO THE THERAPEUTIC STATE

For the past several centuries the criminal law has been the major tool of the state—as contrasted with the church, family and peer groups—for enforcing conformity upon those who refused or were unable to abide. The criminal law in its origins failed to differentiate the various classes of nonconformists. A deviant status and a deviant act were equally deplorable.

To be poor, to be unemployed, to be a vagrant, to be drunk in public or to be mentally distracted was as much an offense as to commit a violent crime. And whether poor, diseased or delinquent, all those charged with either deviant condition and status or with deviant acts were grouped together for similar treatment.

But just as the response to those charged with common criminal activity has undergone many changes since the beginnings of the criminal law in the 12th century, so the social sanctioning institutions for those suffering from mental illness and similar deviant conditions have equally reflected ideological change. The Middle Ages exhibited a great intolerance for all forms of deviation. Widespread poverty, disease, mass movement of populations and religious fanaticism made intolerable the lot of the mentally ill and any other socially displaced persons. In Europe the mad were often executed as witches, chained, or thrown into gatehouses and prisons, where they might furnish horrible diversion for the other prisoners. Those more fortunate were driven out of the city enclosures and forced to roam over distant fields. In northern Europe two modes of ritual exclusion were developed: the mentally distracted were crowded into "ships of fools" (das Narrenschiff) and shuttled from port to port, or were taken on pilgrimages to holy places and abandoned there.

Whereas the Middle Ages drove out the insane, the Renaissance confined them. Some historians see this change not as a chance development. Many cloisters and monasteries began to be abandoned by their former occupants at that time, and the drastic abatement of leprosy brought about the vacating of the more than 19,000 leprosaria, the special medieval institutions in which lepers were committed. The vacated facilities provided the space for the next step in the treatment of the socially unfit in Europe: confinement.

Still, until late in the last century, Western society by and large had refused to differentiate among the common criminal, the vagrant, the indigent, the immature and the insane. All continued to be subject to criminal-type procedures, and the traditional sanctions—execution, bondage, transportation and, later, confinement—applied equally to the sound and to the insane, to the violent criminal offenders and to the meek social misfits whose only crime was indigency and an inability to care for themselves.

In the middle of the 19th century appeared a major new trend regarding selected classes of deviants whose offense was primarily one of status rather than activity. The first group to so benefit from special attention was the insane. The first American institution designed exclusively for the mentally ill dates back to Williamsburg, Virginia in 1773, yet the second hospital, in Lexington, Kentucky, was not built until 1824. Then all at once, at the end of the 1860s, special asylums designed to afford the mentally ill relief from the more severe sanctions of the criminal process began to spread all over the country. The mentally ill person, incapable of *mens rea*, ceased being a criminal and became a patient.

It took some 30 years more before similar institutions were advocated and were introduced for the benefit of the youthful delinquents, who were also veiwed as proper exceptions, because of chronological immaturity, from criminal responsibility. Professing a dedication to the rehabilitative ideal, the juvenile court system was born in Illinois in 1899 and rapidly spread throughout the country.

Some 30 years later a new territory was annexed by the growing therapeutic movement. In the 1930s special concern arose regarding those described as suffering from psychopathy, i.e. various types of habitual offenders, especially those suspected or charged with sexual deviance. Unable to identify and classify these deviants through the traditional psychiatric nomenclature (as was done with the insane) or the chronological immaturity rationale (which was applied to juvenile offenders), the unifying principle for the latter group became their "moral" as distinguished from their "mental" abnormality. Psychopaths, and especially sexual psychopaths, were thus singled out for special and allegedly nonpenal or therapeutic attention on the basis of their particular proclivity or propensity for repeated criminal behavior.

The next 30 years produced a new addition for the therapeutic expansion. Drug addicts were the beneficiaries of the new territorial expansion. While the earlier therapeutic developments were the result of legislative action, the new expansion was the product of a judicial decree. Addressing itself to various social controls of drug addiction, the Supreme Court of the United States ruled in 1962 in the case of *Robinson v. California* that addicts suffer from an illness, and that while they may be quarantined for treatment in "hospitals" they may not be subjected to punishment in "prisons."

Efforts were made at the end of the 1960s to extend to alcoholics this same constitutional doctrine, which holds that any punishment is "cruel and unusual" if applied to those who, because of illness, lack the capacity to control their conduct. This time, however, the high court was unwilling to expand its intervention in the social controls scheme of deviance (*Powel v. Texas*, 1968). The question of whether alcoholics should be treated as criminals or as patients was thus left to the discretion of the different states.

What is it that differentiates the newer mental illness, juvenile delinquency, psychopathy, drug addiction and alcoholism programs from the mainstream of criminal justice? In its quest for social order criminal law has functioned primarily as a system for assessing individual blame and for meting out penalties that fit the severity of the offense and the degree of guilt. Under the newer noncriminal or "therapeutic" system applicable to the mentally ill, delinquents and addicts, little or no emphasis is placed upon an individual's guilt of a particular crime. But much weight is given to his physical, mental or social shortcomings.

In dealing with the deviant under the new system, society is said to be acting as "parens patriae," a term derived from the English concept of the king's role as the father of the country. In this role, society allegedly seeks not to punish but to change or to socialize the nonconformist through treatment and therapy.

Who is subject to the powers and sanctions of the therapeutic state? An increasing number of deviants have come under the therapeutic model. Some 24 million Americans are estimated to suffer from mental illnesses and defects. There are some 75 million juveniles under age 18, and more than 1.5 million of them are arrested and processed annually under the authority of the juvenile justice. There is an uncertain number of people who are subject to the authority of the psychopathy laws—many of them doing nothing more than engaging in unorthodox sexual practices with consenting adult partners. Some 8 million in our midst are estimated to be alcoholics, and probably as much as 25% of the younger population, although not necessarily addicted, have been exposed to habit-forming drugs.

PERSPECTIVES ON THE THERAPEUTIC STATE

Like the five blind men, each grasping a different part of the elephant and each describing a different beast, so the perceivers of the therapeutic state have seen in it diverse realities. Some have viewed it as a humanistic boon. Others have portrayed it as the first rational endeavor for the scientific control of deviant behavior. Still others have compared it to the infamous Star Chamber proceedings, dispensing arbitrary punishment without the safeguards of due process. Widely diverse elements in society have joined together under the therapeutic banner for an allegedly joint endeavor. While all profess to subscribe to the overall nonpenal philosophy, each has had some particular aims which it sought to accomplish, ranging from the greater tolerance of deviation and the deviant to the institution of more stringent societal control and preventive measures.

Some generalized comments are made above on the forces which have given the therapeutic orientation an increasing role in our response to deviance. A more complete inventory is required, however, for a better comprehension and assessment of this development. In listing the major causes for dissatisfaction with the traditional criminal law, to which the new therapeutic alternatives are the response, one must point out that the weight to be attributed to each of these diverse factors remains indeed a function of one's own ideological inclination.

The Search for Individualized and Humanitarian Programs

With industrialization and the popularization of government, there developed a movement for social reform and humanism. New classes obtained a voice by which they could proclaim their dissatisfaction with the harsh past treatment of offenders. Individualized treatment was seized upon as being more humane as well as more effective. A shift to the therapeutic or medical approach permitted an emphasis upon the individual offender rather than upon the offense.

Filling the Moral Guilt Vacuum

Both canon law and English law based criminal punishment on the existence of moral guilt. The early recognition that certain classes of offenders were incapable of guilt because of defective mentality resulted in their exemption from criminal sanctions. The same exemption was extended to juveniles, considered chronologically immature. As determinism and modern psychiatry became more widely accepted—raising increasing doubts as to the capacity for guilt of other classes of offenders—noncriminal sanctions had to be sought for the quarantining of those who might be not-guilty, yet who continued to be viewed as socially dangerous. The therapeutic state permitted social sanctioning and controls without a need to rely upon the concept of guilt.

The Inadequacy of Criminal Sanctions

The positivists, who ruled European criminology in the second half of the 19th century, pointed to the inconsistency and futility of the classic penal approach. Punishing one according to a "tarrif" based on the severity of his offense, they urged, fails to assure his reformation and his future law-abiding behavior. They called for the abolition of traditional sentences and the institution of a medical model. Enrico Ferri voiced his position most effectively:

> It would be as absurd to say that a murderer should remain in prison twenty years rather than fifteen or thirty as it would be to say in advance that a sick person should stay in a hospital ten days rather than twenty or fifty. As a sick person is kept in the hospital [for] just as long a time as is necessary for his cure, and as the insane patient remains in the asylum all his life unless cured . . . so it should be with the delinquent.

By disowning punitive goals the therapeutic state was able to remove the traditional constraints requiring proportionality in the imposition of penalties. Acting in the name of therapy, the state is permitted also to utilize sanctions not otherwise available.

Prevention in Lieu of Suppression

Criminal law traditionally has required an overt act on the part of the offender before state intervention was justified. Thoughts alone and propensity to action, regardless of how vile, were not punishable. The introduction of the therapeutic model, viewing the deviant as a man suffering from a dangerous malady, allowed state intervention as soon as the dangerous status or condition was diagnosed. No longer did the state have to await and react to a harmful act. A prediction of future dangerousness was sufficient to call into effect preventive measures. The therapeutic approach thus permitted prophylactic interventions not possible under the penal process.

THE EVILS OF THE THERAPEUTIC APPROACH

The new conceptualization of deviance as the equivalent of an illness and of the deviant as a person lacking in mental capacity and control produced a new scenario for the interaction between society and its deviants. The conventional and intentional public abuse and cruelty were no longer justified in the absence of the offender's guilt. But with his guiltlessness the latter suddenly found himself also to be a non-person, subject to neglect and debasement by those professing to act in his own best interest.

The Procedural Void

Defining the deviant as one lacking mental capacity or maturity seemed to suggest that he did not require and could not benefit from the traditional due process safeguards designed to give the criminal offender an opportunity to be heard. Similarly, since the state proclaimed its desire to act on behalf of the mentally disabled deviant, instead of seeking to penalize him, the usual protections against the state's police and penal zeal did not seem appropriate.

While the dread of an unjust conviction has been a major force in shaping the safeguards of the criminal process the same concern was long absent in the therapeutic realm. As a consequence, the requirement of a specific listing and proof of charges, a hearing before an independent tribunal, the right to counsel and the right to be heard were long inapplicable to the supposed beneficiaries of therapy. The outcome of this procedural leniency is demonstrated by the fact that, of 135,000 first involuntary commitments to mental institutions in 1965, some 6,500, or 5 %, remained undiagnosed at the end of the year, and another 1750 were found to be totally without mental disorder.

The Definitional Vagueness

Since therapeutic intervention and sanctions were to be triggered by a diagnosis of the deviant's general "illness" status rather than by a particular overt act as is the requirement in the penal process, the substantive definitions of the underlying and triggering "illnesses" were to become the control mechanism against societal excesses. How and by what criteria were these illnesses to be defined? Were the criteria to be derived from general scientific knowledge? Were they to be found in psychiatry, psychology, sociology or religion? Were they to be legislatively or administratively arrived at? How were due process, equal protection and fairness to be guaranteed?

The definitions which were produced frequently remained vague and uncertain. "Being in need of treatment" became a sufficient test and justification for the confinement of an adult to a mental institution. "Being ungovernable and beyond parental control" sufficed as a criterion for the confinement of a juvenile to a delinquency institution. And "the propensity to commit crimes" or "to be addicted to drugs" sufficed for the incarceration of psychopaths and addicts to special hospitals.

Legislatures relinquished their responsibilities to the administrators. And the administrators looked to the therapists for guidance. Were the psychiatrists, the psychologists and the others charged with treatment to be given the power to define their unwilling wards?

With terminology so vague and all-encompassing the opportunities for error were multiplied. But only in recent years have the hazards of this therapeutic vagueness and expansionism been realized. Research evidence presented before the 1971 Kennedy Foundation Symposium on Mental Retardation suggested, for example, that nearly 75 % of the children classified as mentally retarded were marginal and mistaken cases. Yet the attachment of the therapeutic label not only sufficed for initial state intervention but the stigma, once attached, became difficult to remove during one's lifetime.

Once the label of mental illness, delinquency, psychopathy or addiction was attached, an immediate presumption of social dangerousness sprang into being. And the ill deviant was not only entitled to treatment, he was required to take it. Only recently, in the debate and divesting action of the American Psychiatric Association in connection with the homosexuals, is a new professional awareness of the hazards of therapeutic labeling fully displayed.

The Danger of Abuse

The label of insanity, delinquency, addiction and psychopathy can become a dangerous weapon. At the beginning of this century in America the founder of the Christian Science Church, Mary Baker Eddy, was charged with mental illness for imagining herself a new prophetess in a scientific age. Zhores Medvedev and other political dissenters in the Soviet Union have been confined for political heresy. The benevolence of the treaters or therapists in these and many other cases has been in doubt.

Dissenters, protesters, rebels and other malcontents have frequently found it much more difficult to resist the state in her claimed therapeutic and benevolent role than to withstand its penal assault. And as long as state sanctions can be more readily employed in the name of therapy then in the name of punishment, the dangers of therapeutic abuse are to be expected.

More Stringent Social Controls

Acting under its therapeutic mantle affords the state greater social controls that are available under the criminal process. No longer need the penalty be proportionate to the offense. A dangerous or undesirable deviant may be incarcerated for long periods of treatment, even for minor offenses. Gerald Gault, whose case I argued before the United States Supreme Court, was sent away for 5 years to a juvenile institution for making an obscene telephone call which would have been punishable with a maximum fine of $50 or 2 months in jail in the case of an adult. Frederick C. Lynch, whose case I also argued, sought to plead guilty to a charge of passing a bad check. The maximum penalty in the District of Columbia could have been a jail sentence of 12 months. Under the court's therapeutic options Lynch was confined in a mental institution for an indeterminate period. Tired, he committed suicide.

More Drastic "Treatments"

Penal institutions are restrained by the constitutional prohibition of cruel and unusual punishment. But no similar safeguard exists against cruel therapy. The history of the therapeutic state is heavily documented with such therapies as shock treatment, lobotomies (the total number of cases exceeding 50,000), sterilizations (exceeding 70,000 operations) and other drastic measures of social control. Most of these sanctions, notably, were never attempted and would not have withstood the requirements of due process in the old fashioned penal process.

The recent film version of *Clockwork Orange* provided a shocking version of the potential excesses of the therapeutic promise. Traditionally we have sought to reform the criminal through his own inner self-reappraisal. But the criminal, even though subject to penalties, had the option of remaining himself. The involuntary therapeutic process possibly seeks to completely redo and invade the inner man. Some may claim that this cure is worse than the disease.

Neither is the fear of therapeutic excesses the brainchild of a few who are inclined to paranoia. Already at this time there are more than four persons subjected to noncriminal incarceration and treatment for every one sent to the traditional prison. The therapeutic state is evidently marching on.

FROM THE DOMINANCE OF THE SAVERS TO ENVIRONMENTAL MODIFICATIONS

Much has been written about the overreach of the criminal law beyond strict public safety into areas of morality, health and welfare. The plea is made for a rational and narrow approach to criminality, under which neither traditional morality nor harm to oneself but only direct harm to another person would justify state intervention with deviant behavior. What is now readily apparent is that the overflow and overreach from the criminal process have also affected the therapeutic state. Indeed, especially in recent years there has been a tendency to relieve the criminal process of its responsibility for diverse groups of minor deviants and at the same time broaden the boundaries of the compulsory therapeutic state by transferring these groups to it. But if indeed victimless crimes, such as adult homosexuality, gambling, prostitution and alcoholism, should be excepted from state intervention, then their transfer from the criminal to therapeutic sanctions is a mere facade. The change of labels becomes nothing but a sham; and the psychiatrists, psychologists and other "counsellors" now assume the role of the keepers of the new therapeutic prisons.

I have previously urged attention to the increased hazards posed to individual rights and to the pluralistic goals of our society by the therapeutic state. The leaders of the Mettachine Society, for example, when pleading the cause of homosexuality, have viewed the "illness" label as a more insidious threat than the previous criminal penalty. Similarly memorable is the voice of the alcoholic hero of one of the famous court test cases: "No one is going to put me in the looney business. I'm perfectly all right, but I just like to drink."

Recognizing the need to restrain the zeal and often too arbitrary discretion of the state as therapist (much as the police functions of the state had to be curbed previously), I have undertaken to formulate a new therapeutic bill of rights. The bill's principles are rather modest. They insist upon procedural due process even when the state proclaims its benevolent rather than punitive goals. They insist that the substantive criteria for state intervention be made more precise and certain, and that a diagnosis of a person's general condition or status (and the attachment of a peuso-scientific label) not be sufficient by itself to lead to a conclusion of his dangerousness and to result in his involuntary confinement.

Indeed, there should be proof of clear, direct and present danger to others before therapy is imposed. I have urged moreover that the state should never be entitled to use compulsion in order to improve a person. In the words of John Stuart Mill, "The only purpose for which power can be exercised is to prevent harm to others. His own good, either physical or moral, is not a sufficient warrant." Finally, the claim of therapy should not justify the indiscriminate use of all so-called therapeutic means and measures. Certain measures (such as lobotomies and sterilization) must be considered too extreme. The state should not be permitted to do in the name of treatment that which it cannot do as punishment.

While 2 years ago, when *The Right To Be Different* was published, I feared the expanding energies of the therapeutic missionaries and felt the urgency for a new bill of rights, I view the situation differently now. Some limits have since been imposed upon therapy. The writings of Thomas S. Szasz and others are responsible for a greater public consciousness of the therapeutic hazards. Even before that, legislative reforms were similarly oriented, including the Ervin Mental Commitment Act in the District of Columbia. There have been restricting Supreme Court decisions, such as *Gault* and *Powel v. Texas*. I have noted in the air a decline in the prophetic zest of the therapeutic state and its disciples.

But the time has come for us to go further. We cannot merely concern ourself with the substantive and procedural reformation of the therapeutic state. We must seek to reassess its total programmatic role in the field of deviance. And when realistic stock is taken of the therapeutic model we should be honest enough to admit to the false and excessive promises of therapy. From an etiological viewpoint we still fail to understand the true nature of many of the so-called behavioral or deviance illnesses, much less know how to effectively treat them. There are no readily available therapies for alcoholism, addiction, homosexuality and psychopathy. Some of the available therapies, moreover, we cannot afford, either financially, socially or constitutionally. What then is the road ahead?

Having reshaped the image of the offender from a self-possessed evildoer to a predominantly predetermined patient, we must go on to yet different conceptions of deviance and new ideologies of response. There is a major need to shift our attention from behavioral emphasis and control to environmental factors and to environmental modification. There is much need for a shift from the medical to the welfare model, in which basic social services are furnished to those needing them without the requisites of therapeutic labels or compulsion.

Shelters for larger numbers of derelict alcoholics might be more desirable than treatment facilities for a select and unwilling few. Meaningful employment opportunities for prisoners upon release are likely to be more significant than all the counseling and treatment offered within the walls. Restructured and relevant vocational schools, rather than high investment in complex and intensive psychological programs, should be offered to those young persons who are unable to cope with the current uniform academic emphasis.

Instead of seeking expensive remedies for the cure of alcoholics and drug addicts, the environment around them should be modified and corrected. Organized and other crime should be made less profitable by removing its monopoly for furnishing deviant needs. The incentive for corrupting the innocent, and the not so innocent, should be lessened by making the state a major provider of all irresistible vices—gambling, alcohol and drugs—to those addicted to them. In the final analysis, the past models of penal and therapeutic response to deviance need to be greatly modified through a new and greater emphasis upon a welfare and support model. And we should have enough faith in human nature, and we are sufficiently wealthy, to take the chance that we will not be overrun with loafers, bums and other undesirables.

The call for greater environmental emphasis is not totally new. In anecdotal form it goes back to the heroes of positivist criminology in 19th century Italy. The story is that in response to the increasing number of Romans who failed to heed the legal prohibitions against urinating in the streets of their city, the city fathers introduced a new schedule of severe punishments to deter those who had not been previously deterred. When even this sanction failed to completely attain the desired effects, the renowned Cesare Lambroso was consulted. He is reputed to have suggested that by definition those who fail to be deterred by punishment must be viewed as ill, and for them more suitable nonpenal sanctions and institutions must be built. But it was Enrico Ferri, a young criminologist at the time, whose counsel was finally accepted. Objecting to Lambroso's medical diagnosis, Ferri took note instead of Rome's cold winter climate. He recommended the construction of public urinals. This particular deviance of the Roman citizenry declined much after the appropriate structures were completed.

The lesson is one that should not go unheeded in present times. The therapeutic state has made many contributions to the understanding and humanization of the social response to deviance. But we cannot afford a one-to-one therapist-to-deviant solution. We must have more massive approaches, environmental, preventive in nature and broadly applicable.

chapter 8

The Right to Treatment: Some Comments on Its Development

MORTON BIRNBAUM, LL.B., M.D.

In May 1960, I wrote an article in the *American Bar Association Journal* entitled "The Right to Treatment" that proposed what was then a novel concept (1). It advocated the realistic recognition, definition, enforcement and implementation of the legal right of a state mental hospital patient to adequate care and treatment. For convenience I called this concept "the right to treatment." It was pointed out that although our society undoubtedly recognized a moral right to treatment, our law had not realistically recognized this concept, especially for the involuntarily civilly committed state mental hospital patient.

An editorial in the same issue of the *Journal* condemned the understaffing, overcrowding and otherwise generally inadequate treatment then existing in our state mental hospitals as "a wrong which demands correction." Emphasizing that a legal precedent could work wonders, the editorial, entitled *A New Right*, then went on to strongly emphasize, as a necessary method of correcting this wrong, the recognition and financial implementation of this new legal concept (2).

Throughout the 1960s, although the need for this right continued, no court recognized this constitutional concept. On seven separate occasions the United States Supreme Court refused to hear cases involving this question, although the facts of grossly inadequate and inhumane care and treatment were clear and were undisputed by the state hospital personnel who were the defendants in these actions. For example, on four separate occasions, the Court repeatedly refused to hear a Florida case, *Donaldson v. O'Connor* (3), in which there was only one doctor and one nurse for 1,000 patients, where patients were often not seen by any doctor for more than 2 years and were being often brutally assaulted physically and even sexually by illiterate aides who were in full charge of the wards, and where many of the buildings were in a state of obsolescence, some having been built more than 150 years before. And on three other separate occasions, the Court again repeatedly refused to hear a New York case, *Stephens v. La Burt* (4), in which there was only one doctor for more than 500 patients, where the patient had not been seen by any doctor for more than 1 year, and where a ward attendant who was in full charge of a ward—and was subsequently found to be himself criminally insane—routinely committed sodomy upon helpless, bedridden elderly patients, even murdering one patient during such an attack.

These cases involved civilly committed patients who were not accused of committing any crime, who had not been convicted of the commission of any crime, and who had not committed any violent act before or during the entire 13 years of institutionalization for the Florida patient, and before and during the entire 34 years of institutionalization for the New York patient. They were both involuntarily civilly committed solely because of an alleged need for hospital care and treatment.

After an auspicious kickoff, therefore, the concept of the right to treatment gained no ground for a decade. Where is this concept now, 14 years later?

Until a series of decisions that started in March 1971 in the case of *Wyatt v. Stickney* (5), it had gone *nowhere* and done nothing as far as civilly committed state mental hospital patients were concerned. Since 1971, because of the *Wyatt* decisions, it has been *somewhere* and done something. It has, as a minimum, brought about certain needed improvements in basic custodial care—food, clothing and shelter—for some state mental hospital patients.

At present in 1974, it is really impossible to do more than speculate as to whether its present paths are definitely leading to better or worse psychiatric and other medical care in our state mental hospitals. I can only say now what I have repeatedly stressed before, that this concept has a potential both for use and abuse; perhaps this is a characteristic of almost all needed social reforms. In the future, it can lead almost *anywhere* and do almost anything as far as altering the needed care given to state mental hospital patients.

Realistically, of course, it may do nothing for the patient while taking up quite a bit of the time of our courts and increasing state mental hospital expenditures. Or hopefully, it may be the dawn of a new day for the state mental hospital as a vital, integral and necessary part of the therapeutic mental health continuum. Or it may cause the state mental hospital to be, even more than today, the wastebasket for the chronic severely mentally ill from the community and from the community mental health facilities unwilling or unable to manage these individuals.

In this presentation I shall discuss these "nowhere, somewhere, and anywhere" developments of this concept. I shall do this primarily through the discussion of certain legal cases involving the right to treatment in which I was personally involved as an attorney during the last 14 years. These developments will be examined against the background of the rejection mechanisms used by our society, and particularly by our subcultures of law and medicine, against the severely mentally ill, and especially against the involuntarily civilly committed.

When following this discussion, the reader should remember that I was personally—perhaps too personally—involved in these cases. As Learned Hand once noted, an advocate comes to these discussions with the sword of Luther, and certain comments could undoubtedly be more reasoned. For a more reasoned, less passionate and more scholarly approach, you must look to Dr. Robitscher, who comes with the book of Erasmus. I strongly suspect that if the legislatures, courts and professional groups read the necessarily hurried opinions of the judges less, and the well-thought out comments of Dr. Robitscher more, they would usually see well-conceived, practicable approaches to solving many important perplexing problems in this area. Although I have not read the presentation by Dr. Robitscher that follows (Chapter 9), I am sure that it will be both creative and constructive, as were his past papers (6), and that it will offer far better solutions to problems in this area than do the developments that I shall discuss.

Before reviewing these developments, I should like to set forth what I consider to be the basic minimum requirements that should be satisfied before one can say that a right to treatment has been realistically recognized.

BASIC REQUIREMENTS OF RIGHT TO TREATMENT

At the outset it is important to realize that realistic recognition of a legal right to treatment requires more than a bare-bones recognition of the right. Such recognition gives only a moral right to treatment. A realistic legal right to treatment requires recognition, definition, enforcement and implementation of this concept. For, as Justice Oliver Wendell Holmes pointed out, "Legal obligations that exist but cannot be enforced are ghosts that are seen in the law but that are elusive to the grasp." (7) Recognition of the legal right to treatment—perhaps creation of the right is a better phrase in this discussion—can come about by judge-made law involving, in these cases, constitutional interpretation. Or such recognition or creation of the right may be brought about through legislative enactment of a statute.

Personally, I should prefer that the legislature rather than the judiciary take the lead in establishing and enforcing a right to adequate treatment, as it is the legislature and not the judiciary that has the primary responsibility of enunciating the will of the people. Furthermore, the legislature has the opportunity to attempt to build a comprehensive plan of action and to coordinate it with the necessary legislative appropriations, while the judiciary is limited to a step-by-step development of the area.

As to definition of the right, I have always advocated that, initially, the hospital meet certain readily available objective standards. For example, in January 1971, when I was a co-counsel for the plaintiffs in the *Wyatt* case, among the standards that I suggested to the court were that that the hospital be accredited by the Joint Commission on Accreditation of Hospitals; that it be certified by the Social Security Administration as eligible for Medicaid and Medicare payments; that staffing ratios and physical facilities meet past and present American Psychiatric Association (APA) standards; that all professional personnel be licensed; that there be regularly recorded progress notes reflecting patient-physican consultation; and, that adequate alternative extra-hospital facilities be readily available both to avoid unnecessary admission and to facilitate discharge (8).

It is important to realize that an improvement in conditions will benefit not only the type of involuntary patient who usually initiates litigation to enforce the right to treatment or other claimed rights. Also benefited will be the more regressed and seriously disturbed patient who constitutes the overwhelming majority of the hospitalized mentally ill and who, whether voluntarily or involuntarily hospitalized, usually accepts very poor care without any significant complaint. If one appreciates the extent and the nature of the problem posed by these seriously regressed patients, as well as by the helpless aged, the mentally retarded, the severe epileptics and other neurologically and severely physically disabled who also form a significant portion of state mental hospital patients, one can understand why I have advocated objective institution-wide standards as the initial and primary method of defining the right. By contrast, those—usually lawyers (9)—who in the past concentrated on the small minority of involuntary patients who may litigate this right tended to emphasize individual subjective standards as the primary method of definition.

This proposal does not require that the court routinely supervise the treatment plan for individual patients. It does not require individuals in the hospital who do not wish to be formally treated to undergo such treatment.

My discussion until now is an excellent example of what I call "sanism," a concept that I shall discuss in detail below. The minimum standards for adequate treatment will be O.K. as a start for "them"—that is, the state mental hospital patients. If, however, I or one of my family—that is one of "us"—becomes sick, I know what standards I want and probably will get, i.e. the far higher level of treatment of Taylor Manor Hospital, the Menninger Clinic, or some other fine nonpublic mental hospital.

As to enforcement, as the primary method I have advocated the ready availability of habeas corpus or a similar administrative remedy. If one is not getting at least minimally adequate treatment according to certain objective standards, then the patient should be able to leave the hospital at will. Why else has he been hospitalized?

Alternative methods of enforcement are an injunction or other court order ordering that treatment standards meet certain minimum standards, and an action for damages.

As to financial implementation of the right, I have always suggested that federal funding to supplement state funding is essential; therefore I have advocated that the present Medicaid and Medicare exclusions and limitations applicable only to state mental hospital patients be ended (10). This would provide about $1.5 billion of new federal funds annually for state mental hospital patients.

Of course, one of the most difficult problems is the implementation of this right by adequate numbers of competent professional personnel. This might be solved in the foreseeable future if the total number of available physicians, nurses, etc. continues to increase rapidly, if government medicine continues to replace and further finance private medicine, if far higher competitive salaries and fringe benefits are offered, and if the state mental hospital is integrated into, rather than segregated from, community mental health facilities and nonpublic mental hospitals.

Some of the complex problems inherent in properly recognizing, defining, enforcing and implementing this right may be clarified by briefly describing the concept in terms in the overall legal picture.

THE PLACE OF THE RIGHT IN THE OVERALL LEGAL PICTURE

In the field of mental hospitalization, the traditional primary concern of the substantive law—the area of the law that concerns itself with what is being regulated—involves basically two questions. First, is the person mentally ill? Second, if so, should he be hospitalized, or continue to be hospitalized, either voluntarily or involuntarily, or should he be placed in an alternative extra-hospital facility such as his home, a foster home, a halfway house, an old age or nursing home or a correctional facility, or should he be allowed to roam the streets completely unsupervised? The procedural law—the area of the law that concerns itself with how the substantive law is regulated—in this field involves as a primary issue, the formal and informal problems associated with voluntary and involuntary hospitalization.

The fundamental innovation of the recognition of the concept of a right to treatment is that the additional question of adequate care is presented as an area of proper concern. If this right is properly recognized, the primary determinations of substantive law in this field will involve the following questions: first, is the person mentally ill; second, if so, should he be (or continue to be) hospitalized, either voluntarily or involuntarily, or should he be (or continue to be) in an alternative extra-hospital facility; and third, if this person is to be (or continue to be) hospitalized, will he receive adequate care and treatment in this institution?

The concept of the right to treatment, therefore, is not directly involved with the question of whether a resident rate of one person in a mental hospital per 100 general population, per 1,000 general population or per 100,000 general population is needed or preferred. This concept only claims that whatever the number of patients in these facilities, they should receive a basic level of adequate treatment.

Neither does this discussion address itself to the important problem of when and which alternative facilities are to be preferred over mental hospitals. I should like to note, however, that fine nonpublic mental hospitals such as Taylor Manor Hospital and the Menninger Clinic do not limit their service to their immediate geographical neighbors. Neither are they located in medical skyscrapers in the center of the city. Whether within the community or within the hospital, the primary issue should be the quality of the facility for the problem concerned.

SOME LEGAL, MEDICAL AND SOCIAL NEEDS FOR, AND GOALS OF, THE RIGHT TO TREATMENT

Some Legal Needs and Goals

It is not generally appreciated that there is a basic unmet legal need for this concept.

If the hospital is able in general to provide proper care by means of an adequate staff and satisfactory physical facilities, the staff will not only be able to properly decide and effectuate the conventional primary medical decisions of whom, where, when and how to treat. The staff will also be able to properly decide the secondary substantive and procedural legal-medical questions of whom, when and how to admit to, or discharge from, the state mental hospital.

Realistically, however, the average state mental hospital too often does not provide adequate care and treatment, the legal goals of rational and just decisions as to whom and how to admit or discharge cannot properly be reached by an overburdened staff. This is true not only when the legal decision is an informal administrative decision made by staff members in an emergency room, a ward examination or a staff conference. It is just as true when it is a formal judicial decision made in a court of law. For in reality, in most cases a judge bases his legal decision upon the medical opinion of a hospital staff member.

I also think that it is interesting to speculate that, as no jurisdiction in our nation has a realistic right-to-treatment provision in its involuntary commitment statutes, and as too many state hospitals too often provide inadequate care, are not the involuntary commitment statutes throughout the entire nation an unconstitutional deprivation of due process of law? Whether or not the courts will so hold if the question is presented to them is, of course, yet to be decided.

In 1972 I initiated a proceeding in the U. S. District Court in Manhattan to declare the entire New York involuntary civil commitment statutes unconstitutional because they lacked a realistic right-to-treatment provision and because the average New York state mental hospital was not providing adequate care. However, as this proceeding was part of another complex attack on certain Medicaid exclusions of state mental hospital patients, the attack on the New York statutes was discontinued at that time. My litigation and other activities are essentially both a one-man activity and personally financed, as I receive no fee or subsidy; therefore, I am forced to choose whatever I believe is most important in the long run.

I shall now go on to discuss some medical needs for, and goals of, the right to treatment. At the outset of this discussion, however, I wish to emphasize that no adverse criticism of any state mental hospital personnel is intended by any comment in this paper, for the inadequate staffing and other aspects of improper care are not their doing but rather are the doing of our society. Our society therefore should be grateful to, rather than adversely critical of, the personnel who continue to work in these institutions under the present trying conditions.

Some Medical Needs and Goals

The most obvious primary goal of a legal right to treatment is to improve the often inadequate care and treatment now accorded to too many of the 300,000 Americans now in our state mental hospitals and to too many of the 700,000 Americans treated in these facilities every year.

Throughout the nation, cases of inadequate care and treatment in our state mental hospitals are being recurrently brought to public attention, which proves that this problem is neither new nor limited to one state (10). For example, in the 1970s one can still find ratios of one doctor (usually unlicensed) to 800–900 patients in state mental hospitals in Alabama, Connecticut and Florida. Again as late as the 1970s, pellagra, a vitamin deficiency disease that itself can cause severe mental illness, was found among patients in all six Maryland state mental hospitals because of inadequately financed dietary programs.

Admittedly, the level of care in many state mental hospital systems is improving. This improvement, however, should not lead to any false sense of optimism. For in summarizing its most recent review of state and local mental health and hospital programs, the Joint Information Service of the American Psychiatric Service and the National Association for Mental Health concluded:

> A word should be said about the ranking of the states. In no case should a high standing lead to complacency. It appears to be the consensus among mental health professionals that *even the top ranking state programs fall short of adequacy;* consequently, the ranking should be viewed as extending from "less than adequate" downward. (11) (Emphasis added.)

The full extent of the problem can better be appreciated by noting that, while the total number of resident patients in these facilities decreased from a high of 559,000 in 1955 to 339,000 in 1970, this still meant that one of every 593 Americans was a resident patient in these hospitals at the end of 1970. Furthermore, in spite of the decreasing number of resident patients by about 39% from 1955, the real work of these institutions is increasing. The number of admissions and readmissions, for example, increased from 185,000 in 1956 to about 339,000 in 1970, an increase of about 112%. At the same time the number of discharges increased from 145,000 in 1956 to about 400,000 in 1970, an increase of 175%. From 1968 to 1970 alone, the number of patients treated annually in state and other public mental institutions rose from 800,000 to 850,000 (10).

The time needed for the daily care of first admissions, readmissions and discharges of short term patients (whether acutely or chronically ill) is more than the time needed for the daily care of long term chronic patients; therefore the burden on the state mental hospital system that treats the sickest, the most disabled and the poorest mental patients is becoming increasingly heavy. This development is occurring in spite of the continuing increase in the number of community mental health centers and in the number of beds in the psychiatric units of general hospitals.

In summary, the more than 700,000 Americans treated annually in our mental hospitals remain the primary unsolved national problem in the delivery of adequate health care.

Some Social Needs and Goals

The two main underlying themes of this paper will be developed in some detail in the following discussions of social needs for the right and of the various cases.

First, it is submitted that our society's rejection mechanisms against the severely mentally ill, and especially against the involuntarily civilly committed, have limited and may well continue to limit the realistic establishment of a legal right to treatment. These rejection phenomena prevent any comprehensive rational approach to the proper legal, medical and social treatment of the most severely mentally ill, both within and without the mental hospital. For convenience I have called the mechanisms of these rejection phenomena "sanism."

The second underlying theme of this paper is that hopefully the realistic recognition of the right to treatment will significantly counteract the sanist rejection phenomena that exist throughout our entire society and that are directed against the severely mentally ill. For the right to treatment is not only an end in itself but is rather like other important reforms in this field. The increasing use of voluntary rather than involuntary admissions and the increasing utilization of the open rather than the closed hospital ward are merely steps in effecting relief for the enormous disability associated with mental illness which is unnecessarily imposed by our society.

In the following discussion I shall discuss how, in general, sanism pervades our entire society. Then I shall point out how, unfortunately, it appears to be surprisingly strong in law and medicine. Probably one of the strongest sanist bastions of these rejection phenomena that oppress our nation's most severely mentally ill is to be found where one would least expect to find it: in the U. S. Supreme Court.

AN AMERICAN TRAGEDY: SANISM IN OUR SOCIETY

I believe that it will facilitate the discussion of this subject if one tries to view this area from the viewpoint of the severely mentally ill—that is, from the viewpoint of the oppressed—rather than from the viewpoint of myself and the other members of society, who are the oppressors. For it seems to me that only from the viewpoint of the oppressed can one properly understand our society's pathological sanist mechanisms of oppression. Analogous to the claims of blacks that they are oppressed by the bigotry of our racist society, and analogous to the claims of women that they are oppressed by the bigotry of our sexist society, so can the severely mentally ill, and particularly the involuntarily civilly committed, claim that they are invidiously and irrationally oppressed by the bigoted thinking, feeling and behavior patterns of our sanist society.

Sanism is the irrational thinking, feeling and behavior patterns of re-

sponse by an individual or by a society to the irrational behavior (and too
often even to the rational behavior) of a mentally ill individual. It is
morally reprehensible because it is an unnecessary and disabling burden
that is added by our prejudiced sanist society to the very real affliction
of severe mental illness.

The recognition of the rejection phenomena of sanism is of course not
new with this paper. For example, Dr. Robert Hunt, a New York state
mental hospital superintendent, described "The enormous disability associated with mental illness which is to a large extent superimposed, is
preventable and is treatable." (12).

It should be clearly understood that sanists are bigots. A bigot is defined by Webster's New International Dictionary (third edition) as "One
[who is] obstinately and *irrationally*, often intolerantly, devoted to his own
church, party, belief, or opinion" (emphasis added). Furthermore, as
Supreme Court Justice Thurgood Marshall, who is an expert on racism,
has stated, racism "is oftentimes deliberate, and sometimes unintentional.
Nevertheless, the consequences are the same." (13) By analogy, therefore,
it is of no consequence to the oppressed mentally ill whether the sanism
of our society is deliberate or unintentional.

In his provocative study of racism in America entitled *Beyond Black
and White*, Dr. James P. Comer, a black psychiatrist who is the Associate Dean of Yale Medical School, discussed in some detail the bigoted
thinking, feeling and behavioral patterns that lie behind what Dr. Comer
termed "the white mind syndrome." In that discussion he described and
analyzed our society's pathological racist mechanisms of oppression.

By substituting the term "sane" wherever Dr. Comer uses the term
"white," and "sanist" where he uses "racist," one can begin to appreciate
and understand our society's pathological sanist mechanisms of oppression:

> Observers . . . are often perplexed by the ability of the [sane] mind to remain
> impervious to [sanist] realities. . . .
>
> I now understand the phenomenon . . . as a collective defect in the national
> ego and superego; a blind spot that permits otherwise intelligent people to see,
> think and act in a [sanist] way without the expected level of guilt and pain.
> The syndrome is what I call "the [sane] mind."
>
> To many observers, this failure to see, acknowledge or understand the pecu-
> liar experience and special problems of [the mentally ill] is [sanism], pure and
> simple. [Sanism] it is, but simple it is not. The [sane] mind is a complex aber-
> ration. . . . [It] is the unwanted product of growing up in a society where [san-
> ist] viewpoints are transmitted from generation to generation by people and by
> their institutions.
>
> To avoid anxiety and guilt, it has been necessary over the years for many
> [sanists] to deny that [the] human and constitutional rights of [the mentally ill]

have been violated. But the violation has been so flagrant that denial alone is not enough. So the [sane] mind adds rationalization and justification.

Through these psychological mechanisms, the [sane] mind has managed to establish the notion that no consequential violation has ever taken place. (14)

It should be understood that personally I am quite conservative, and the term "oppression" normally is neither part of my vocabulary nor of my conscious thinking. Its utilization first came into my conscious thinking one evening while I was reading Dr. Comer's book. Gradually I realized that our society's irrational mechanisms of oppression of blacks which Dr. Comer was describing were similar in operational procedures to the operation of our society's irrational mechanisms of oppression of the involuntarily civilly committed.

My long-time friend and law school classmate Florynce Kennedy, a black feminist lawyer, has been telling me for years that I really do not understand what she terms the pathology of oppression. Although I probably continue to be diametrically opposed to her politically, I understand her better when she says that our society oppresses state mental hospital patients by "niggerizing" them. We lower their own esteem and that of their families by unnecessary and oppressive measures. She firmly believes—as I do not—that unless they openly and forcefully protest, as have blacks, prisoners, homosexuals, etc., the involuntarily civilly committed will not receive their just due.

As primary evidence of the sanism that pervades our entire society, the severely mentally ill need only point to the too often grossly inadequate conditions that frequently exist in our state mental hospitals. These inadequate conditions, which are due primarily to insufficient funding by our state legislatures, are well known and routinely accepted.

Then those oppressed need only point to the further acceptance of what too often may appear to be a modern day Bedlam throughout our society, as shown by the simple fact that Medicaid excludes only almost all state mental hospital patients from its benefits among all our nation's poor and infirm. It is not unexpected that a sanist society elects a sanist Congress that enacts sanist Medicaid legislation.

As mentioned before, the recognition of the rejection phenomena is of course not novel with this discussion. For example, after first noting that inadequate treatment in state mental hospitals rarely caused a significant and continuing public outcry, a lawyer, Professor Henry Weihofen, and a psychiatrist, Dr. Manfred Guttmacher, commented on the intrapersonal factors involved:

The fixation on illegal commitment to the exclusion of the many other tragedies connected with the insane is but another instance of man's neurotic self-interest. Most people defensively feel that insanity can never come to them. An old term for insanity, "alienation," clearly portrays this. It is remote like some decimating plague in distant India. But they can conceive of normal people like themselves being unjustly committed. What may happen to *me* is more important than what is happening to others. (15)

From the viewpoint of the oppressed, I believe that one of the most insidious forms of sanist oppression occurs in a segment of our society in which one would expect to find it least: among psychiatrists and other mental health professionals. For it is to these personnel that our sanist society has traditionally told the oppressed to turn for succor from their very real afflictions.

AN AMERICAN MEDICAL TRAGEDY: SANISM IN MEDICINE

Dr. Alfred Bay, formerly superintendent of Topeka State Hospital, has pointed out that many "new, refreshing or even exotic ideas" were merely "many of the practices of patient treatment in the mid-19th century that have only recently been discovered." He goes on:

> Why is it that gains so laboriously made became lost? Perhaps it is, as Richard Neutra says, because it is difficult to empathize with the mentally ill. It is unnatural, he says, even impossible, to share the feelings of someone who does not talk about the same subject at the end of a sentence as he did at the beginning, who sees and responds to things we do not see, whose mood, reason and very identity may change from moment to moment. These unfortunate people are uncanny, disconcerting, and inevitably alien to us. They invite rejection. . . .
>
> Perhaps, with our rapid transportation, we shall be unlikely in the future to reject patients by removing them far from our communities, but rejection can take many other forms. Political, for instance, in the declaration that psychiatry is atheistic, subversive and socialistic, and concerns itself with brainwashing and group indoctrination. Or economic, since psychiatry has to compete with military preparedness, urban renewal, education, and other important programs for public money. *But the subtlest of all is professional rejection, which only the frankest self-inspection will reveal.* What about our eagerness to decentralize, to deploy our patients in the community, and to forget the sickest, chronic patients and concentrate instead on the curable, the socially maladjusted, and the emotionally lame? Is this really the professional manifestation of a fantasy that if we just ignore the whole problem of the severely and persistently psychotic patient, the problem will disappear? (16) (Emphasis added.)

Cannot one point to those mental health professionals who refuse to associate themselves in any way, even part-time, with any state mental institution, who work only with the less sick and the "emotionally lame," and who press only to divert both public and private funds away from the state mental hospital system as some sort of "Uncle Sigmund" or

"Uncle Freud," pejorative terms analogous to the pejorative term of "Uncle Tom" as used by those oppressed by racism?

From the viewpoint of the oppressed, it must be tragic to realize that rejection mechanisms against them exist throughout our society, as shown in a primary manner by inadequate state and federal appropriations for necessary care and treatment in our state mental hospitals. It must be even more tragic to realize that sanism is so entrenched in the area of society in which one might expect to find it least: in American medicine, and in particular among psychiatrists and other mental health professionals. It is undoubtedly equally, if not even more, tragic to find that bigoted sanism is so firmly entrenched in our law, and especially in the thinking, feeling and behavioral patterns of the justices of the U. S. Supreme Court.

AN AMERICAN LEGAL TRAGEDY: SANISM IN THE LAW

From the viewpoint of the oppressed, one can readily recognize, as a primary example of pathological sanist oppression in our society, the obvious fact that no jurisdiction contains a realistic right-to-treatment provision in its involuntary civil commitment statutes.

Even more disheartening to the oppressed must be the bigoted sanist philosophy of the Supreme Court. As discussed in greater detail below, since 1960, on seven separate occasions, the Supreme Court refused to hear cases arising from New York and Florida state mental hospitals involving, *inter alia*, the claim that denial of adequate care and treatment to involuntary civilly committed state mental hospital patients is a deprivation of their liberty without the due process of law required by the Fourteenth Amendment to the Constitution. The failure of the Supreme Court to hear these cases without giving any reason for so deciding is surprising only if one is unaware of the sanist philosophy of the Court. *It has never even heard one case involving a civilly committed mentally ill patient who had committed no crime* except some minor cases during the last century and at the beginning of this century when the real issue was property rights and the question of the patient's civil rights was incidental (17).

The fact that the Court has begun to hear cases involving those accused of committing criminal acts who are also alleged to be mentally ill, e.g. *Jackson v. Indiana* (18), is only a reflection of the Court's proper concern with those accused of looting, plundering and raping who are subsequently involuntarily criminally committed to a public mental hospital. It is not a reflection of the Court's insight into its own sanism.

With all due respect to the Court, it is submitted that, analogous to the insight of Dr. Comer into racism, the justices lack the sociological and psychological insight into their own prejudicial sanist thinking, feeling and behavior patterns against the severely mentally ill, and particularly against the involuntarily civilly committed.

In view of the Court continually turning its back upon the hundreds of thousands of Americans treated annually in our state mental hospitals and who desperately need the help of the Court, from the viewpoint of one of the oppressed—for example, an involuntarily civilly committed patient who receives grossly inadequate care—is it not quite puerile for Arthur J. Goldberg, who as a justice of the Court during the 1960s participated in condoning and in effect continuing these abominable sanist practices by our society, to hortatorily pontificate:

> Whatever the justification for avoiding decisions on the merits of a case in other times, the tenor of the modern world demands that judges, like other men, frankly confront even the most controversial and troublesome judicial problems. . . .
>
> The courts did not invite these cases, but, having been presented with them, they ought to decide them in accordance with their function as the ultimate guardian of constitutionally protected fundamental rights. The Court's obligation is to be the guardian of our constitutionally protected individual liberties. The Justices of the Court must act forcefully and review scrupulously threatened infringements. (19)

From the viewpoint of an oppressed involuntarily civilly committed patient, like Donaldson or Stephens, these high-sounding phrases are only a meaningless passel of words. For the sad reality of sanism is that all of the humane and learned justices of both the Warren and the Burger courts, whether of the so-called liberal or the so-called conservative tendencies, have been unanimous in only one area of civil rights, i.e. in agreeing in effect that the civil rights of the involuntarily civilly committed mental patient are not protected by the United States Constitution.

Realistically, of course, I realize that most members of our society quite properly hold the Supreme Court justices in such high regard that these allegations of sanist bigotry—even if it is unconscious and unintentional on their part—will receive the same warm reception accorded to the little boy who claimed that the Emperor wore no clothes.

One simple observation may help you realize that in reality the Emperor wears no clothes. Judge Russell, the moderator of this morning's panel, is a black and I am a Jew. If I told you—and if it were true—that the Supreme Court had never heard and openly decided even one case involving a black or a Jew, and if this were true in spite of the fact that numerous cases had been presented to the Court ranging from denial of right to vote, to denial of right to any government job, to denial of right to go to a public school, etc., and if it were obviously true and well known that blacks and Jews were not able to vote, to hold any government job, to go to any public school, etc., would not you see this as de facto racism and antisemitism on the part of the Court when Judge Russell and I made this claim to you? Furthermore, would not our claims be valid whether this racism and antisemitism were unintentional and unconscious rather than intentional and conscious?

Further evidence of the sanism of the Supreme Court is not only that they invariably decide these cases against the involuntarily civilly committed. Even more is that they have never written opinion setting forth in detail the claims that they have denied or the reasons why they denied these claims; therefore, they have not even attempted to awaken the conscience of our nation to its irrational sanism.

Again from the viewpoint of the irrationally oppressed involuntarily civilly committed state mental hospital patient, it is important to realize the scope and the depth of the irrational sanist bigotry against the institutionalized mentally ill which these sanist decisions of the Supreme Court reflect. Because the Court has never openly heard and decided any case involving the civil rights of the involuntarily civilly committed, the hundreds of thousands of Americans who are involuntarily civilly committed annually, who have never committed any criminal act and who only ask for adequate care and treatment are still treated as modern day common law outlaws beyond the pale of any constitutional protection. In the eyes of our sanist Supreme Court, the flag and its protections fly over our nation's Atticas—our state penal institutions—but not over any of our nation's modern day Bedlams—our state mental hospitals.

From the viewpoint of the oppressed involuntarily civilly committed patient, as tragic as the sanism of the Court is the sanism shown by leading civil liberties groups. For example, the American Civil Liberties Union (ACLU), while handling numerous cases to improve conditions in prisons for common convicted criminals who have murdered, raped and plundered, had never handled any aspect of even one case involving a civilly committed patient who had committed no crime, until 1970 when it filed an *amicus curiae* brief in the previously mentioned *Donaldson* case. Similarly, the national offices of the National Association for the Advancement of Colored People (NAACP) never filed any brief in even one case involving an involuntarily civilly committed patient who had committed no crime until 1973 when it filed an *amicus curiae* brief in the *Legion v. Weinberger* (Richardson) case discussed below.

Again from the viewpoint of one oppressed by sanism, the foregoing undoubtedly constitutes, at the very least, *prima facie, de facto* sanism throughout the law, and especially in the U. S. Supreme Court. My own explanation of the actions of the Supreme Court is the irrational fear of the involuntarily civilly committed that pervades our entire society.

Repeatedly I have tried to show that mental hospitalization rates have varied more than 1,000 % from state to state. Furthermore, these variations occur in spite of data showing that there is no concomitant variation in the incidence or prevalence of severe mental illness. Neither is there any concomitant variation in the commitment laws of these jurisdictions; therefore, I conclude that these variations are due primarily to social factors rather than to legal or medical (individual psychopathological) factors (20–22). These arguments have been of no avail for, as Mr. Justice Holmes clearly pointed out in his classic study, *The Common Law:*

> The life of the law has not been logic; it has been experience. The felt necessities of the time, the prevalent moral and political theories, intuitions of public policy, avowed or unconscious, even the prejudices which judges share with their fellow men, have had a good deal more [to do] than the syllogism in determining the rules by which men should be governed. (23)

A personal experience that illustrates how valid was Holmes' observation, and how too often attempts at rationality are of no avail when sanism is involved, is the following.

Several years ago, while waiting to argue an appeal in the *Stephens* case, I listened to the arguments of the earlier cases on the calendar. The first case involved a recidivistic armed robber appealing from his third conviction for armed robbery. Counsel began her argument by surprisingly conceding to the court that her client had probably been properly convicted in the two previous convictions; that he had probably committed other armed robberies for which he had never even been arrested, much less convicted; that if released he probably would commit other armed robberies; and that the evidence introduced in his trial that resulted in his third conviction undoubtedly proved that he had actually committed the crime. However, she properly and skillfully argued that much of the evidence introduced in the trial was not admissible because of a claimed unconstitutionally obtained confession and because of an alleged unconstitutional search for and seizure of the weapons and the loot. Of course, no judge upbraided counsel for seeking the release of this common hoodlum on procedural grounds.

The second case involved a recidivistic heroin pusher appealing from his second conviction for heroin distribution. He had been arrested after the police, while pursuing him and in order to get him to stop, had crashed into his car. Search of the car revealed a substantial quantity of uncut heroin. Here again counsel skillfully and properly raised questions as to the admissibility of the evidence because of an unconstitutional search and seizure. The police informant was a known drug addict who had previously given the police unreliable information. Accordingly, the fact that the search warrant was based solely on this addict's information posed a major constitutional question about which the learned judges asked probing questions of defendant's counsel. And here again, of course, no judge upbraided counsel for urging that a known heroin pusher go forth—solely on procedural grounds—to continue to peddle his wares that have destroyed so much of our nation's youth.

The third case involved a recidivistic pimp, and the questions on appeal involved primarily the admissibility of confessions of codefendants and accomplices and of evidence seized after searches of persons and premises. The evidence showed not only that the defendant was a pimp but that most of his prostitutes were heroin addicts whom he kept in line both by supplying them with heroin and by brute force. And here again, no judge upbraided counsel for skillfully and properly urging that this brutal pimp be released to pursue his activities.

The fourth case involved a habeas corpus proceeding brought by a 66-year-old inmate of Creedmoor State Hospital in Queens, New York, who had been involuntarily civilly incarcerated for more than 32 years because he suffered from paranoid schizophrenia and who was not considered to be dangerous to himself or to others, who claimed that he should be released as he no longer needed involuntary hospitalization, and that even if he did in theory need this involuntary hospitalization, as he was receiving grossly inadequate treatment, he should be released.

This last case was the *Stephens* case. I was the attorney. Instead of the scheduled 15 minutes allowed by the court, the oral argument lasted well over an hour; however, unlike the queries of the applicability of concepts of due process of law that were posed by the judges to the lawyers for the armed robber, the heroin pusher and the brutal pimp, the sanist judges posed no questions as to the applicability for Stephens of constitutional safeguards. The questions and comments concerned the dangers to the public order and to the community if an insane man were to be discharged simply because he was not receiving adequate treatment. These judges repeatedly posed questions of me asking if I were seriously recommending that this insane man simply be released from "the hospital"; yet none of the sanist judges ever openly mentioned Stephens' undisputed claims that there was only one doctor to more than 500 patients; that no doctor had examined him for more than a year; that the only aide on duty at night on Stephens' ward had been arrested for sexually assaulting and killing a helpless, bedridden fellow inmate of Stephens; and that Stephens routinely worked without any pay for 7 days a week, 52 weeks a year, year after year, as a porter, general handyman and kitchen helper.

The foregoing episode merely describes the tip of the iceberg of sanist thinking, feeling and behaving that determines the decisions reached by our judges. It is of no importance to those oppressed by this irrational sanism whether this oppression is unconscious and unintentional, rather than conscious and intentional. For, to paraphrase Justice Marshall's previous mentioned comment on racism, "[Sanism] is oftentimes deliberate, and sometimes unintentional. Nevertheless, the consequences are the same."

Against this background of sanism pervading our entire society, and in particular, law and medicine, I shall discuss what I call the "nowhere, somewhere, anywhere" development of the concept. I shall first discuss the constitutional and statutory developments of the *nowhere* era of the 1960s: a period of time when the concept went nowhere and did nothing for the severely mentally ill state mental hospital patient. Then I shall proceed to discuss certain constitutional and statutory developments of the *somewhere* era of the early 1970s up to the present day. This is a period of time when the right has gone somewhere and done something for the state mental hospital patient. Only future evaluation will enable us to correctly assess where the concept is now. Finally, I shall conclude this presentation with comments on the future *anywhere* era of the right—a period of time when the right may go anywhere and do anything for the mentally ill. Whether it will do a lot or nothing, and whether it will do harm or do good, remains to be seen.

SOME DEVELOPMENTS IN THE "NOWHERE" ERA OF THE SIXTIES

This presentation will show primarily that sanism has limited the capacity of the right to respond significantly to certain unmet important legal, medical and social needs of severely mentally ill state mental hospital patients. Again, to inject some realism into this discussion, I shall comment primarily from the viewpoint of the irrationally oppressed, involuntarily civilly committed state mental hospital patient.

Some Constitutional Developments

THE STEPHENS CASE IN NEW YORK. The first case I should like to discuss is that of Edward J. Stephens, who in 1960 was 62 years old and had been an involuntarily civilly committed patient for more than 30 years at Creedmoor State Hospital in New York City. He first contacted me in May 1960 after reading in the Sunday *New York Times* about my contention that there is a constitutional right to treatment. He asked me to aid him in his efforts to be released and to obtain proper care and treatment.

On 12 separate occasions I presented his claims before New York and federal courts, including the U. S. Supreme Court on three occasions. No court consented to hear his claim of inadequate care and treatment.

In 1960 this man was one of more than 500 inmates in a building of Creedmoor State Hospital that was staffed by only one physician. Accordingly, the physician-inmate ratio inside the hospital was less than that of the surrounding area of New York City, and it was also less than that of Sing Sing Prison, then a New York maximum security prison. Also, in the entire year prior to his contacting me, there was not even one note on his chart by any doctor, nurse or attendant. He worked 7 days a week in the kitchen for which he received no pay, only better sleeping accommodations. Yet hospital authorities denied that these conditions constituted inadequate care and treatment, and no court granted a hearing on his complaint of inadequate treatment.

During this period, when the courts stood by and did nothing, an elderly bedridden patient on Stephens' ward was found dead one morning, and an autopsy revealed that he had been choked to death. This helpless man had been killed during a sexual assault by the sole attendant in charge of the ward at night. It turned out that this attendant had for a long time made a practice of routinely assaulting helpless bedridden patients. The attendant was subsequently committed to Matteawan, a New York state mental hospital for the criminally insane. Undoubtedly, a primary factor in the continuance of these assaults over a period of time was an insufficient number of proper personnel on the ward.

From the viewpoint of the judges who rendered these 12 decisions denying his claim for adequate care, Stephens had a fair hearing and a just decision on each occasion. From the viewpoint of the dead inmate, of Stephens and of the 500 other inmates on his ward, these were merely additional examples of the courts holding that they were beyond the pale of constitutional protections.

Shortly after the last hearing, solely because of a change in administrative policy and not because of any medical or legal development, he was discharged to a residential hotel and transferred from the state hospital rolls to the welfare rolls.

Until now I have discussed this case from the substantive aspects, and now I should like to mention some procedural aspects of this matter. My discussion is directed to the old Section 86 of the New York Mental Hygiene Law and to its similarly worded successor (24). For whenever the problem of inadequate treatment in New York state mental hospitals was raised, the New York and federal courts pointed to Section 86 as the primary remedy. If one complained of improper care and treatment in a New York state mental hospital, however, he soon found:

1. That Section 86 provided no separation of functions in that the one who investigates, the one who prosecutes, the one who is the plaintiff, the one who hears and determines and the one who is the defendant are all one and the same legal person, the Commissioner of Mental Hygiene; and

2. That Section 86 provided for an inadequate remedy in that:

a. If the Commissioner found overcrowding, understaffing and other evidence of inadequate care, he was given no way of obtaining additional personnel, funds or buildings to improve conditions;

b. The patient could never obtain his freedom no matter how inadequate was his care and treatment; and

c. The enforcement procedures contemplated by the statute are far too complex and are unrealistic.

From the irrational sanist viewpoints of the humane and learned Supreme Court judges who repeatedly held this statute to meet the requirements of procedural due process of law under the Fourteenth Amendment, Stephens had a fair hearing and a just decision on every occasion.

From the viewpoint of the involuntarily civilly committed New York state mental hospital patient who received inadequate treatment, this is merely another example of sanist oppression. I submit to you that in any field of law, except one involving state mental hospital inmates, this statute would be held to be unconstitutional, either on its face or as applied to these patients.

I know of no other case in American law in which the Supreme Court or any other court has held it to be a fair and constitutional hearing for one who complains that a constitutional right has been violated to be compelled to appoint someone else—here the Commissioner of Mental Hygiene or his agent—to investigate, prosecute and appear as *plaintiff* in an action to secure his constitutional right; then to be compelled to continue to participate in this charade wherein the Commissioner of Mental Hygiene or his agent, wearing his second face, appears as a *judge;* and then to be continue to be compelled to participate in this fiasco wherein the Commissioner of Mental Hygiene or his agent, now wearing his third face, appears as a *defendant.* Only sanism can explain how the Supreme Court judges could repeatedly delude themselves that this was a fair hearing as mandated by the due process clause of the Constitution.

From the viewpoint of those oppressed by the sanism of the Court, the *Donaldson* case equally illustrates—if not even more so—the irrational sanism of the Court.

THE DONALDSON CASE FROM FLORIDA. In May 1960, also as a result of the Sunday *New York Times* column on the *American Bar Association Journal* article on the right to treatment, I also received a letter from one Kenneth Donaldson, then a 51-year-old involuntarily civilly committed inmate since 1956 of Florida State Hospital located in Chatahoochee,

Florida. He also asked me to aid him in his efforts to obtain his release on the grounds that he did not need involuntary institutionalization and that he was receiving inadequate treatment. Since then, on 18 separate occasions, his claims were presented to various Florida and federal courts, including the U. S. Supreme Court on four separate occasions. Through the last adverse decision by the Supreme Court in 1970, no court granted his petition for a writ of habeas corpus in spite of the fact that *from 1969 on, he had had town privileges so that he could go back and forth into Chattahoochee at will.*

In May 1961, more than 6 months after the Supreme Court declined to hear his first appeal to that court, and in effect told him that there was no constitutional right to treatment, the Committee of State Institutions of the Florida Legislature made a report on conditions at Florida State Hospital. This detailed report proved the validity of Donaldson's claim. It showed that there was only one doctor for more than 1,000 inmates in Donaldson's section of the institution, that the buildings were in a complete state of obsolescence, that disturbed inmates were commonly "choked down" to subdue them and that some of the attendants who were in complete charge of giving care to inmates could neither read nor write. This report was part of Donaldson's papers in subsequent proceedings, as were later reports further proving inadequate treatment.

From the point of view of the sanist judges who on 18 occasions denied his claim for a writ of habeas corpus to see if he was getting adequate care, Donaldson had a constitutionally required fair hearing and a just decision on each occasion. From the viewpoint of Donaldson and the 1,000 other inmates in his section under the care of one doctor, most of whom, like Donaldson, had not been seen by the doctor for more than 2 years, the courts were simply treating them like modern day common law outlaws beyond the pale of the Constitution.

In July 1971, after the fourth refusal by the Supreme Court to hear his case, Donaldson was granted an unconditional release by the hospital. This was either because a federal judge finally set a pre-trial hearing to see whether the writ of habeas corpus should be granted, or because of a change in administrative policy.

After his discharge from Florida State Hospital following 14 years of involuntary incarceration, Donaldson took a train back to his boyhood home in Syracuse, New York. There he immediately obtained a full-time position as a night clerk in a hotel. He worked there continually for more than a year, after which he left that job to devote his full-time efforts to writing a book about his hospital experiences. He rejected the suggestion of others that he go on welfare, and he supports himself solely from his Social Security allotment.

To simplify matters, the foregoing discussion of the *Donaldson* case concerned itself primarily with the concept of the right to treatment. As proof of how deeply sanism is part of the philosophy of the U. S. Supreme Court, however, it should be noted that the constitutional issues presented to the Court in this matter concerned themselves with every major facet of substantive and procedural law. For when I submitted Donaldson's petition for certiorari to the Supreme Court in 1970, his primary claims were exactly those that had been submitted to the Court in 1960 and again in 1962 and again in 1967.

Donaldson claimed that he was entitled to the Great Writ—the writ of habeas corpus—so that for the first time since his involuntary civil commitment in 1957, a court would fully examine his claims that:

a. After 14 years of involuntary civil commitment, after 18 attempts for a writ of habeas corpus before more than 30 different judges, he was entitled to at least one judicial hearing in the nature of habeas corpus to review the staff doctors' decision that he still needed involuntary civil commitment. In 1970, it should again be noted, Donaldson was not on a locked ward and he had not only ground privileges but full town privileges since 1969, and he went back and forth from the hospital to the town of Chattahoochee at will during the day. Again it should be noted that Donaldson was not accused of committing any crime and had never been convicted of the commission of any crime. Furthermore, he had not committed any act of violence either before or during his 14 years of institutionalization.

b. As he did not receive adequate treatment in Florida State Hospital in that *inter alia* there was still only one doctor to more than 900 patients during 1970, he could not be involuntarily civilly committed in this "hospital."

c. He had not received a fair hearing in the lower Florida courts because in the initial proceedings, he was compelled to proceed involuntarily *pro se*—as his own lawyer. In spite of the fact that he was legally declared mentally incompetent, in spite of the fact that it was undisputed that he was a pauper who could not pay a lawyer, in spite of the fact that he had repeatedly requested the court to appoint a Florida lawyer to represent him, no lawyer was appointed in the initial proceedings; therefore Donaldson initially had represented himself. For common criminals, the Supreme Court decided in *Gideon v. Wainwright* (25) that when a felony was involved, it was constitutionally required that paupers have court-appointed counsel. Although Donaldson had already "served" 14 years, no counsel was appointed.

d. At his initial commitment in 1957, he was unable to prove that he did not even then require involuntary civil commitment in that he did not have a proper hearing before a judge, and he had no access to proper counsel and to an expert witness on his behalf before he was "locked up."

In 1967, the U. S. Court of Appeals for the Fifth Circuit specifically stated that it affirmed the decision of the lower U. S. District Court in denying Donaldson's petition for the writ because Donaldson should first go to the lower Florida courts. There he should avail himself of the state habeas corpus procedure specifically available to state mental hospital patients.

In his papers to the Circuit Court, Donaldson had specifically pointed out that he had tried on several occasions to get the writ in the lower Florida courts. The Circuit Court paid no attention to these claims. The Supreme Court denied certiorari to review the Circuit Court's decision. With no other alternative, Donaldson then went back to the lower Florida courts to again petition for the writ under the Florida statutes specifically applicable to state mental hospital patients. Again habeas corpus was denied, and again the Supreme Court refused to grant certiorari.

The simple fact remains that for 14 years, on 18 separate occasions before every Florida and federal court having jurisdiction over the granting of the writ, and before more than 30 different state, federal and U. S. Supreme Court judges, he was unable to obtain a fundamental writ of habeas corpus to even once review the decision of the hospital doctors that he continued to need involuntary institutionalization. From the viewpoint of one oppressed as was Donaldson, these events are stark proof of the sanism of our courts. The fact that on four separate occasions the Supreme Court saw no wrong in this denial of the Great Writ is further *prima facie* proof of the de facto irrational sanism of the Court.

In 1970, before it denied certiorari for the fourth time, the Court had asked the State of Florida to file a reply brief. Furthermore, groups such as the ACLU, the Connecticut Chapter of the Psychologists for Social Action, the Medical Committee for Human Rights and the New York Chapter of the Lawyers Committee for Civil Rights Under Law all filed *amicus curiae* briefs supporting Donaldson's position; therefore it must be assumed that the Court was aware of the issues involved. After more than 8 months of deliberation, the Court denied certiorari in accordance with its policy of never having openly decided any issue involving the civil liberties of any involuntarily civilly committed state mental hospital patient who was not accused of committing any crime.

Sanist legal scholars, of course, can prattle that denial of certiorari does not mean a decision on the merits by the Supreme Court. From the viewpoint of an oppressed involuntarily civilly committed inmate—here, Donaldson—I can only repeat, and parapharase, what Judge Thurgood Marshall said to me in 1962. At that time Judge Marshall was a member of the bench of the U. S. Court of Appeals for the Second Circuit, and I was arguing the *Stephens* case before him. I had told Judge Marshall that a prior denial of certiorari to Stephens by the Supreme Court was not a decision on the merits. I was told that for Stephens (and this would apply to Donaldson), it was a decision on the merits because it was a final decision for Stephens on that appeal to the Court.

Until now I have discussed certain constitutional events in the "nowhere" era of the sixties. I shall now discuss some statutory developments during this "nowhere" era—a time when the concept did nothing for the civilly committed state metal hospital patient.

Some Statutory Developments

DISTRICT OF COLUMBIA CODE: ROUSE V. CAMERON. In March 1961, pursuant to the suggestion of Dr. Winifred Overholser, then Superintendent of St. Elizabeth's Hospital in Washington, D.C., I was invited to testify on the concept of the right to treatment before the Subcommittee on Constitutional Rights of the Committee on the Judiciary of the United States Senate. This subcommittee, whose chairman was Senator Sam J. Ervin, Jr., was then considering revisions of the District of Columbia Mental Health Code.

In my testimony (20) I advocated a statute that would recognize, define and enforce the right to treatment in a manner similar to what I have set forth at the beginning of this chapter. While the first revisions proposed by the subcommittee introduced some provisions for recognition, definition and enforcement of the right, the final revision sent to, and enacted by, Congress in 1964 contained only a precatory phrase concerning recognition of the right. It contained no definition or enforcement provisions; therefore, knowing the legal ability of Senator Ervin and his staff, I concluded that it was only intended to be a moral right to treatment and not a realistic legal right.

Accordingly, I was quite surprised in October 1966 to read in the first *Rouse v. Cameron* decision (26) that the U. S. Court of Appeals for the District of Columbia, in a decision written by Chief Judge David L. Bazelon, had held that a statutory right to treatment existed under the revisions of the District of Columbia Mental Health Code. This landmark case marked the first significant breakthrough in this area. While a statutory right was recognized, it was not (and still has not been in my opinion) adequately defined, effectively enforced and properly implemented. The question of whether there is a constitutional right to treatment was not decided in *Rouse*. By deciding that there was a statutory right to treatment, the *Rouse* court avoided deciding the more basic issue of whether there is a constitutional right to treatment.

My opinion of the first *Rouse* opinion, however, is that it represents not only a worthwhile potential for use of the right, but also a dangerous potential for abuse. For in a habeas corpus proceeding involving the right to treatment, under the *Rouse* guidelines the institution must not only show that it has an adequate staff, physical facilities, etc.—it must also show "the suitability and adequacy of . . . [the] therapy for *this* petitioner." (27) This last requirement compels the trial court to receive such detailed testimony on diagnosis, prognosis and treatment that most of the time of staff physicians, nurses and other needed personnel may well be spent in testifying and preparing to testify in courtroom proceedings, rather than in attending to the needs of the hospital's patients.

So far I have given what I consider to be a conventional sanist approach to this matter. But from the viewpoint of the oppressed involuntary civilly committed patient, what does one see? A pre-eminent legal scholar such as Senator Ervin drafts a statute that contains only a precatory clause that has only moral, not legal, force. It can only serve to placate the conscience of a sanist Congress. It cannot serve to help the oppressed patient.

Following this, an equally pre-eminent legal scholar such as Judge Bazelon takes a precatory statutory clause that a first year law student knows should have no legal effect, and to avoid a constitutional issue, seeks to weave this precatory phrase into the fabric of a realistic statutory right to treatment. From the viewpoint of the oppressed inmate, the issue was important enough not to call for evasive tactics but rather for a realistic constitutional approach to the problem.

In *Rouse*, a statutory precatory phrase whose history shows that it was not intended to be a realistic right was theoretically converted into a potentially effective right through judicial efforts. By comparison, the history of the proposed Pennsylvania "Right to Treatment Act of 1968" (28) shows the difficulty of openly enacting a valid right to treatment statute in the milieu of sanist legislative bodies.

THE PENNSYLVANIA RIGHT TO TREATMENT STATUTE. In early 1967 the Pennsylvania AFL-CIO mounted a massive effort to obtain the passage of legislation establishing a statutory right to treatment in that state. Because of this effort, legislation drafted by a group of consultants, including myself, was introduced in both houses of the General Assembly and was made the subject of several days of joint hearings (29). Unfortunately it was never reported out of the legislative committees.

Pennsylvania's proposed "Right to Treatment Law of 1968" would have been the first comprehensive attempt by any legislative body in the United States, if not in the world, to regulate the important substantive problems of adequate care and treatment for patients in public mental institutions. The objective of this bill was to provide some basic minimum level of care for all patients as a matter of right rather than of selection. Its provisions would have established a Mental Treatment Standards Committee which would have in turn drafted minimum personnel-patient standards equal at least to those of the APA in the past. Similarly, the statute provided for a standard on the minimum number of consultations and physical examinations to be required within a given period of time. The committee would also have been barred from setting requirements on methods or quality of treatment, but the proposed statute established a Patient Treatment Review Board to investigate, hear and decide questions of adequate treatment. Another innovation was a method by which inmates might obtain private care through public funds if an adequate staff were not available. Unfortunately, the Pennsylvania General Assembly failed to enact the statute.

The Pennsylvania proposal could be validly criticized on several grounds. Among them are the lack of any provision for counsel to represent the patient who appeared before the proposed review board, and the fact that the board did not have the power to order and enforce the most effective statutory remedy, i.e., the discharge of the patient. While a writ of habeas corpus was theoretically available, it would seem more effective if the board itself could order the patient's release when inadequate treatment was being provided.

Regardless of the minor imperfections embodied in the Pennsylvania draft, the state legislature rather than the judiciary seems the proper instrumentality to establish a realistic right to treatment. Only the legislature has the means to set up a comprehensive scheme and to coordinate it with necessary legislative appropriations; the judiciary, as in the *Wyatt* case, is limited to a step-by-step development. Unfortunately, however, until recently it seemed a fact of life that neither the Congress nor any state legislature would take it upon itself to deal with this problem unless the Supreme Court recognized a realistic right to treatment.

Up to this point I have discussed the "nowhere" era of the concept of the right to treatment. Realistically, during this period, the concept contributed nothing to the improvement of the care of the involuntarily civilly committed. I have, however, discussed the constitutional and statutory developments in this era as a way of focusing on the recognition of what I consider to be the basic problem in this field. This fundamental problem is that sanism throughout our society, and especially in the field of law and medicine, irrationally, unnecessarily and invidiously oppresses the severely mentally ill.

SOME DEVELOPMENTS IN THE "SOMEWHERE" ERA OF THE
EARLY SEVENTIES

Beginning with the *Wyatt v. Stickney* case in 1971, the "somewhere" era was ushered in. For since that decision, the right has begun to go somewhere, and it has begun to improve care—even if only on the custodial level initially—for some state mental hospital patients. *Wyatt* is the landmark case in this area because it marks the first time that a court recognized the constitutional right to treatment, defined it by objective standards and then proceeded to enforce it by injunction.

Some Constitutional Developments

THE WYATT CASE IN ALABAMA. In March 1971, in the case of *Wyatt v. Stickney*, a class suit involving more than 5,000 patients in a state mental hospital in Alabama, U. S. District Court Judge Frank M. Johnson, Jr. held that involuntarily civilly committed patients are entitled to adequate care and treatment, or else they are being deprived of their liberty without due process of law as required by the Fourteenth Amendment to the Constitution.

It is usually overlooked that a significant breakthrough occurred when the defendants, led by Dr. Stonewall B. Stickney, the Alabama Mental Health Commissioner, conceded at the outset of the proceedings that the patients has such a right. *Wyatt* therefore not only marked the first time that an American court clearly recognized this concept: it also marked the first time that state mental hospital personnel agreed during litigation that their patients have this right.

In subsequent orders, the scope of the hearings was extended to include the other Alabama public mental hospital and the state institution for the mentally retarded. It should be noted that problems of the retarded are very similar to, and interrelated with, those of mental hospital patients. Therefore all patients, both voluntary and involuntary, in the state mental institutions in Alabama were included in the court's follow-up orders.

Recognition, however, was only child's play compared to the problems faced by the court in defining, enforcing and implementing the right. As one of the original co-counsel for the plaintiffs in the Wyatt case, I assisted in drafting the post-trial brief that contained the plaintiff's suggestions as to recognition, definition, enforcing and implementing the concept. Judge Johnson's original opinion in that matter merely recognized the right. It was not until almost a year later that he held hearings on defining, enforcing and implementing the concept. In April 1972, more than a year after the original decision, he handed down an opinion that defined the right (30). Specific enforcement and implementation provisions were absent and, in reality, still are.

As to defining the right, a significant contribution was that *Wyatt* set forth objective standards, rather than the subjective standards of *Rouse*.

Admittedly, one may validly criticize these standards on several points; however, as an initial step, they represent a significant and much-needed contribution.

Judge Johnson adopted standards that were drafted primarily by the *amici curiae* who entered the case after the March 1971 decision. These *amici* have now formed the Mental Health Law Project. The standards range from staff-patient ratios to frequency of linen changes. The court rejected other readily available objective standards that were already drafted by various professional groups, and which I had originally submitted to the court when the proceeding was initiated. The standards which I suggested would have required much more professional supervision and treatment than those adoped by the court.

The court also rejected the much higher standards recommended on behalf of the plaintiffs by Dr. Jack Ewalt, Chairman of the Department of Psychiatry of Harvard Medical School. He suggested staffing standards similar to those at the Massachusetts Mental Health Center, a Harvard teaching hospital. Dr. Ewalt's recommendations were the least sanist of all. For he suggested that "they," the state mental hospital patients, should receive treatment under the same standards as applied for "us" when we become severely mentally ill.

As I was the co-counsel who arranged for the expert witnesses for the plaintiffs, I should like to relate some background material. I had first arranged for Dr. Harry Solomon, former Chairman of the Harvard Psychiatry Department, to be our main and lead-off witness. Subsequently he informed me that he could not be present at the adjourned date of the hearings. On very short notice I telephoned Dr. Ewalt out of the blue and asked him if he would be an expert witness. I knew he had been the Director of the Joint Commission on Mental Illness and Health and that he had prepared its report entitled *Action for Mental Health* (31). Fortunately he not only agreed to come but even before I could get around to telling him that there were no funds for fees, etc., he said that the only terms on which he would come would be that he would pay all his travel and hotel costs and accept no fee. Dr. F. Lewis Bartlett, our other main witness, also paid all his own expenses. All the plaintiff's counsel were also paying their own expenses and were receiving no fee.

As to enforcement of the concept, the court chose injunction as the method of enforcing these objective standards; however, it has been sparingly used. Habeas corpus hearings were not ordered if the standards were not met, and no one suggested actions for injuries due to inadequate treatment under the federal civil rights laws.

While the number of resident patients has fallen dramatically, there has been no follow-up to see how the ex-patients have been faring in their communities.

The primary unsolved problems in *Wyatt* are implementation of the right, both from a personnel and a financial aspect. Two years after the *Wyatt* decision ordering certain objective standards, one finds that custodial care—food, clothing and shelter—is probably improved. Undoubtedly more maids, porters and other nonprofessional personnel are available. On the other hand, it is probable that the needed psychiatric and other highly professional personnel and the needed psychiatric esprit de corps—admittedly grossly inadequate before—are not significantly more adequate now. Dr. Stickney and his assistant, Dr. James Folsom, both native Alabamans and both qualified psychiatrists, have been replaced by lay administrators. In March 1974 an editorial in *Psychiatric News* (32), the official newsletter of the APA, pointed out that Bryce State Hospital, an Alabama state mental hospital, had been unable to recruit even one of five needed psychiatrists for many months; therefore, as Dr. Stickney pointed out at the Hospital and Community Psychiatry meeting in Miami in September 1973, recruitment of professional personnel has not significantly improved.

Since the original *Wyatt* decision in March 1971, numerous other right to treatment cases have arisen throughout the nation. While most courts have adopted the reasoning of *Wyatt*, these courts are all lower trial courts; none is a higher appellate court.

The defendants in *Wyatt* have appealed to the U. S. Court of Appeals for the Fifth Circuit. In this appeal the Circuit Court may affirm or reverse in whole or in part, or it may send the case back for further determinations. Although it was originally argued in December 1972, no decision has been handed down as yet—16 months later, at this writing. The delay in deciding the *Wyatt* appeal is especially significant in view of the fact that, by order of the Circuit Court, the appeal in the Wyatt case was combined with the appeal in the case of *Burnham v. Dept. of Public Health of Georgia* (33). In the *Burnham* case, a different U. S. District Court had held that there was no constitutional right to treatment.

THE BURNHAM CASE IN GEORGIA. In August 1972 in this case, a class suit involving all patients in all of the six Georgia state mental institutions, U. S. District Court Judge Sidney O. Smith, Jr., held that these patients did not have a constitutional right to adequate care and treatment. Judge Smith therefore did not even recognize the right. Before denying that this right existed, however, Judge Smith described a significant improvement in the level of care being provided for Georgia state mental institution patients during the last decade.

As with the *Wyatt* case, on appeal the Circuit Court may affirm or reverse in whole or in part, or may send the case back for further determinations.

The next development that I shall discuss is another method of enforcement of the right. This method is by suing for money damages under the federal civil rights laws for injuries sustained due to inadequate treatment. It can be used as an alternative or as a supplement to an injunction or habeas corpus.

MONEY DAMAGES AND DONALDSON V. O'CONNOR AGAIN. Conventionally, money damages serve both to compensate an injured party for injuries and damages and to deter future perpetration of similar wrongs. When I first advocated the right to treatment, I discussed the use of money damages under tort law—when there was no sovereign immunity—as a method of enforcement. This requires that the state allow itself to be sued, but it does not require recognition of the right. Subsequently I discussed the possibility of suing under federal civil rights laws. This however would necessitate, as a pre-condition, recognition of the concept of the right to treatment as a constitutional right.

My own lack of interest in this remedy stems from a basic belief that money damages cannot in any real way compensate for years of inadequate care and treatment in a state mental institution. Second, my own observations have been that, in general, malpractice awards have not significantly improved care in any area of medicine. Third, when damages have been awarded to state mental hospital patients still in the hospital, they have been awarded only for physical injuries, e.g. a patient falls off a stretcher because of being improperly strapped on and is paralyzed secondary to cervical spinal cord injuries. Realistically, in order to collect for injuries suffered because of lack of psychiatric treatment in a state hospital, usually one must be out of the hospital, i.e. must be an ex-patient.

However, as a reaction to the gross injustice of the 1970 decision of the U. S. Supreme Court in the *Donaldson* case which for the fourth time denied certiorari to Donaldson, I initiated further proceedings in the U. S. District Court in Tallahassee, Florida. This complaint was a class action on behalf of Donaldson and the 6,000 other patients in Florida State Hospital at Chattahoochee. It claimed that any of the 6,000 patients who were involuntarily civilly committed should be able to leave at will because they all received inadequate treatment. It also claimed damages for Donaldson and all the 6,000 other patients under the federal civil rights laws. The supporting papers for both these claims cited *Wyatt v. Stickney.*

For the first time in more than 14 years, a court set down this matter for a preliminary hearing, to determine whether the District Court would issue a writ of habeas corpus. Either because of the court's action or because of a change of administration at the hospital, or both, Donaldson was unconditionally discharged before the return day for the preliminary hearing. Subsequently the court dismissed the class action for habeas corpus and for damages for civil rights violations. As he had been discharged, Donaldson's habeas corpus petition may have become moot; however, he was allowed to file an amended complaint claiming money damages for violation of his civil rights, in particular his constitutional right to treatment.

Because of the time needed for the handling of the *Legion v. Richardson* case, I have participated almost in name only since then in this matter. I left the future handling of this case to Bruce Ennis of the ACLU, who had been associated with me in the prosecution of this matter. He and his associate, Eugene Du Bose, proceeded to bring the case to trial. Donaldson was awarded a unanimous jury verdict of $28,500 as compensatory damages for inadequate treatment and $10,000 as punitive damages. These substantial damages were awarded only against two hospital doctors. Because limitations in the scope of the civil rights laws restrict against whom damages could be levied, damages were awarded neither against Florida State Hospital nor against the State of Florida. Neither were damages awarded against the sanist Florida, federal and Supreme Court justices who refused to grant even one writ of habeas corpus over a 14-year period to an involuntarily civilly committed patient, even when this patient had full and unrestricted town privileges.

As this case has also been appealed by the defendants to the U. S. Court of Appeals for the Fifth Circuit, I do not wish to comment on it in any more detail; however, the potential of this decision to drive state hospital doctors out of these facilities is obvious.

It is my guess that one of the primary reasons for the appellate court not deciding the *Wyatt* and *Burnham* appeals after more than 16 months is the potentiality of numerous civil rights actions for money damages if the recognition of the right is affirmed. A realistic solution would be to bar this type of remedy in the future unless injuries warranting punitive damages were involved.

To summarize these constitutional developments in the "somewhere" era of the early 1970s, all of the well-known right to treatment cases are being prosecuted in U. S. District Courts claiming violations of the federal civil rights laws. Most of the cases, e.g. *Wyatt* and *Donaldson*, have held that there is a constitutional right to treatment. Some have refused to recognize this right, e.g. *Burnham*. None of the well-known cases are being prosecuted in state courts.

Those federal trial courts that have recognized the right, have proceeded to define it and then enforce it, either by injunction or by damages: e.g. *Wyatt* and *Donaldson*, respectively. No court has ordered a state legislature to specifically appropriate increased funds to financially implement the enforcement of the right.

Most important, it should not be overlooked that no federal appellate court has yet openly decided whether or not to recognize this constitutional right. Even if the constitutional right exists, the federal appellate courts will then have to decide when it can be litigated in the first instance only in a state court, only in a federal court, or in either. Then these federal appellate courts will have to proceed from the comparative child's play that is recognition of the right to defining, enforcing and implementing the right.

The development that I shall now discuss is in my opinion the most important, but probably the most unappreciated and unrecognized, potential development in this area. It is primarily statutory rather than constitutional—that is, legislative rather than judicial— which is the method that I prefer. The seed for this development that was planted in the "nowhere" era of the 1960s questionably has begun to blossom in the present "somewhere" era, and I believe that it will bear fruit and be the controlling development in the future "anywhere" era.

It was to partake in and foster this development that I discontinued my original participation in both the *Wyatt* and *Donaldson* cases. During the last 3 years I have directed all my legal efforts toward this area. This development is based on the simple fact—generally unappreciated and unrealized—that Medicaid and Medicare statutes are in reality federal right-to-treatment statutes. These statutes recognize, define, enforce and implement the right. If made fully applicable to state mental hospital patients, they would constitute important initial steps in offering legislative solutions to many of the perplexing problems in this area.

Some Statutory Developments

As a lawyer, physician and social scientist who was interested in sociolegal aspects of medicine, I started working in the area of national problems in the delivery of adequate health care in the 1950s, before it became as fashionable a study as it is today. My fundamental thinking was, and is, that the federal government should start with the needed improvement in the care and treatment of catastrophic illnesses, e.g. severe chronic mental illnesses, which the average afflicted individual and family cannot or will not handle adequately. In my opinion this general plan is to be preferred over current provisions and proposed planning that often include full coverage for even relatively minor health problems (I call this cold and bunion health care planning) that almost all our population can and does handle adequately. At the same time, politically popular health care delivery plans, such as the original Kennedy-Griffiths proposal, have excluded almost 90 % of the patients treated annually in the state mental hospitals.

Accordingly, although I was engaged in general practice and was not a psychiatrist, I became interested in the problems of state mental institutions. For this was the sole area of catastrophic illnesses in which the government had had primary jurisdiction for the provision of total care for more than 100 years, and it was an area in which it was universally agreed that an improvement in care and treatment was needed. I formulated, and then began to advocate, the concept of a legal right to treatment for patients in state mental hospitals. I also pointed out that solutions to the problems of providing adequate care for state mental hospital patients would help solve similar problems in other areas of government-supported chronic medical institutionalization, e.g. for the mentally retarded and the aged.

In 1965 the number one unsolved national problem in the delivery of adequate health care was the generally low level of care and treatment given to our state mental hospital patients. Accordingly, I was quite surprised that in 1965 the initial Medicaid legislation that theoretically was to provide for all our nation's poor and infirm totally excluded only one group among our nation's poor and infirm: state mental hospital patients under 65. I was especially surprised because of the background for this Congressional exclusionary plan.

Historical Backgrond Prior to Enactment of Congressional Plan of Medicaid

By 1965, when Medicaid was first enacted, certain classic studies such as *Social Class and Mental Illness* (34) by Professors August S. Hollingshead and Frederick C. Redlich, respectively Chairmen of the Departments of Sociology and Psychiatry at Yale University, had confirmed what was already well known: that a two-tier system of care and treatment was being provided for our nation's hospitalized mentally ill. The lower tier, which made up the majority of the hospitalized mentally ill, consisted of the sicker and poorer patients, who were disproportionately frequently black and who had been usually involuntarily civilly committed. These patients were receiving grossly inadequate care and treatment in under-financed, overcrowded and understaffed state mental hospitals, in buildings that were frequently antiquated and often were fire and health hazards. Funds for these state mental institutions came almost entirely from state governments. The funds provided by the patients and their families were so minimal that realistically speaking they could be considered nonexistent.

The upper tier, a minority of the hospitalized mentally ill, consisted of the less sick and wealthier. These patients were rarely black and were invariably voluntarily hospitalized. They usually received adequate care and treatment in well-financed, physically adequate and fully staffed nonpublic mental hospitals. Funds for these facilities came from the patients and their families, from charitable contributions by members of the community and from various federal, state and local governmental sources.

In 1955 Congress had appropriated $1.5 million for a comprehensive study of the nation's number one unsolved problem in the delivery of health care: the failure to provide adequate care for the mentally disabled, particularly for those mentally disabled institutionalized in our state mental hospitals. In 1961 the Joint Commission on Mental Illness and Health, the group established by Congress to study this problem, issued its report entitled *Action for Mental Health*. This report recommended the following:

> *Expenditures for public mental patient services should be doubled in the next five years— and tripled in the next ten.*
>
> Only by this magnitude of expenditure can typical state hospitals be made in fact what they are now in name only—hospitals for mental patients.
>
> Therefore, *we recommend that the States and the Federal government work toward a time when a share of the cost of state and local mental patient services will be borne by the Federal government, over and above the present and future program of Federal grants in aid for research and training.* The simple and sufficient reason for this recommendation is that under present tax structure only the Federal government has the financial resources needed to overcome the lag and to achieve a minimum standard of adequacy. . . .
>
> Certain principles should be followed in a Federal program of matching grants to states for the care of the mentally ill:
>
> The *first principle* is that the Federal government on the one side and the State and local governments on the other should *share in the costs* of services to the mentally ill. (31)

In 1965, in the face of these findings and recommendations, Congress enacted the initial Medicaid legislation, Title XIX of the Social Security Act of 1935, as amended. Because this statute totally excluded state mental hospital patients under 65 years of age from Medicaid benefits, it assured the continuance of the invidious two-tier system of care for the nation's hospitalized mentally ill. This is simply another example of how a sanist Congress elected by a sanist society handles this most complex problem in planning to deliver adequate health care to our nation.

During discussions about the *Wyatt* case during 1971, George Dean, the chief counsel for the plaintiffs, and I decided to challenge the constitutionality of this Medicaid exclusion at the end of the February 1972 hearings on this matter.

Wyatt Developments on Medicaid Exclusions

Under present Medicaid sharing formulas, Alabama, being a poorer state, receives back 75 % of its Medicaid disbursements from the federal government. If Alabama state mental hospitals met federal standards and if the Medicaid exclusions of state mental hospital patients under 65 were ended, it meant that Alabama could quadruple its expenditures on its state mental hospital system without increasing state appropriations. To my way of thinking, this meant that Alabama would be able financially to implement the right to treatment.

Dean, however, subsequently decided not to challenge the constitutionality of the Medicaid exclusion. He believed that the state mental institution system was basically bad and should be done away with in favor of alternative community facilities. My arguments that a sufficient number of alternative facilities were not available were of no avail. I then decided not to participate any further as co-counsel for plaintiffs and attempted to interest various groups participating as *amici curiae* in this challenge of the Medicaid exclusions. They believed, however, as did Dean, that the state mental hospital system should be abolished and that increased funding would only perpetuate an evil.

I then discussed this matter with Dr. Stonewall Stickney, the Alabama Mental Health Commissioner, who believed as I did that it was a realistic approach to financially implementing the right to treatment. He discussed this matter with Governor George Wallace, who also approved of the idea; however, the Alabama Attorney General's office did not believe it to be feasible to prosecute this challenge at that time.

After Judge Johnson ruled against allowing me to bring on this challenge in the *Wyatt* case because he was ready to hand down his decision establishing standards, etc., I decided to return to New York and bring on a test case there. Accordingly, I initiated the *Legion v. Richardson* case.

Legion v. Richardson (Weinberger) (35)

In this case which I initiated in the U. S. District Court for the Southern District of New York in July 1972, the plaintiff was John Legion, a pseudonym. He was a 30-year-old poor, uneducated, black, involuntarily civilly committed paranoid schizophrenic patient at Brooklyn State Hospital, a New York state mental hospital. Prior to his involuntary institutionalization, Legion was on welfare and received both cash welfare, payments for food, clothing and shelter, and Medicaid benefits for both physical and mental illnesses. In New York, a wealthier state, the contributions to both cash welfare payments and Medicaid were 50% federal, 25% state and 25% local governments.

Because Legion was involuntarily civilly committed, he was institutionalized only in a state hospital, as the nonpublic mental hospitals did not accept involuntarily civilly committed patients. Because he was institutionalized in a state mental hospital, Legion lost his Medicaid benefits for both his mental and physical illnesses. He also lost his cash welfare benefits for food, clothing and shelter.

It was claimed that in this state hospital he did not receive adequate care and treatment because of insufficient state funding. If Medicaid and welfare benefits available to, and utilized by, Legion in the community were available to him in the hospital and were claimed by the state, funds available to treat Legion would have been doubled. He would have been the beneficiary of the prior state expenditure plus an equal amount of federal matching funds.

Furthermore, Legion claimed that he was involuntarily civilly committed because of a concatenation of factors: he was severely mentally ill, was poor, was uneducated and was black. He claimed that if he were equally severely mentally ill but were richer, educated and white, it would have been very probable that he would have been voluntarily hospitalized at the superior facilites of the psychiatric ward of a general hospital or of a psychiatric hospital affiliated with a general hospital. In these superior facilities, if he did not have adequate funds, he would have been eligible for Medicaid because he was medically indigent: i.e. he could not meet necessary medical expenses. In many states, for Medicaid there is no requirement of being financially indigent, i.e. on welfare; therefore, even if he were the son of a millionaire, Legion could obtain Medicaid in a nonstate mental hospital if his personal funds were insufficient.

Furthermore, it was shown that not one cent of the federal taxes paid by Legion's family go towards paying for, and improving, the inferior level of care received by their son in a state mental hospital. Instead their federal taxes contribute to the superior level of care provided in a nonstate mental hospital for the less sick, wealthier, probably white and voluntarily hospitalized patient; in addition, it was shown that the state could go against the financial resources of Legion's family to pay for the inadequate level of care given to Legion in the state mental hospital. No one, however, claimed against the financial resources of the wealthier patient's family because he was covered by Medicaid in the superior psychiatric facility.

Legion did not claim that he was entitled to Medicaid for any custodial care received in the state hospital. He claimed that he was entitled to Medicaid benefits only if the state mental hospital provided active treatment, and only if this active treatment was provided at a cost less than or equal to that provided by the nonstate mental hospital facility. Furthermore it was shown that, while there are no data showing an increased incidence or prevalence of severe mental illnesses among blacks as compared to whites, hospitalization rates in state mental hospitals of blacks often are more than 300 % that of comparable white groups. This is primarily because for the poor, uneducated, very sick black, whether he goes voluntarily or involuntarily, the state mental hospital, rather than the nonpublic mental hospital, is the only facility available.

It was claimed that all of the foregoing constituted a violation of Legion's rights to due process and equal protection of the law under the Fifth Amendment.

Legion sued on his own behalf and on behalf of all the more than 600,000 Americans under 65 years of age treated annually in our state mental hospitals. The original defendant was Elliot Richardson, then Secretary of the Department of Health, Education and Welfare, who was replaced in that post by Caspar W. Weinberger. Legion asked that the Medicaid exclusion of state mental hospital patients be declared unconstitutional. It was then requested that benefits be extended to all the state mental hospital patients now excluded—at a potential annual expenditure of $1.5 billion of additional federal Medicaid funds. In the alternative, it was asked that the entire Medicaid statute be declared unconstitutional.

A three-judge District Court was convened to decide the constitutionality of this exclusion. This court granted the defendant's motion to dismiss the complaint without hearing any evidence on the plaintiffs' claims.

In its opinion, the court unanimously held that the Medicaid exclusion was a rational discrimination for Congress to make. In its sanist decision, however, there is no mention that Legion was involuntarily civilly committed, that because he was involuntarily institutionalized the committing judge or doctor could send him only to a state mental hospital, and that solely because he was sent to a state hospital he was deprived of both his Medicaid benefits for physical and mental illnesses and of his cash welfare benefits in food, clothing and shelter.

The U. S. Supreme Court affirmed this decision, with only Justice

Blackmun noting probable jurisdiction and voting for oral argument. As I believe that the decision was incorrect and was sanist, I am now considering further petitioning of Congress to end this exclusion, filing a formal complaint with the United Nations Human Rights Council concerning this Congressional sanism—also pointing out how widespread sanism is throughout the world—and lastly, initiating a new proceeding *ab initio*. Of course, my future actions are controlled by limitations of time and money. My course has been eased appreciably by the fact that 16 *amicus curiae* briefs were filed in the *Legion* appeal to the Supreme Court.

"*Amici Curiae*" in the Legion Case

The major national health care groups that filed separate *amicus curiae* briefs in this case were the American Medical Association, the American Nursing Association, the American Orthopsychiatric Association and the APA.

The major national black health care groups that filed separate *amicus curiae* briefs were the Association of Black Psychologists, the Black Psychiatrists of America and the National Medical Association. The major national black civil rights groups that filed separate *amicus curiae* briefs were the Congress of Racial Equality, the NAACP, the National Black Feminist Organization, the National Conference of Black Lawyers and the National Urban League.

The states that filed separate *amicus curiae* briefs were Ohio, Oregon and Pennsylvania. The National Health Law Program also filed a separate *amicus curiae* brief.

Although supreme in the law, the Supreme Court lacks the medical and sociological expertise to evaluate either the medical or sociological irrationality or the racially discriminatory effects of the Congressional decision to exclude our nation's Legions from Medicaid benefits. By granting the motion to dismiss, the District Court barred not only itself but also the Supreme Court from the knowledge and benefits derived from receiving expert medical and sociological opinions attacking both the medical and the sociological irrationality and the racially discriminatory effects of this Medicaid exclusion. The 16 *amicus curiae* briefs presented to the Supreme Court the expert medical and sociological opinions that it needed to properly hear and determine the matter. All *amici* concluded that the Medicaid exclusion of our nation's state mental hospital patients was medically and sociologically irrational, that the exclusion is racially discriminatory in effect, and that the motion to dismiss should not have been granted.

The Sanist Supreme Court Has Condoned in Medicaid What It Would Have Condemned in "Educaid"

With all due respect to the Supreme Court, from the viewpoint of the oppressed involuntarily civilly committed state mental hospital inmate, one can claim that the Court's approval of a two-tier system of federal reimbursement for the institutionalization of our nation's mentally ill is only the latest illustration of the sanism of the Court. The sanist absurdity of the Congressional plan immediately becomes apparent if one starts by imagining the following "translation."

A few years ago [we are supposing] Congress investigated the nation's education programs and found that a two-tier system existed in the education of our nation's children. In the upper tier, Congress found that the private school system gave a superior education to a smaller number of wealthier and initially more intelligent students, that these children were rarely black, and that they had a choice among several private schools; furthermore, that this superior education was given in excellent physical plants, by well-trained teachers and in small classes.

In the lower tier [we continue to imagine], Congress found that the public school system gave an inferior education to a larger number of poorer and initially less intelligent students, who were often black, and that these children were compelled to attend these inferior schools by local laws. Furthermore, that this inferior education was usually given in overcrowded and antiquated buildings that too often were fire and health hazards, and in large and too often unmanageable classes. And that too often the least educable students were taught by inadequately trained foreign-educated teachers, usually with a poor command of English, who had been given special state teaching licenses that could be utilized only in the worst of these schools.

Upon learning these findings [we imagine], Congress passed educational assistance statutes, entitled "Educaid," that established a federal reimbursement plan that provided for federal-state sharing of tuition payments in the upper tier private school system for those upper tier students whose parents were either financially indigent (i.e. on welfare) or educationally indigent (i.e. not on welfare but having difficulty paying rapid increasing private school tuitions, especially for several children in one family). At the same time the inferior lower tier public school system was totally excluded from receiving any federal reimbursement under Educaid, no matter if its students were financially or educationally indigents.

Further [we imagine], Congress enacted companion legislation providing federal reimbursement for a federal-state sharing program that again provided only the upper tier private school system with payments on behalf of the educationally indigent for school health programs, for lunches, for textbooks and other educational supplies and for recreation—again, totally excluding public schools from these programs.

[We continue to imagine that] the total cost of tuition per pupil in the private school system averaged about seven times the cost of education in the public school system, and the actual contribution of the state alone to this federal-state reimbursement Educaid plan for an educationally indigent person cost twice as much as the total cost to the state of educating a student in the public school system.

Then [we strive to imagine] this entire federal reimbursement plan for the educationally indigent in the upper tier private school system was paid for primarily by the poorer parents of the more numerous students in the inferior public school system. Therefore, these poorer Americans were taxed to pay solely for the superior education received in private schools by the initially more intelligent children of wealthier citizens. [We further imagine that] because of an insufficient number of seats in the private school facilities, the question of who should be admitted was delegated by Congress solely to the present staff members of these schools. And the private school staff continued to admit under the Educaid programs the same students as before, i.e. children of wealthier families, those who were more intelligent, who were rarely black, etc.

Definitely, the invidious hypothetical Congressional reimbursement plan which ensured any such continuance of this two-tier system of the education of our nation's children would be held unconstitutional by this Court.

State mental hospital patients have suffered the invidious and arbitrary discrimination complained of in the *Legion* case simply because they are poor and are severely mentally disabled. Accordingly, they have been considered to be politically powerless by our Congress. In spite of its initial defeat in the Supreme Court, the bringing of the *Legion* case and the entrance of politically influential *amici* in this case may eventually contribute to a far-reaching Congressional victory.

Recent Congressional Developments

To summarize Congressional developments, therefore, it can be said that prior to 1965 there was no significant supplemental federal funding for our state mental hospitals. The original Medicaid statute, enacted in 1965 to benefit our nation's poor and infirm, specifically excluded state mental hospital patients; however, as patients over 65 years of age in state mental hospitals received no significant Medicare benefits, the Long amendments to the Medicaid statutes were passed. These amendments made state mental hospital patients over 65 eligible for Medicaid benefits.

In theory, these benefits are substantial, for they now amount to more than $250 million annually. In fact, however, as they usually go into the state's general funds rather than directly to the state mental hospital system, these substantial sums have been diverted to other state purposes, e.g. education, roads, parks, etc., rather than being applied to improve care and treatment in the state mental hospitals. Furthermore, even if directed somewhat to the state mental hospital system, the effect of these federal funds has been diluted as they have been distributed not only among the over 65 patients but also among the under 65 patients; and the patients under 65 constitute 90% of those treated annually in our state mental hospitals.

Since 1972, patients under 21 are eligible for Medicaid benefits. This age group, however, only constitutes about 40,000 patients annually. These funds are also either diverted from the state mental hospital or diluted among the far greater number of patients who are over 21 and under 65.

Not only the initial Medicaid statute specifically excluded almost all state mental hospital patients from benefits. As the exclusion was either taken for granted or overlooked, it was not surprising to find that until 1974 all later proposals for the extension of federally subsidized general health care to additional segments of our population similarly specifically excluded state mental hospital patients from general coverage. Even the original health care plan proposed by Senator Kennedy—the Kennedy-Griffith bill (36), which is the most widely discussed proposal and which is conservatively estimated to cost $40 billion annually if enacted—also contained this sanist exclusion. During the last month, however, the Kennedy-Griffith health care proposal was specifically amended to provide for a limited 45-day period of active treatment in a state mental hospital. Similarly, the new national health care proposal offered by President Nixon and introduced in March 1974 (37) contained a similar provision for a limited 30-day period of active treatment in a state mental hospital. Finally, the Kennedy-Mills proposal that was introduced in April 1974 (38) also contained a provision for a limited 30-day period of active treatment in a state mental hospital.

The potential significance of these changes in national health insurance proposals should not be underestimated. All of these health care proposals now recognize the right to treatment, set up objective standards by which the right can be defined, enforce it by giving or withholding federal funds, and financially implement it for a limited period by supplementing state appropriations with federal funding.

Furthermore, even if these new national health proposals are not enacted, the fact remains that both the Administration and influential Senators and Representatives are considering the inclusion of state mental hospital patients for federal national health insurance benefits; therefore the present Medicaid statute may be amended to end, or modify, the present exclusion of state mental hospital patients.

In the present "somewhere" era in 1974, therefore, there has occurred a comparative avalanche of national health insurance proposals that specifically include state mental hospital patients. This has come about probably because of the push of *Wyatt v. Stickney* bringing the problem out into the open, because of the effects of the distribution of the *amici curiae* briefs in the *Legion* case, accompanied by detailed follow-up discussions among the leadership of the AFL-CIO and among various influential Senators and Representatives, and perhaps because it is simply a right whose time has come.

It should also be noted that these proposals are being made in spite of the fact that various groups interested in the mental health field opposed the goals of the *Legion* case and refused to join in. These groups included the Mental Health Law Project, the ACLU, the Civil Rights Division of the U. S. Department of Justice and the Legal Defense and Education Fund of the NAACP. This last group is distinct from the NAACP. All of these groups refused to join in because it is their goal to destroy the state mental hospital system, in spite of the fact that there is an insufficient number of adequate alternative community mental health facilities.

In view of these recent Congressional developments, I believe that it can be validly prophesized that there will be a right to treatment, in more than name only, in the foreseeable future; therefore some observations about developments in the future "anywhere" era are warranted.

COMMENTS ON SOME "ANYWHERE" ERA DEVELOPMENTS

Admittedly, simply increasing state and federal funding of state mental hospitals may not result in an improved level of care and treatment for the patients in these institutions; however, the patients in these hospitals should be given the same opportunity to find out if money alone will do the job that Congress has given to all the other of the nation's poor and infirm who are covered by Medicaid but who are not in state mental hospitals.

Admittedly, the right to treatment may do very little to improve state mental hospital care in the face of the increasing civil service welfare-like mentality that is found among too many government employees. This philosophy of getting almost everything and doing very little in return increasingly appears to be pervading all branches and levels of government bureaucracy, especially if one looks at it from the viewpoint of a New York City resident.

Admittedly, state mental hospital psychiatry may still remain unpalatable to highly trained professional personnel because of a lack of prestige in state hospital work, because salaries are not really competitive with earnings in private practice, in community facilities and in nonstate mental hospital practice, because of a lack of professional satisfaction, because of the continual harassment of lawsuits, whether valid or not, etc.

Admittedly, the concept of the right to treatment may not necessarily result in an increase in the number of adequate alternative facilities to the state hospital; however, whether in the community or in the hospital, it is the quality of care that is the issue, not the place of care.

The recent history of the care of the severely mentally disabled, whether mentally ill or mentally retarded, shows that initially this care was provided by the family. When the family was inadequate, it was provided by the community in poorhouses and foster homes, and when these community facilities were deemed to be scandalous and inadequate, reformers like Dorothea Dix and John Conolly urged the utilization of public mental institutions as humane alternatives to the inadequate community facilities.

Now that the community mental facility advocates are the most vocal, it behooves us to ask what we are doing and where we are going. We can look at England, where decreased utilization of the public mental hospital system has resulted in inadequate community care of chronic psychotics, turning them into "rootless wanderers" (39). We can look at Canada, where the foster home system has been criticized as constituting the new back wards for the chronic schizophrenics (40). We can look at California where, in association with the decreased utilization of the state mental hospital system, acts that in the past were characterized and condoned as being due to mental illness are now being characterized and condemned as being due to criminal intent (41) and where studies show that the back alleys of the community now substitute for the former back wards of our state hospitals (42). In general we can look throughout the United States, where increases in community welfare rolls because of the addition of the mentally disabled are often due to decreases in state hospital rolls—too often, with no real benefit to the patient, to his family or to the community.

Admittedly, enforcement provisions in the present Medicaid statute and in the proposed national health insurance programs do not adequately ensure that supplemental federal funding will not be diverted from the state mental institution system into general state funds. Present "maintenance of state effort" requirements decree only that, after a state receives these substantial funds, it shall maintain its total appropriations at the same level as before it received this federal reimbursement; therefore, in spite of inflation and the periodic raises given to employees, etc., "Many of the mental hospitals providing service to Medicaid recipients are required to function within their pre-established yearly allocations, regardless of the magnitude of Medicaid reimbursable claims." (43)

Recent disclosures have shown that even "progressive" states readily divert these funds. For example, in 1970 New York state began to receive substantial Medicaid funds for the residents of its state schools for the retarded. The state diverted all these monies to its general funds and froze the level of appropriations for its state mental institutions; therefore, because of inflation increasing the cost of food, housing and shelter and because of increased salaries and benefits to employees, the real appropriations for the state institutions decreased and the level of care provided for the institutionalized mentally retarded fell even from its prior inadequate level. Similarly, Ohio voluntarily decertified several of its state mental hospitals as being eligible for Medicaid and Medicare funds for patients over 65 years of age when it was shown that adequate care was not being provided for these patients; this measure also permitted the diversion of these substantial supplemental federal funds for other state purposes, e.g. roads, education, parks, etc.

I believe that these abuses can be prevented either by amendment of the various national health insurance plans to assure that these federal funds go directly to improve the level of care in the state mental hospital system, or by *Wyatt* types of proceedings, or both.

CONCLUSION

In this presentation I have discussed certain developments in the area of the concept of the legal right of a state mental hospital patient to adequate care and treatment. These developments have been traced from the inception of the concept of the right to treatment through the "nowhere" era of the 1960s through the present "somewhere" era of the early 1970s and towards the future "anywhere" era.

I have pointed out that a realistic right to treatment is needed to improve what too often is inadequate care for these patients. Furthermore, I have emphasized how realistic recognition of the concept may help deter and offset our society's irrational oppression of the most severely mentally ill, a phenomenon that I have termed "sanism."

REFERENCES

1. Birnbaum, M. The Right to Treatment. *A.B.A.J.* 46: 499, 1960.
2. Editorial. A New Right. *A.B.A.J.* 46: 516, 1960.
3. *Donaldson v. O'Connor*, 400 U.S. 869 (1970); *Donaldson v. O'Connor*, 390 U.S. 971 (1968); *Donaldson v. Florida*, 371 U.S. 806 (1963); *In re Donaldson*, 364 U.S. 808 (1960).
4. New York *ex rel. Anonymous v. La Burt*, 385 U.S. 936 (1966); United States *ex rel. Stephens v. La Burt*, 373 U.S. 936 (1966); New York *ex rel. Anonymous v. La Burt*, 369 U.S. 428 (1962) (J. Douglas dissenting).
5. *Wyatt v. Stickney*, 325 F. Supp. 781 (M.D. Ala. 1971).
6. Robitscher, J. The Right to Treatment: A Social-legal Approach to the Plight of the State Hospital Patient. *Villanova Law Rev.* 18: 11, 1972.
7. Holmes, J. In *The Western Maid*, 257 U.S. 419, 433 (1922).
8. Birnbaum, M. Some Remarks on "The Right to Treatment," *Ala. Law Rev.* 23: 623, 1971.
9. Halpern, C. R. A Practicing Lawyer Views the Right to Treatment. In Symposium: The Right to Treatment. *Georgetown Law J.* 57: 673, 782, 1969.
10. Birnbaum, M. The Right to Treatment—Some Comment on Implementation. *Duquesne Law Rev.* 10: 579, 1972.

11. Joint Information Service of American Psychiatric Association and National Association of Mental Health, eleven indices 8, 1971.
12. Hunt, R. Ingredients of a Rehabilitation Program. Reprinted in *An Approach to the Prevention of Disability from Chronic Psychoses.* Report of the 34th Annual Conference of the Milbank Memorial Fund Proceedings, 1957, Part I, at 9,21, 1958.
13. Marshall, T. Foreword. In Willie, C. V., Kramer, B. M., and Brown, B. (eds.). *Racism and Mental Health,* xi, 1973.
14. Comer, J. P. *Beyond Black and White,* 1972, pp. 117–118.
15. Guttmacher, M., and Weihofen, H. *Psychiatry and the Law,* 1952, p. 302.
16. Bay, A. Hospitalization Phase. *Ment. Hospitals* 16: 43, 1965.
17. *Simon v. Craft,* 182 U.S. 427 (1901); *Dexter v. Hall,* 82 U.S. 9 (1872).
18. *Jackson v. Indiana,* 406 U.S. 715 (1972).
19. Goldberg, A. High Court Strength. *N. Y. Times,* Nov. 17, 1971, p. 47, col. 3.
20. Birnbaum, M. Statement on The Right to Treatment. Presented at Hearings on Constitutional Rights of the Mentally Ill before the Subcommittee on Constitutional Rights of the Senate Committee on Judiciary, 87th Congress, 1st session, Part 1, p. 273, 1961.
21. Birnbaum, M. Some Comments on "The Right to Treatment." *Arch. Gen. Psychiatry* 13: 34, 1965.
22. Birnbaum, M. A Rationale for the Right. In Symposium: The Right to Treatment. *Georgetown Law J.* 57: 752, 1969.
23. Holmes, O. W., Jr. *The Common Law,* 1881, p. 1.
24. New York Mental Hygiene Law, § 13.19.
25. *Gideon v. Wainwright,* 372 U.S. 335 (1963).
26. *Rouse v. Cameron,* 373 F. 2d 451 (C.C.A., D.C. Circ. 1966).
27. *Rouse,* 459.
28. S.B. 1274 and H.B. 2118, Pennsylvania General Assembly, 1968 session.
29. Hearings on S.B. 1274 and H.B. 2118: The Right to Treatment Law of 1968 before Joint House and Senate Committees on Public Health and Welfare, 1968 session.
30. *Wyatt v. Stickney,* 344 F. Supp. 373 (M.D. Ala. 1971).
31. Joint Commission on Mental Illness and Health, Action for Mental Health, 1961.
32. Editorial. Unanswered. *Psychiatr. News,* Mar. 6, 1974, col. 1., p. 2.
33. *Burnham v. Dept. of Public Health of Georgia.* 349 F. Supp. 1335 (N.D. Ga. 1972).
34. Hollingshead, A. S., and Redlich, F. C. *Social Class and Mental Illness,* 1958.
35. *Legion v. Richardson,* 354 F. Supp. 456 (S.D., N.Y. 1973); affd., *sub nom. Legion v. Weinberger,* 1973 (J. Blackmun noting probable jurisdiction and voting for oral argument).
36. S. 3 and H.R. 22, 93rd Congress, 1st session.
37. S. 2970 and H. R. 12684, 93rd Congress, 2d session.
38. H.R. 13870, 93rd Congress, 2d session.
39. Editorial. Rootless Wanderers. *Br. Med. J.* July 7, 1973, col. 1, p. 1.
40. Murphy, H. B. M., Pennee, B., and Luchins, D. Foster Homes: The New Back Ward? *Canada's Ment. Health* 20: Suppl. 71, p. 1, 1972.
41. Abramson, M. F. The Criminalization of Mentally Disordered Behavior: Possible Side-effect of a New Mental Health Law. *Hosp. Community Psychiatry* 23: 101, 1972.
42. Aviram, U., and Segal, S. P. Exclusion of the Mentally Ill: Reflection on an Old Problem in a New Context. *Arch. Gen. Psychiatry* 29: 126, 1973.
43. Financing Mental Health Care under Medicare and Medicaid. Research Report 37, Office of Research and Statistics, Social Security Administration, U.S. Dept. of Health, Education and Welfare 33, June 1971.

chapter 9

Implementing the Rights of the Mentally Disabled: Judicial, Legislative and Psychiatric Action

JONAS ROBITSCHER, J.D., M.D.

Those of us who want to define and implement the rights of the mentally disabled have a terrible task.

Terrible because it must be done in the face of neglect and inertia.

Terrible because in the process of trying to improve the rights of the mentally disabled we come face to face with tremendous human misery.

Terrible because in the process of trying to improve the status of the mentally disabled we find conflicting interests and conflicting priorities, all with their own validity, which make it difficult to know where we should put our efforts.

And terrible because we have so few allies in this effort. Other civil rights efforts, even when initiated by an elitist group, are eventually supported and then taken over by the group-in-interest which has gained enough cohesiveness and self-direction to carry on on its own. The mentally disabled are different, and we must expect always to do the fighting for them.

The mentally disabled do not have minority pride, like blacks. They do not organize like grape pickers, or agitate like students, or rebel like prisoners. They passively wait for action to be taken on their behalf.

I know of only one report in the literature of a riot in a mental hospital and that was small scale: in a 10-bed unit, and the unit was devoted to the care of delinquent adolescents. Most of the mentally disabled cannot protest effectively (1).

Some of the characteristics of the condition of mental disability are seclusiveness, apathy, withdrawal, isolation, suspicion, irrationality and old fashioned "orneriness." So the mentally disabled are not well equipped to fight for their own rights or even to help us in securing for them the benefits of a rights-conscious society that has made great strides in implementing the human rights of other groups. The mentally disabled depend on the good offices and the unselfish efforts of other segments of society to improve their position, to rescue them from the kind of despotism that psychiatry and the state, from the best and from the worst of motives, have imposed on them.

Starting with the case of *Heryford v. Parker* in 1968 (2), a long series of innovative and provocative court decisions is midwifing new rights for the mentally disabled; these judicial actions are in response to long neglect and to the failure of other reforming efforts, and they are based on a strong antipsychiatric bias which may be deserved but which has been expressed by the courts in ways which complicate mental health administration and treatment.

Heryford v. Parker is a federal case involving the continued holding of a mentally retarded man under the terms of a Wyoming statute which provided that the proposed patient "may be represented by counsel." The case guaranteed the right to counsel at each stage of the proceedings, even when the parents of the proposed patient have not expressed a desire for a lawyer, on the ground that the "difference" between civil and criminal commitment is not a real difference; the extent of the deprivation of civil rights is similar in either case. Beginning with this case, courts have been increasingly willing to equate the benign, well-intentioned psychiatrist with the malevolent and punitive jailer; a number of courts have now expressed the idea that one role is very like the other, at least so far as the effect on the patient/prisoner is concerned. As a result, courts have grafted onto the mental health system a number of new rights and protections which make the administration of mental health institutions much more difficult but which do not necessarily solve the problems in the field.

The mental health system is a domestic equivalent of Vietnam. We see the chance for solution of some problems if we put effort at certain strategic points, but our analysis of the situation turns out to be deceptively simplistic, and after we have made the effort we find that we have only become further embroiled, we see that the problem is larger and more complicated than we had thought. The more we become involved in psychiatric reform, the more we understand how much more remains to be done.

Legal reformers are only the last of a series of groups to have tried to improve the mental health system. Public disinterest in and distaste for the mentally ill, combined with a denial of their problems, have caused many gains to be lost when reforming spirit waned. Worse than that, some of the reforms which have been secured in the past, such as the shift from judicial to medical commitment, at a later point have been evaluated not as gains but as setbacks. The present wave of court-imposed reforms is also in danger of losing effectiveness because of the mistaken view that a court victory necessarily gets translated into effective help for patients and because some of the gains bring losses with them.

None of the previous reforming efforts have achieved for a continued period of time what patients need most: the time and interest of a concerned therapist. The present reform movement is also failing to achieve that goal.

Meaningful change in psychiatric care can emanate from only four sources: the doctors who run the show; the consumers, by which I mean both patients and the concerned public; the legislatures which set up the rules of the game and appropriate the funds; and the courts which decide whether legal minimums are being met.

Doctors and patients are the two parties in the best position to produce meaningful change. When doctors decide that patients are being unfairly treated and when patients demand more attention to their rights, changes can result. But doctors have generally not been interested in psychiatric reform. F. Lewis Bartlett has documented the decreasing importance of the state mental hospital superintendent in organized psychiatry (3). Despite the fact that the American Psychiatric Association (APA) was started as an association of hospital superintendents, it now devotes only the slightest fraction of its attention to state hospital patients, whose rights are at risk, who are without meaningful alternatives, who do not have the money to pay for private care and who must be satisfied with what the state offers. We can think of this as a group of 275,000 patients, the population of state hospitals, some of whom are technically voluntary patients but all of whom are subject to similar treatment. We can think of this as a much larger group, since there is a continual turnover: statistics in terms of patient care episodes compiled by the National Institute of Mental Health give the figure of 745,259 for state and county mental hospitals in 1971; the figure represents residents at the beginning of the year plus total additions to the facilities during the year (4). These are the people who have no alternatives when psychiatry treats them badly.

Even that small segment of modern psychiatry that is primarily concerned with hospitalized patients does not emphasize rights of patients; psychiatrists are not interested in psychiatric reform. Many psychiatrists see the present system if not as exemplary at least as tolerable. Some doctors seem to gain pleasure and satisfaction from the very inequality of their relationship with patients, from the authoritarian position from which they operate, and they see more rights for patients as an infringement on their special status. Indeed, so meager are the returns from public mental hospital psychiatry in terms of salary and prestige that the enjoyment of the exercise of psychiatric authority may be one of the main rewards of this kind of psychiatric practice. We cannot expect the major thrust for psychiatric reform to come from the doctors who man public institutions, although we can note that some doctors who have had such positions have in earlier times led the fight for patients' rights.

Psychiatrists were responsible for the first great effort at psychiatric reform. The First Psychiatric Revolution started when Phillipe Pinel in 1793 removed the chains and shackles from 53 lunatics. His campaign for the moral treatment of the insane—kindness, understanding, and a minimum of physical restraint—led to a new approach to mental hospitalization. But in spite of this reforming movement, 25 years later Pinel's disciple Esquirol wrote after an inspection tour of French mental hospitals: "These unfortunates, who experience the worst human misery, are treated worse than criminals and reduced to a condition worse than animals." (5) Although Thomas Kirkbride and other names in early psychiatry are associated with psychiatric hospital reform, it is hard to think of many prominent modern psychiatrists who have made a primary concern of the improvement of the conditions of psychiatric hospitalization and the implementation of patients' rights. The spokesmen for modern psychiatry, the APA and the Group for the Advancement of Psychiatry (GAP), have devoted little energy to the public mental hospital patient. One notable exception is Harry Solomon, who when he was president of the APA in 1958 delivered a presidential address detailing the deficiencies of the public mental hospital system and the shortages of doctors, nurses and other personnel.

Solomon's words are worth repeating today to indicate how little has been accomplished since he said them and to contrast his concern over these matters with the lack of concern of those who have led the APA in the intervening years:

> After 114 years of effort, in this year 1958, rarely has a state hospital an adequate staff as measured against the minimum standards set by our Association, and these standards represent a compromise between what was thought to be adequate and what it was thought had some possibility of being realized. Only 15 states have more than 50% of the total number of physicians needed

to staff the public mental hospitals according to these standards. On the national average registered nurses are calculated to be only 19.4% adequate, social workers 36.4% and psychologists 65%. Even the least highly trained, the attendants, are only 80% adequate. I do not see how any reasonably objective view of our mental hospitals today can fail to conclude that they are bankrupt beyond remedy.

In many of our hospitals about the best that can be done is to give a physical examination and make a mental note once a year, and often there is not enough staff to do this much. (6)

In the intervening years Solomon's remarks have been quoted by nonpsychiatric reformers—Morton Birnbaum has quoted them often—but organized psychiatry has not picked up on his campaign. Organized psychiatry has not been interested in the involuntarily committed public patient; the residency training programs of the university-affiliated departments of psychiatry avoid public hospitals if private hospitals are available for residency training. The leaders of the APA and GAP are interested in the private practice, not the public practice, of psychiatry. The few psychiatrists who are most prominent in psychiatric reform, including Thomas Szasz, F. Lewis Bartlett and Ronald Leifer, are not members of but are in opposition to the Psychiatric Establishment, as are such nonpsychiatrists as lawyer-physician Morton Birnbaum, law professor Alan Dershowitz, lawyers Bruce Ennis and Charles Halpern, Judge David Bazelon and sociologist Erving Goffman.

So the initial attempt at psychiatric reform, led by psychiatrists, did not continue as an important force. The next attempt was the reforming effort of former patients such as Mrs. E. P. W. Packard and Clifford Beers, and representatives of the public such as Dorothea Dix. Public efforts have helped but have not prevented the continuation of injustices. We eulogize the efforts of these campaigners for psychiatric reform, but in spite of their contributions we find that the present situation still stands in need of tremendous efforts, that psychiatry still has its Atticas, which go by such names as Partlow, Searcy, Chatahoochee, Fairview, Matteawan and Elgin State.

Public efforts did lead to an interest in psychiatric reform on the part of legislatures; they spurred the passage of laws designed to protect patients, such as the judicial commitment laws of the late 19th century and later laws designed to make therapy more available, such as the medical commitment laws of this century. Legislative interest in the mentally disabled has become more sophisticated during recent decades. At an earlier period a legislature could satisfy itself that it was doing its best for the mental hospital patient by building bigger and more isolated hospitals; now legislatures concern themselves with more subtle questions: by requiring as North Carolina has that the dangerousness of a patient be shown by overt acts and not by the unsupported clinical impression of the examiner, by requiring as California has that dangerousness be reassessed at frequent intervals so that there is a necessity to release patients who no longer meet the criteria of commitability (7). But legislatures do not have the time or the expertise to do a thorough job in the mental health field, and they shirk their duty in their most important function, the appropriation of funds. The basic anomaly in the mental health field is the disparity between the cost per day of maintaining a patient in a public and in a private hospital; if mental disability is to be considered a disease and is to be treated in accordance with the medical model—which is one of the most controversial questions in legal psychiatry but which is the course advocated by the Psychiatric Establishment—then a dual care system in which private and public patients get different quantities and qualities of treatment cannot be justified. In spite of an avowed interest in mental patients, legislatures continue to fund mental hospitals at inadequate levels.

Some legislatures have pioneered in progressive mental health legislation, particularly when additional procedural safeguards for the patients require no increased expenditures. But the legislative approach has proved ineffective. A legislature in session for a short period of time and with many competing interests will not pass the kind of laws that will produce therapy-oriented, procedurally safeguarded mental hospitals. Legislatures are always willing to pass laws which state that "the individual dignity of the patient shall be respected at all times and on all occasions . . ." (8), or "the policy of the state is that no person shall be denied care and treatment for mental disorder . . . " (9), or "each patient . . . shall receive care and treatment that is suited to his needs and such care and treatment shall be administered skillfully, safely, and humanely with full respect for his dignity and personal integrity . . . " (10); it is only the appropriations that might give meaning to these phrases that legislatures are reluctant to pass.

Since psychiatric efforts, the efforts of patients and the public, and legislative attempts to improve mental hospitals have failed, or have succeeded only in part, lawyers have increasingly taken up the burden of initiating reform. The movement for legal redress for patients who are treated unfairly had its impetus with Thomas Szasz, a psychiatrist whose books are more familiar to law students than they are to psychiatric residents and whose ideas have had a great impact on nonpsychiatrists who are interested in legal psychiatry. Szasz came to the fore as a champion of the mental patient at a time when legal psychiatry was oblivious to civil rights issues. If we look at the writings of the leading legal psychiatrists of

20 years ago, the main themes expressed are either anti-civil libertarian (give psychiatrists more power and they will deal more adequately with the problems of commitment, they will clear up the problems of the criminal offender; psychiatric experts can be best utilized not in an adversary setting like other kinds of expert witnesses but as arms of the court, making final decisions regarding dispositions for judges in a position immune from hostile cross examination), or else they indicated a lack of interest in and awareness of rights problems (one of the most popular themes in legal psychiatry has been the false promise that, if psychiatrists and lawyers can only learn to understand each other's terms, to speak the same language, all the complex problems resulting from their clash of interests will somehow be resolved).

Lawyers have been forced into the field of patients' rights largely because our early leading legal psychiatrists not only failed to see the many civil rights issues in the field but created civil rights issues by their endorsement of the idea that more psychiatric authority over more types of people and greater respect for the expertise of the psychiatrist and his greater utilization as an arm of the court would be the answer to problems of crime, deviant behavior, the adversary battle in the court room and other thorny issues. The APA has until recently denied any Right to Treatment for state hospital patients, and it has undercut efforts to implement this right. GAP, the unofficial but powerful organization which states that it speaks for psychiatry, has issued reports on such large issues as what psychiatry can do to prevent nuclear war and to screen political candidates so that our leaders have the imprimatur of psychiatric approval, but it has not been concerned with such close-to-home issues as psychiatry's mismanagement of the problem of competency to stand trial or the problem of sexual offenders who are placed in double jeopardy by serving a sentence for their crime and then being transferred for an indeterminate period to a hospital for the criminally insane.

Not a spokesman for psychiatry but a psychiatric outcast, Thomas Szasz has been the lawyers' leading authority for the proposition that in the name of psychiatry and of health we deprive people of their rights. More than any other psychiatrist, he has pointed out that in the area of incompetency to stand trial, great injustices have been done to people who: (a) may not have been guilty of crimes with which they have been charged, or (b) may have been guilty of only a very minor offense, and (c) may meet the legal standards of competency to stand trial but who are seen as not competent by legally unsophisticated psychiatrists who may be ignorant of how simple the legal criteria are to meet. These patients then spend years and perhaps lifetimes in the worst kinds of mental institutions, the hospitals for the criminally insane. Szasz has documented the two most prominent examples of the political use of psychiatric power in the United States: the case of Ezra Pound and the case of General Edwin Walker. He has described the tyranny of the psychiatrist that may result when special laws are passed, such as sexual psychopath or defective delinquency laws, which give medical labels to deviants who have been considered criminal and thus subject these deviants to indeterminate sentences, which last until the psychiatrist is satisfied that the deviant is "cured." Szasz has documented the role of the psychiatrist as a double agent: appearing to the patient in the role of a physician and also serving the court or some other civic body as its expert. He has alerted the law to the inexactitude and the controversial character of psychiatric diagnosis.

Szasz is not the most popular of psychiatrists with his fellow psychiatrists; lawyers see him in a more kindly light. He follows his ideas about abuse of psychiatric authority so far that he leaves most psychiatrists behind him: he opposes all involuntary commitment and would give those whom we call mentally ill the right to harm themselves if they desire. However one feels about Szasz, the current legal literature in forensic psychiatry takes off from his writings, and he is quoted and cited more frequently than any other psychiatrist.

A number of years ago I wrote that the three most influential psychiatric reformers of today were Szasz, Birnbaum, and Bartlett (11). All three have been influential in psychiatric reform through the agency of lawyers and court cases rather than through the acceptance of their ideas by psychiatry. They delineated the great vacuum in which civil rights were lacking, and when psychiatry did not move in to fill the empty space, it was inevitable that the law and lawyers would become involved.

Morton Birnbaum, internist and lawyer, not a psychiatrist although often mistaken for one, is the author of an original concept, that there is a constitutionally guaranteed Right to Treatment for involuntarily committed mental patients, since restoration of liberty depends upon the opportunity for therapy[1] (12). He first presented this idea in an article that appeared in the *Journal of the American Bar Association* in 1960 (13). Birnbaum was aware of dangers in his approach. The chief danger as he saw it was that courts would get too involved in the internal administration of mental hospitals, so he emphasized the need for simple standards that would be ipso facto proof that a patient was not being given adequate treatment, the standard of the ratio of patients and physicians being most important. His original plan called for the same patient-personnel ratios

---

[1] Birnbaum has written, "Although I am not a psychiatrist, because of my interest in socio-legal aspects of medicine, this concept has been the subject of a great deal of study, thought and work on my part starting in the 1950's. . . ." (12)

for public hospitals that the APA required for private mental hospitals. Birnbaum wanted extremely limited intervention on the part of the courts.

As Birnbaum sees it, the recognition of the Right to Treatment

> ... requires that a public mental institution meet certain minimum numerical standards for staffing and physical facilities. This right should be enforced by writs of habeas corpus or equivalent administrative remedies and should require that a minimum number of consultations and physical examinations be conducted on all inmates within a given period of time. These are elements of the standards courts should use in determining whether or not treatment is adequate.

He adds that the standards are not intended to be panaceas.

The idea was endorsed by lawyers (14); it was opposed by psychiatrists. After Judge David Bazelon in the District of Columbia case of *Rouse v. Cameron* gave a limited recognition of the concept of the Right to Treatment (although not on the constitutional grounds suggested by Birnbaum) (15), the APA undercut his position in important ways.

In February 1967 the Council of the APA approved a reactionary position statement on the Right to Treatment (16). The statement acknowledged that there were staff shortages in state hospitals but categorized Birnbaum's proposal of a writ of habeas corpus remedy for patients deprived of therapeutic help as "tantamount to an oversimplified gospel of perfection." It said, "Clearly, in the perspective of the over-all mental health manpower shortage in our country, one must settle for something less until personnel shortages can be overcome." The formula which the APA went on to specifically endorse, an old formula dating back to the Model Draft Act of 1952, was that patients are entitled to treatment only "to the extent that facilities and personnel are available." (17) By adopting this position statement the APA was saying that organized psychiatry felt no responsibility for the improvement of the public mental hospital system; it was inviting the kind of response from the courts that has since been expressed in *Wyatt v. Stickney.*

In 1969 the APA dealt the Birnbaum concept a second blow by discontinuing its formulation of minimal acceptable patient-staff ratios for private mental hospitals.[2] This was the method by which evaluation of care could most simply have been measured.

The 1971 case of *Wyatt v. Stickney* (18) not only recognized the concept

---

[2] APA Standards for Psychiatric Facilities (1969) omit any recommended objective personnel ratio. The 1958 edition of these standards had required a ratio of 1:30 for admission and intensive treatment services; 1:150 for continued treatment and geriatric services, and 1:50 for mental hospital medical and surgical services, with ratios also established for clinical psychologists, registered nurses, occupational therapists, psychiatric social workers and others.

of a constitutionally guaranteed right to treatment but also endorsed Dr. F. Lewis Bartlett's concept that hospital patients should not be subjected to institutional peonage (19). Bartlett, a psychiatrist who works in the mental hospital system of his state, Pennsylvania, feels that unpaid and low paid patient labor leads to a kind of hospital system that is so inexpensive to the state in cost per day per patient that there is little incentive to push the patient out as soon as possible. Indeed, the incentive may be to hold good patient-workers—bakers, food preparers, laundry workers, maintenance men—since their services are vital to the institution and are secured free or almost free. Not until the mental hospital system recompenses patients for work done and thus gets on a cost-accounting basis comparable to other hospitals will this motivation for the prolongation of psychiatric hospitalization be removed. Bartlett has also led a campaign, recognized by the court in *Wyatt*, to have institutional physicians meet the same requirements for licensure that other physicians in the state must meet; he would like to put an end to the use of the mental hospital as a place of detention not only for patients but for doctors who because of incompetence, lack of training in accredited institutions or lack of language skills would not be employable elsewhere (19). Like Birnbaum's proposal, the ideas that patients should be paid for work done on behalf of the hospital and that psychiatrists should be able to communicate with their patients seem to have earned more support in legal than in psychiatric circles.

Judicial activism has taken over the field of psychiatric reform. A series of surprising decisions has established important precedents which lawyers are familar with but which psychiatrists continue to ignore. Although the United States with its separate jurisdictions is able to shrug off the effects of momentous court decisions, if only temporarily, because they do not affect our whole population, these cases are being quoted in other cases; the ripple effect is at work here.

One of the most important concepts in the new cases, a concept that has been generally ignored by psychiatry, is our obligation to provide for patients "the least restrictive alternative." This is a concept borrowed from other fields of law by Judge David Bazelon in *Lake v. Cameron* (20), a District of Columbia case involving a 60-year old woman who was found wandering about by a policeman and eventually was committed to Saint Elizabeth's Hospital as an insane person. Mrs Lake was suffering from a senile condition and had been diagnosed as having a chronic brain syndrome. Testimony indicated that she was not dangerous to others and would not intentionally harm herself, but she was prone to "wandering away" and needed constant supervision. Judge Bazelon's opinion was that it does not appear from the testimony that the appellant's illness re-

quired the complete deprivation of liberty that results from commitment
to Saint Elizabeth's as a person of "unsound mind." Bazelon said that,
since Mrs. Lake did not know and lacked the means of ascertaining what
other facilities—public health nursing care, community mental health
and day care services, foster care, home health aide services or private
care financed by welfare—might be available to her, the responsibility
was the hospital's to show that there was no less restrictive alternative
available. When the case was remanded to the District Court for a determination of that question, no less restrictive alternative was produced,
and Mrs. Lake was denied her release from Saint Elizabeth's; nevertheless, the case stands for the proposition that involuntarily committed patients are entitled in that jurisdiction to the help of the hospital administration in finding some other method of dealing with their problems; the
hospital has the duty not only of running its own services but also of di-
verting patients to other services.

Perhaps the start of the series of cases in which the courts began to
question how psychiatrists ran their affairs was *Heryford v. Parker* (2), a
1968 Federal case arising in the Tenth Circuit concerning the commitment of a mentally deficient man to the Wyoming State Training School
for the feeble-minded and epileptics. He had originally been committed
at the age of 9 at his mother's initiation and on the certification of a physician and a psychologist; there had been no opposition. Seventeen years
later when he was 26 he was released to the custody of his parents, and
2 years later, under the authority of the original commitment, he was returned to the training school against the wishes of his parents. Three
years later they initiated proceedings to secure the release of their son.
The court stated that the original commitment was not valid because
the boy had not been represented by a lawyer and the mother had not
expressly waived her son's right to a lawyer: ". . . The fundamental
right to have counsel is involved and failure to have counsel at every step
of the proceedings may result in indefinite and oblivious confinement and
work shameful injustice." But the case stands for more than the proposition that legal counsel is a right at every step in any commitment proceeding unless expressly waived; it also stands for the proposition that
the logic of preceeding cases having to do with juvenile delinquents, particularly *In re Gault* (21), the famous Supreme Court case which gave
juveniles some of the same criminal law safeguards accorded to adults,
also applies in a mental health setting.

> Like Gault, and of utmost importance, we have a situation in which the
> liberty of an individual is at stake, and we think the reasoning in Gault em-
> phatically applies. It matters not whether the proceedings be labelled "civil"
> or "criminal" or whether the subject matter be mental instability or juvenile

delinquency. It is the likelihood of involuntary incarceration—whether for punishment as an adult for a crime, rehabilitation as a juvenile for delinquency, or treatment and training of a feeble-minded or mental incompetent—which commands observance of the constitutional safeguards of due process. (2)

Although most psychiatrists are not aware that they have been so labeled, the court has said that it sees psychiatrists as hardly distinguishable from jailers.

Other recent cases of importance deal not with the civilly committed but with New York State prisoners who had been transferred from prisons to Matteawan and Dannemora Hospitals for the criminally insane while serving their sentences and who were considered too dangerous to be released when their prison sentences expired. Although psychiatrists from Matteawan and Dannemora testified that these men were too dangerous to be transferred to regular ("civil") hospitals, the courts ordered the transfers made (22). This remarkable "in vivo" experiment has produced a series of sociological papers by Steadman (23) which demonstrate by follow-ups of these end-of-sentence men that they were not particularly dangerous, that psychiatrists had badly overestimated their potential for dangerous behavior. Thomas Szasz, Alan Dershowitz, Bruce Ennis and other civil libertarians will not let us forget that the so-called Baxstrom Operation, the transfer of 967 inmates out of the two maximum security mental hospitals to nonmaximum security mental hospitals, resulted in the need for a retransfer back to the hospitals for the criminally insane of only seven patients by the end of the first year. It also led to discharge from the "civil" mental hospital of a large percentage of these patients. So psychiatry will be hearing about *Baxstrom v. Herold* and the follow-up of the Operation Baxstrom patients for a long time.

Testimony concerning the Baxstrom case patients was heard by the United States District Court for the Middle District of Pennsylvania in the case of *Dixon v. Commonwealth* (24), a case concerning the patients at Fairview State Hospital, the Pennsylvania counterpart of Matteawan and Dannemora. The patients at this institution included defendants not competent to stand trial as well as prisoners who had become psychotic during their incarceration and defendants who had been acquitted on the grounds of criminal irresponsibility. The court was impressed by evidence from the Operation Baxstrom studies concerning the deficiencies of psychiatric prognostications. It commented on the fact that because of insufficient funding on the part of the Pennsylvania legislature, only 3% of inmates in this institution were receiving "any therapeutic psychiatric treatment." But this court went further than merely ordering patients out of the institution into other institutions; citing the *Gault* case and *Heryford v. Parker*, the court said that the medical commitment procedure in Pennsylvania, a commitment on the certification of two physicians, lacked the procedural due process safeguards that should go with a deprivation of liberty. The court expressed approval of decisions which state that committing procedures and rules of commitment should be the same in a civil proceeding as in a criminal or a quasi-criminal case. Because of the *Dixon* case, Pennsylvania has had to return to the judicial commitment of patients with its expense, delay, lack of dignity, and its demands on the time of psychiatrists—all of which is perhaps not too high a price to pay for a stricter observation of patients' rights but which does make great demands on psychiatric hospitals and their personnel as well as on patients and their families.

When I began my psychiatric residency in Pennsylvania in 1956 I was told that Pennsylvania had one of the most modern and humane commitment laws of any state. It was modern and humane because it did not require that a patient be subjected to the stigma of a public court procedure and because it recognized that psychiatry had become such a well-accepted medical discipline that the signed statements of two physicians, rather than a full-fledged court trial, could determine the status of the patient.

I was told that the old judicial commitment procedure had fallen into disfavor because it placed the patient in a position of public exposure, it forced him to be part of an adversary process which was not appropriate for a civil determination dealing only with the patient's best interest, it left the determination in the hands of a jury of laymen whose decision on a medical matter might not be the best decision, it downgraded the status of the medical authority. It was a procedure that was expensive, inefficient, unscientific and cruel.

I was also told that the patient had little to fear under our streamlined procedure. He still had his great rights, conferred by "Magna Carta," the right of a writ of habeas corpus, so that any injustice done could be remedied. But what of patients who had the right to pursue the writ of habeas corpus but either did not know of their right or did not pursue the right diligently or effectively? There was no problem: the lack of the ability of the patient to work effectively toward his release was one of the indications that hospitalization was really needed or, alternatively, that although on a conscious level he "wished out," on a less conscious level he really wanted the safety and protection of the hospitalized status.

Psychiatrists were easily persuaded by this kind of logic several decades ago, although to modern ears it sounds like a variation of the old medieval practice of trial by ordeal: if the subject sank instead of floating it proved he had not deserved to be set free.

The court in the *Dixon* case decided that the medical commitment, in spite of the fact that psychiatry had considered it more modern and more humane than the judicial commitment, was in violation of the United States Constitution; as of the date of the court's order, April 22, 1971, there were to be no more medically committed patients in Pennsylvania. All patients were to be discharged or newly committed with due procedural safeguards within 60 days. Prior to such new commitment, each patient was to be evaluated, using appropriate psychiatric, psychological and social work personnel; he was to be aided in contacting his nearest relatives; a treatment program was to be developed for him and discussed with him and his family. A new commitment must not be sought without an attempt to have the patient submit to a voluntary arrangement, "including the minimum restraint considered necessary by the facility."

The court order protects the subjects of involuntary commitment by a whole series of rights: the subject shall be informed of his right to counsel, and an attorney shall be appointed for him; he shall be entitled to independent expert examination, at the expense of the state in the event of his inability to pay, and communication between the patient and his independent expert shall be privileged; he shall be entitled to a full court hearing at which he has the right to subpoena witnesses and documents and to confront and cross examine all witnesses; the standard for commitment shall be reliable evidence that establishes clearly, unequivocally and convincingly that the subject of the hearing poses a present threat or serious physical harm to other persons or to himself. If the subject is to be placed at the hospital for the criminally insane, the state shall have the burden of proving that there is no facility or part of a facility where he can be alternatively placed. The commitment cannot be for more than 6 months.

The court further ordered that there should be a verbatim transcript and full record made of the commitment proceedings with the right of appellate court review, including assistance of counsel and record and transcript without cost in case of indigency. The order also required the transfer of patients out of Fairview, following the Baxstrom Operation model.

A more far-reaching case, the most far-reaching case on civil commitment recently handed down, a case that should be familiar to all psychiatrists but which has been overlooked as part of the general psychiatric syndrome of ignoring the social and legal matrix in which psychiatry operates, is *Lessard v. Schmidt* (25), also a federal case dealing with the commitment laws of one state, in this case Wisconsin. Like the court's ruling in the *Dixon* case, this court, the United States District Court for the Eastern District of Wisconsin, finds the medical commitment law of a state invalid when it fails to provide the kinds of procedural safeguards

that the criminal law provides. But the court goes further than the *Dixon*
case court in the safeguards that it requires and in its antipsychiatric
point of view.

One of the characteristics of many modern law cases is the misreading
of history to justify a court's decision. Court opinions are usually based
on the preliminary drafts of a busy clerk who may or may not be skilled
in the historical method. The court in *Lessard* says that the American
practice of committing patients for their own welfare is in contrast to the
English practice which allowed a lunatic to be committed to the care of
a friend, to manage his own property during lucid intervals and to generally exercise his civil rights. The court says that there was "thus a very
real difference between the English practice, which could only be for the
benefit and protection of the incompetent, and which was only effective
during periods of insanity," and the American practice "which resulted
in total, and perhaps permanent, loss of liberty." Anyone familiar with
the descriptions of English psychiatric practice in the novels of Charles
Reade, Charles Dickens and Wilkie Collins knows that American and
British commitment practices did not have that divergence.

The problem with inaccurate history as expressed in court decisions is
that it then becomes part of the official record of the case and is seized
upon by other courts as justification for their decisions; we can expect to
find this misleading contrast between American and alleged British
practice reappearing in cases of the future.

The decision also quotes from John Stuart Mill's *On Liberty*. The passage quoted is the one that has been used by the political left to justify
violations of laws which seem oppressive and to promote social change.

> The only freedom which deserves the name, is that of pursuing our own good
> in our own way, so long as we do not attempt to deprive others of theirs, or
> impede their efforts to obtain it. Each is the proper guardian of his own health,
> whether bodily, *or* mental and spiritual. Mankind are greater gainers by suf-
> fering each other to live as seems good to themselves, than by compelling each
> to live as seems good to the rest. (26)

This expression of opinion by John Stuart Mill represents the source of
much debate in jurisprudence; it has been criticized on the grounds that
it subordinates social welfare to the rights of the individual, and that it is
Utopian because it does not recognize that some varieties of freedom
cause an impingement on other potential freedoms. Mill himself has been
criticized because of inconsistencies in his philosophy. This high-minded
but essentially vague philosophy is out of place in a judicial decision.
In *A Theory of Justice* John Rawls gives a more balanced point of view:

> It is important to recognize that the basic liberties must be assessed as a

whole, as one system. That is, the worth of one liberty normally depends upon the specification of other liberties, and this must be taken into account in framing a constitution and in legislation generally. While it is by and large true that a greater liberty is preferable this holds primarily for the system of liberty as a whole, and not for each particular liberty. Clearly, when the liberties are left unrestricted they collide with one another. (27)

Rawls uses as an example the right of free speech. Certain rules of order are necessary for intelligent and profitable discussion. Without the acceptance of reasonable procedures of inquiry and debate, freedom of speech loses its value. One liberty must be balanced against another.

> The best arrangement of the several liberties depends upon the totality of limitations to which they are subject, upon how they hang together in the whole scheme by which they are defined. (27)

The analogy of freedom of action and of freedom of speech is close. If psychotic people are free to express themselves as they desire, their actions impinge on the liberties of others. Psychiatry felt that it was doing an act of humanity by seeing that much deviant behavior was classified as symptomatic of mental illness rather than as criminal activity (disturbing the peace, creating mayhem, committing murder) so the psychotic could be prevented from impinging on the rights of others without being stigmatized as criminal and subjected to criminal penalties. But courts now are beginning to deny that any difference exists between the psychiatric approach and the correctional approach to these restraints on individual liberty, except perhaps that the indefinite holding in the psychiatric institutionalization is less desirable than the fixed sentence of a criminal judgment. Some psychotic people can be left to their own devices: they will not harm themselves or others; but when other psychotic people are left free, their rights and the rights of others come into collision. If we are not allowed to use the medical model, the only alternative is to classify this behavior as criminal and allow criminal sanctions to be imposed. This is what Szasz has suggested, and this is where the ruling in *Lessard v. Schmidt* will lead us. A new literature has begun to develop on the criminality of mentally disordered behavior.

The court takes notice of the fact that "many mental illnesses are untreatable," that the recovery rate from chronic paranoid schizophrenia—the diagnosis given to Miss Lessard—is low, and involuntary hospitalization may "greatly increase the symptoms of mental illness and make adjustment to society more difficult." It finds no justification for giving fewer safeguards to the mentally ill than to the criminal defendant when loss of liberty is at stake. The court finds that in many respects the civil deprivations which accompany commitment may be greater than those which accompany a criminal conviction. It cites the Thomas Eagleton affair for the proposition that the stigma of hospitalization will produce difficulties for the committed individual in attempting to adjust to life outside the institution following release. Bruce Ennis is quoted for the proposition that "former mental patients do not get jobs," and in the job market "it is better to be an ex-felon than ex-patient." Although some of the statements made by and quoted by the court may be factual, facts are not cited to support them. Nevertheless, there they are in the decision, available for quoting by courts in future cases in this and other jurisdictions.

But the *Lessard* court has even graver charges against psychiatry:

> Perhaps the most serious possible effect of a decision to commit an individual lies in the statistics which indicate that an individual committed to a mental institution has a much greater chance of dying than if he were left at large. Data compiled in 1966 indicate that while the death rate per 1000 persons in the general population in the United States each year is only 9.5, the rate among resident mental patients is 91.8.

The court concludes:

> It would thus appear that the interests in avoiding civil commitment are at least as high as those of persons accused of criminal offenses. The resulting burden on the state to justify civil commitment must be correspondingly high.

The court then held the Wisconsin two-doctor commitment statute constitutionally defective because:

—it failed to require effective and timely notice of "charges" justifying detention;
—it failed to require a notice to the individual of rights, including the right to a jury trial;
—it permitted detention for more than 48 hours without a hearing on probable cause;
—it permitted detention of longer than 2 weeks without a full hearing on the necessity for the commitment;
—it permitted commitment based on a hearing in which the individual was not represented by counsel, at which hearsay evidence was admitted, and at which the individual was not given the benefit of the privilege against self-incrimination;
—it permitted commitment on the basis of proof of mental illness and dangerousness that was on the basis of the civil law standard of a preponderance of evidence and was thus less than the criminal law standard of beyond a reasonable doubt; and
—it failed to require those seeking the commitment to consider less restrictive alternatives.

The court is saying loud and clear that psychiatrists are like jailers regarding the justification of the detention of a patient. And the law in Wisconsin now, whether observed or not, requires that the same warnings that are given to criminal defendants must be given before the start of psychiatric evaluations:

> Wisconsin may not, consistent with basic concepts of due process, commit individuals on the basis of their statements to psychiatrists in the absence of a showing that the statements were made with "knowledge" that the individual was not obliged to speak. . . . The patient should be told by counsel and the psychiatrist that he is going to be examined with regard to his mental condition, that the statements he may make may be the basis for commitment, and that he does not have to speak to the psychiatrist. (25)

Jackson v. Indiana (28) was a case decided by the Supreme Court in 1972 that dealt not with civil commitment but with an incompetent criminal defendant who under Indiana law was to be held until sane before he could be tried. The court held that because this defendant probably could not improve—he was a retarded mute—he should not be held until competent since that period would in effect be indeterminate (in contrast to a temporary period). Although the case does not involve civil commitment, Justice Blackmun's dictum in this case applies to civil commitment, and it will be quoted often as more and more commitment cases are brought to court:

> The States have traditionally exercised broad power to commit persons found to be mentally ill. The substantive limitations on the exercise of this power and the procedures for invoking it vary drastically among the States. . . . Considering the number of persons affected, it is perhaps remarkable that the substantive constitutional limitations on this power have not been more frequently litigated.

All of these new cases are important, some like *Jackson v. Indiana* because they redress an injustice, others like *Lessard v. Schmidt* because they impose such a great burden on the committing psychiatrist that it is hard to see how he will be able to meet all the requirements that are being imposed upon him. When the Supreme Court finally addresses itself to the question of civil commitment—if it allows itself to become involved in this area—we will see whether some of the restrictions against medical commitment, as in the *Dixon* and *Lessard* cases, will be upheld or will be overruled.

Lawyers involved in commitment work in both Pennsylvania and Georgia have told me that they prefer the medical commitment if patients can be guaranteed prompt and effective legal services so that a habeas corpus proceeding can be accomplished quickly. The money of the patient and the time of the psychiatrist that are saved are both important factors in attempting to preserve the medical commitment, but unless psychiatry devises ways to give patients prompt access to the courts after commitment the medical commitment will be outlawed in other states. The Georgia law is particularly worth noting: commitment by two physicians requires a hospitalization certificate on which is entered the doctor's recommendation. Copies are served on the patient and his representatives accompanied by a "plain and simple" notice that the patient or his representatives may apply for a hearing on the need for hospitalization, by a petition for a hearing which requires only a signature for completion, and by a notice that the patient or his representatives may apply immediately to have counsel appointed if the patient cannot afford counsel. The petition may be filed at any time during a 6-month period; however, if it is not filed within 5 days the certificates of the doctors are authorization for the holding of the patient in a treatment facility (10).

Although, as I have said, all of these new cases are important, *Wyatt v. Stickney* (18) is the new case that goes farthest, raises the most novel points and places psychiatry under the greatest obligation to bring its own house into order, under the threat that order will be imposed upon it it if does not. In some sense the *Wyatt* case marks a coming of age for the psychiatrist: he can no longer hold on to his naive theory that what we do for the mentally disabled represents a gratuity which we bestow upon them. The parallel with social welfare law is clear: originally the recipients of welfare were not considered to have rights to receive welfare.

Wyatt v. Stickney is the great Right to Treatment case in that it deals with commitment, the right to treatment, institutional peonage, the use of foreign physicians operating on institutional licenses, patient-personnel ratios, heating and air conditioning in mental hospitals and a huge variety of other matters. All psychiatrists should be familiar with the 35 Constitutional Standards for Bryce and Searcy Hospitals and the 49 Standards for Partlow State School and Hospital issued by the court in that case. Since some of these Constitutional Standards have many subdivisions, Judge Johnson's order of April 13, 1972 covers hundreds of aspects of psychiatric hospitalization (18).

Here are some of the regulations which the court has said represent the minimal standards for involuntarily committed patients:

> Patients shall have the same rights to visitation and telephone communications as patients at other public hospitals except to the extent that the qualified mental health professional responsible for formulation of a particular patient's treatment plan writes an order imposing special restrictions.

Patients have a right to be free from unnecessary or excessive medication.

Patients have a right to wear their own clothes.

The institution shall provide suitable opportunities for the patient's interaction with members of the opposite sex.

Patients may not be used for labor which involves the operation and maintenance of the hospital unless they are compensated in accordance with minimum wage laws of the Fair Labor Standards Act. (This is a response to the Bartlett institutional peonage campaign.)

The number of patients in a multi-patient room shall not exceed six persons.

There will be one toilet for each eight patients and one lavatory for each six patients. The toilets will be clean and free of odor.

The minimal day room area shall be 40 square feet per patient. Areas used for corridor traffic cannot be counted as day room space.

Adequate heating, air conditioning and ventilation systems shall be afforded to maintain temperatures and air changes; such facilities shall ensure that the temperature in the hospital shall not exceed 85° F. nor fall below 68° F.

Hot tap water shall be maintained at 110° F.

The list continues on and on. These are all listed under Minimum Constitutional Standards for Adequate Treatment of the Mentally Ill, and if the tap water falls below 110°, a Constitutional Standard has been abrogated and presumably a cause of action has arisen.

Under Constitutional Standard 31, which deals with patient records, there are 16 subregulations stating what the record should contain, how often it should be updated, how it should be reviewed and how nurses should indicate that orders have been carried out.

One of the many "sleepers" of this omnibus order is the provision regarding institutional peonage. This states that patients may voluntarily engage in therapeutic labor for which the hospital would otherwise have to pay an employee, provided that the labor is an integrated part of the patient's treatment plan and is approved by a mental health professional responsible for supervising the patient's treatment, that it is supervised by a staff member to oversee the therapeutic aspects of the activity, and that it is compensated in accordance with the minimum wage laws of the Fair Labor Standards Act.

Since the *Wyatt* decision, the United States District Court for the District of Columbia has responded to a suit brought by mental health groups and the American Federation of State, County, and Municipal Employees by ordering that the Labor Department notify patient workers at institutions for the mentally ill and retarded that they are covered by federal labor laws and that they must be paid minimum wages or a portion of minimum wages based on productivity. The Labor Department was given a year to implement all phases of the order (29).

Many, probably most, of the provisions of the 12 pages of regulations are humane and are needed; my question concerns the administration problems that arise when courts impose these as minimum constitutional standards. Courts do such a poor job of maintaining their own minimal constitutional standards concerning jail facilities, length of delay in bringing defendants to trial and setting bail that does not discriminate against the impoverished that I should think they would be reluctant to interfere with internal administration of mental hospitals on this grand scale.

My main complaint is the staffing ratios set by Judge Johnson. They demand the increase in the number of psychiatrists employed by Alabama from four to 42—which is necessary but which cannot be accomplished quickly or easily—but in addition they specify in a very fixed way who of the 207.5 personnel members (only two of whom are psychiatrists) are to look after each 250 patients. The courts specify one unit director, two psychiatrists, four nonpsychiatric physicians, 12 registered nurses, six practical nurses, six aide IIIs, 16 aide IIs, 70 aide Is, 10 orderlies, three clerk stenographer IIs, three clerk typist IIs . . . the list continues through psychologists (one Ph.D., one M.A., and two B.S.s), social workers (two M.S.W.s and five B.A.s) down to one dietician, one food service supervisor, two cook IIs, one cook I, 15 food service workers, one vehicle driver, 10 housekeepers, one messenger, two maintenance repairmen, and 0.5 chaplain for every 250 patients.

When I first saw these ratios I felt that lawyers had imposed impossibly high requirements on the Alabama hospital system; I have since learned that the ratios were arrived at with the consent of the defendants and that the lawyers representing the plaintiffs in this class action suit had hoped for even more personnel. The ratios should have been higher, according to witnesses who testified in the case, *Psychiatric News* (30) recently reported; it described these as "bare-bones" rations and quoted Franklin Clarke, superintendent of Philadelphia State Hospital, as saying, "Frankly, these are abominable staffing ratios. . . ." To my mind, a ratio of almost one staff member for every patient is not "barebones"; the problem is that most of the staff required are not therapists: they are aides, orderlies, stenographers, typists, food service workers and housekeepers. Nowhere in Judge Johnson's order is there any indication that individual psychotherapy has a place in the mental hospitals; only six out of the 207.5 personnel are psychiatrists and psychologists. Judge Johnson's order guarantees that the hospitals will become more bureaucratic, but they do not indicate how the patients will get more or better therapy. The contrary is possibly true.

What happens if hospital administration would like three psychiatrists and a smaller number of food service workers? The order specifies clearly:

"Changes in staff deployment may be made with prior approval of this Court upon a clear and convincing demonstration that the proposed deviation from this staffing structure will enhance the treatment of the patients."

The hospital administration now has its own administration, the Court. And articles are appearing in the literature not only on how psychiatric services can be evaluated for adequacy but how we can evaluate the evaluations. The process of separating the psychiatrist from the patient goes on inexorably as more of the time of psychiatrists is forced into administration and into making hospitals conform to the regulations which are being imposed.

Much of the work that lawyers are doing to protect the rights of patients is needed. Every day lawyers bring cases that are designed to prevent the unjust use of the tremendous power that psychiatrists have at their command. I am focusing here not on these cases, which require support and deserve appreciation, but on the cases in which forces from outside psychiatry are attempting to impose drastic changes well intentioned but not carefully thought out—on the practice of psychiatry, the cases that impelled a recent issue of *Psychiatric Annals* to use as its theme "Psychiatry Under Siege" (31).

I hold no special brief for the state hospital system; it has required tremendous improvement, an interest by that part of psychiatry—private psychiatry and teaching institution-affiliated psychiatry—which has paid it little attention. It has received little attention from the groups that speak for psychiatry, the APA and GAP. State hospitals need improvement. I only question the effect of Judge Johnson's and similar reforms.

Commenting after the *Wyatt* case decision, a spokesman for the American Civil Liberties Union, Bruce Ennis, said that the Alabama case was only "the first in a long series" of mental patients' rights cases. He estimated that only 16 of the 321 state and county mental hospitals in the United States could meet the minimal Constitutional Standards (32).

I think it is worth pausing to look at the fate of Dr. Stonewall Stickney, State Mental Health Commissioner for Alabama, who had welcomed the suit because he wanted legal force to help him in his efforts to improve the Alabama mental health system and who had not opposed many of the charges and claimed that, although an ostensible defendant, he saw the suit as fitting in with his own aims for improvement of the system. Stickney's program for Alabama had included such progressive goals as the decentralization of mental health treatment, the building of regional mental health centers, and the reduction of the population of hospitals by returning to private homes those patients who were simply in need of custodial care or geriatric nursing (33).

Stickney and his co-defendants had proposed conditions that they felt were compatible with a minimal treatment program, although these stipulations were entered into after the court had enunciated the doctrine of a constitutionally guaranteed Right to Treatment, had given the state an opportunity to improve its services and had expressed its disapproval of the lack of improvements. The stipulations were therefore entered into at a time of pressure and represent a bargain from a position of weakness on the part of the defendants. The patient-personnel ratio of 250:207.5 seems particularly hard to justify.

But acceding to the pressure from the court and conceding all these rights did not relieve Stickney of the pressure from his legislature and his Mental Health Board, and as a result of *Wyatt* he was fired. Previously he had fired his deputy commissioner, Dr. James Folsom. The next Commissioner of Mental Health for Alabama was not a doctor, he was the Department's finance officer. The transition from a system dominated by medically trained men to a system dominated by accountants has great significance: it is part of a nationwide pattern of subordinating the role of the psychiatrist, emphasizing administrators and financial experts, and of putting psychiatry on a costs-benefits basis. At the time accountant Charles Aderholdt took the job, one Mental Health Board member made the comment, "Well, we've got a new pitcher, we're still ten runs behind and it's the last inning of this ball game." (33).

Aderholdt lasted a year; he has resigned and the post has gone to another nonphysician, a member of Governor Wallace's cabinet, State Finance Director Taylor Hardin (33). Changes have been wrought, although these were generally initiated by Stickney. By moving patients out and by limiting admissions, the state has cut the population of its mental institutions from in excess of 10,000 to less than 6,000; spending on the hospitals has gone from $14,000,000 yearly to $54,000,000 (34); cost per patient per day has gone from $6.86 per day (with only 50 cents representing the cost for food) to $17.25 and will rise to $25 next year. But the manpower requirements which Judge Johnson states are constitutionally mandated minimums are not being met. Bryce and Partlow Hospitals, which should have 52 licensed physicians, have only 13. Partlow State School and Hospital for the mentally retarded still has only three doctors; their average age is 66 and the eldest is 78. One has cataracts and the other two have had strokes (35).

An expert who has visited Bryce says that not only is there a "frightful shortage of mental health professionals," but that "the staff interviewed, with few exceptions, reflected no awareness of what might constitute a therapeutic experience for patients." One patient who ran errands for the hospital staff was rewarded with points which could be used to buy canteen items; the staff described this as a behavior modification program, but the visiting expert stated, "A more gross distortion of behavior-modification therapy can hardly be conjured up." (35)

Since *Wyatt v. Stickney*, similar right to treatment cases have been brought in other jurisdictions, including New York, Illinois, Massachusetts, Ohio, Minnesota, Nebraska, Tennessee, Georgia and Florida. A whole group of related cases deal with such topics as the right to treatment for children, for retardates, the right to education for children too disturbed for normal classes, the right to compensation for institution-maintaining labor, and damages against psychiatrists both for continuing commitment when treatment was not being provided and for letting patients leave the hospital before they were adequately treated (36). In the Georgia Right to Treatment case, the court did not read the Constitution in the same way that the *Wyatt* court did; it found no constitutionally guaranteed treatment rights (although it said there may be a moral right), and the case was dismissed. On appeal to the Fifth Circuit Court of Appeals, it was joined with the *Wyatt* case appeal (37). So the Circuit Court of Appeals will have to uphold either the Alabama or the Georgia decision. The fact that it is having extraordinary difficulty in resolving this issue is demonstrated by the extraordinary delay between the presentation of final arguments before the court and its decision. Oral argument was heard on December 6, 1972; over a year later the court still had not handed down its decision. The question of whether there is a constitutionally guaranteed right to treatment in absence of specific state statutes giving that right will ultimately have to be considered by the Supreme Court.

Wyatt v. Stickney is the high water mark up to this time of a court's willingness to interfere in the internal administration of a state's mental health system. It is only within very recent times that courts have been willing to probe the internal administration of institutions which are lawfully constituted; the theory has been that the law cannot be an expert in all matters, and the internal administration of institutions has usually been off limits for judicial inquiry. For an example of the more traditional attitude of the court, see a recent New York action for damages, *Ferrici v. State* (38), in which the court refused to consider the internal workings of Matteawan State Hospital because New York State had not waived its liability:

> That part of the claim contending that there was a false imprisonment alleges . . . that claimant was held at Matteawan for approximately 28½ years, that he was confined with little or no attention, and that there were no consultations with qualified medical personnel who in any way tried to help claimant with his supposed psychiatric infirmity. . . . The frequency and amount of

psychiatric treatment and care to be furnished to a person confined to Matteawan State Hospital being an administrative decision and the type of treatment
to be afforded him being a governmental function, liability will not attach for a
failure to make properly such a decision or to exercise properly such a function.
... (38)

Although courts have not shown themselves to be skilled in their own
internal administration—delays in criminal justice and civil cases, mal-
administration of juvenile delinquency homes, and out-of-date prisons all
attest to the poor jobs courts do in maintaining standards in the institutions with which they are particularly concerned—courts have now decided to reverse policy and to interfere in the internal administration of
mental hospitals. This interference was inevitable, because psychiatry had
let hospitals deteriorate to the point where some social action was required.
But the interference does not get to the root of the problem, because there
is no way that a court can mandate a helpful therapeutic relationship, and
the helpful therapeutic relationship is the essential element of all meaningful therapy. The beauty of Morton Birnbaum's original proposal was
that the courts would not be concerned with individual treatment plans
or the kinds of treatment offered; it would assume that well-staffed, well-
funded public hospitals would offer services as good as those provided by
comparable private hospitals, and that therefore the treatment available
to the poor would be equivalent to the treatment available to the rich.
The Birnbaum proposal was designed to put an end to the dual hospital
system in mental health ($6-a-day care for the public patient, $100-a-day
care for the private patient); it was not designed to put judges, lawyers,
and cost-benefit and cost-analysis personnel accountants and finance directors in charge of the mental hospital. Courts have fallen into the trap
that Birnbaum repeatedly warned against: they are in the business of determining the adequacy of individual treatment programs, of setting
mental health policy and of being responsible for every detail of hospital
administration. Psychiatric training is no longer a prerequisite or even a
help for the determiners of hospital policy. Cost accountants, determining
hospital policy, will always prefer drug therapy and behavior modification programs to individual and group therapy, and they will always
prefer programs which can be run by the less trained in preference to
programs requiring psychiatrists and psychologists. In a recent collection
of the experiences of mental patients, one patient describes the beginning
of her recovery, when a woman doctor laid a hand on her knee and said,
"You are going to get better, you know." (39) Kindness, perhaps touch-
ing, saying a few words to the patient—these are functions of a physician
that go out the window in the regime of the cost analyst. They are re-

placed by efficiency, accountability, evaluations, and evaluations of evaluations to the point where no one with a high degree of professional competence has time to spend with patients. State hospital psychiatry has not done a good job of spending time with patients, but at least it held that factor as a therapeutic objective; it hoped to improve hospitals to the point where there would be more time for therapy. Now we have been told by the courts that they will set objectives. The solution has turned out to be a problem.

Wyatt has turned out to be a problem for a number of reasons. Perhaps the most important is that those who have pushed the concept of the Right to Treatment have done so from a divergence of motives: on the one hand to improve the state hospital system and on the other to "bomb out" the state hospital system. Morton Birnbaum, Stonewall Stickney and many others have felt that the concept of the right to treatment would be useful to improve state hospitals, but some lawyers who have taken up the campaign have said that one of the values of the concept is to make public hospitalization so prohibitively expensive that psychiatry will be forced to abandon the traditional system and to rely on treatment in the community instead. Lawyers who have pushed the concept of the right to treatment have the advantage over psychiatrists: they can use this concept in order to impose their mental health plan on a system, and they can do this without psychiatric background on patient needs and without responsibility for the patient whose course of treatment they are determining.

The legal scrutiny of psychiatry is going to get sharper. The Association of American Law Schools recently instituted a Section on Law and Psychiatry; the theme for its first meeting, held in New Orleans in December 1973, was "The Scientific Manipulation of Behavior and the Legal Protection of Freedom" (40). The American Bar Association has created an interdisciplinary Commission on the Legal Rights of the Mentally Handicapped on which psychiatrists and psychologists will probably play a much smaller role than the lawyers, judges and other nontherapist members who outnumber them. Its initial agenda includes the criteria for commitment, the stigmatization of the mentally handicapped, the permissibility of various therapies, including chemotherapy, psychosurgery and electroshock therapy and the related problem of informed consent, and the rights of involuntarily committed patients.

Increasingly, lawyers and legal policy will determine the structure of American psychiatry.

The legalistic approach takes the psychiatrist out of the driver's seat.

The legalistic approach takes the psychiatrist away from what should be his primary concern—interaction with patients—and forces him to spend much of his time in litigation and in the defensive practice of psychiatry in fear of future litigation.

The legalistic approach puts the burden on psychiatrists to prove veritable dangerousness when patients are commited; it prevents the psychiatrist from being helpful to the patient who is demonstrably psychotic but not demonstrably dangerous. The legalistic approach in a few jurisdictions is even putting the psychiatrist to the task of establishing commitability beyond a reasonable doubt, a criminal justice standard (41).

The legalistic approach is equating psychiatrists with correctional personnel.

The legalistic approach is forcing psychiatrists to release patients earlier and at the same time is holding them financially responsible for the damage that such an early released patient sometimes does. The ruling in *Donaldson v. O'Connor*[3] (42), which held that the state of Florida was immune from suit but two state hospital doctors would personally have to pay $38,500 to recompense a patient for inadequate treatment, is not calculated to make recruitment for the state hospital service easier.

The new legalistic approach to psychiatry makes public mental health service an impossible choice of careers for responsible psychiatrists. I have not met any third year psychiatric residents in recent years who plan a career in the public mental health hospital system, even though at an earlier stage in the formulation of career goals many would-be psychiatrists have great hopes that they will be able to be useful in filling the unmet needs in this sector. The growing shortage of public sector psychiatrists is evidenced by the fact that psychiatry is the specialty that recently has had the greatest growth in classified and display advertisements for doctors in professional journals (43).

Law, when it is not acting as an adversary and when it is not being legalistic, can be of tremendous help to psychiatry. A lawyer does not have to be an adversary, an opponent; he can be a conciliator, an advisor, a facilitator. Not all conflicts have to come to blows.

I come to a rather mixed conclusion. I think that the good offices of the lawyer are desperately needed to protect the rights of psychiatric patients and to see that the patients get a better quality of care. On the other hand, the adversary process gives the lawyer many advantages when he

---

[3] The *Washington Evening Star and Daily News* reported on April 20, 1973 that the United States Government had lost a suit and was liable for $100,000 for damages resulting when a patient was released "prematurely"; the hospital had released the patient 55 days before he murdered his wife. The court said the release was "proximately connected" with the murder.

is opposing the psychiatrist in seeking some benefits for a mentally ill person, and sometimes this benefit, particularly if it is unrestricted freedom, may not turn out to be a benefit at all. In his role as a participant in the adversary process, the lawyer has thus become much more active, although in this field many cases still go unrepresented.

The adversary role of the lawyer is only one of his roles, and the real question is whether the lawyer can be effective in a more constructive and cooperative role in the mental health field. Lawyers, particularly in their role as legislators, must see that mental health facilities are properly financed and that psychiatrists are given the manpower to run worthy institutions. Lawyers must maintain a watchdog function and continue to see that the rights of patients are observed, but often this can be done in cooperation rather than as an adversary contest. Lawyers can improve their own psychiatric expertise in order to understand the situation, to understand the mental health system better and to play a more effective role in promoting it; and also so that they can do a more effective job in advising the client, whether the case be commitment, divorce, custody or contract litigation, concerning his own interests. In his role as a part of the adversary process, the lawyer often makes life easier for the patient but makes life more difficult for the hospital administrator. To some extent this is necessary, because in some ways life should be made more difficult for the hospital administrator, but the lawyer is also going to have to find ways to help the administrator.

One of the greatest services that law has performed for psychiatry is the great compilation that the American Bar Association issued in 1961 called *The Mentally Disabled and the Law* (44). For the first time the laws of all our states and the District of Columbia were collected and tabulated, correlated historical background was given to explain their development, and recommendations were given for their improvement. The subjects covered do not include all those of interest in modern legal psychiatry, but all the basic topics are covered: involuntary and voluntary hospitalization, the rights of patients, release from mental hospitals, competency, criminal responsibility, competency to stand trial, sexual psychopathy laws and eugenic sterilization. Until the publication of this book, it was not possible to understand the field of mental health law, and work to attempt to bring order to it could not be begun.

The other great service that law has provided for psychiatry is the protection of individual rights, not in the sweeping class action cases designed to revolutionize mental health practice, but in the unpublicized cases in which individuals caught up in the mental health process are given their day in court or are accorded rights which have been denied. The American Civil Liberties Union and its affiliated organizations have done the most important work in this field; its recent very valuable publication is *The Rights of Mental Patients* (45).

But some other new groups are entering the field. Increasingly there has been recognition that mental patients like other people have legal problems—custody of children, financial snarls, landlord and tenant problems—in addition to grievances against the hospital. The Legal Aid Society of Cleveland has initiated a program which provides legal services through four offices in the four state mental institutions serving that area; among its activities has been help to mental health agencies in the community to incorporate and apply for funding. Although a major aim of this program has been to oppose the hospital administration, the program has been carried on with the cooperation of the hospital, which recognizes that may of its other aims are therapeutic for the patient and that even though some of its actions erode the concept of the omnipotent psychiatrist—as patients' advocates now deal with "past mistakes and improprieties, long buried in the records" which now can be "exposed by prying lawyers who are completely independent of the hospital administration"—the aims of the program are useful to all concerned. These aims are "to provide, for those individuals in the poverty community who are presently identified as mentally ill, the same individual human dignity, the same equal justice under law, and the same increased independent social and political power that the Legal Services program is trying to effect for the general poverty community." (46)

VISTA has been interested in providing more legal services for mental hospital patients; pioneer projects have been initiated in Illinois, Massachusetts, Washington, Minnesota and Missouri. James Sherby, the VISTA attorney assigned to the St. Louis Legal Aid Society, says that "mental health law is changing so fast that many attorneys can't keep up with it." VISTA has supported the Patient Advocacy Legal Service, located at Washington University Law School and directed by Max George Margulis, a former VISTA lawyer. This is a national clearinghouse for information on mental commitment and an agent for commitment reform. The Service collects and digests articles which pertain to mental health law and publishes materials on commitment to help lawyers and law students (47).

The National Center for Law and the Handicapped is funded by the Department of Health, Education and Welfare; its goals are both public education and legal technical assistance. Its projects include a course in "the Handicapped and the Law" developed for the Notre Dame Law School with materials to be made available to others.

The most important new force in the legal approach to mental patients has been the Mental Health Law Project, made up of attorneys and mental health professionals, with the aim of defining and implementing the rights of the mentally ill and the mentally retarded through litigation and other techniques. The project was organized in January of 1972 by, among others, Bruce Ennis, Paul Friedman and Charles Halpern, attorneys specializing in mental health law. The project is sponsored by the Center for Law and Social Policy, the American Orthopsychiatric Association and the American Civil Liberties Union Foundation (48). Although the project carried the burden of the *Wyatt* case and *Donaldson v. O'Connor* and other cases which have been described here as imposing legalistic restrictions on the practice of psychiatry, it has also won other victories which are more palatable to psychiatrists, such as the ruling in *Jackson v. Indiana* which defines for the first time some rights for those declared incompetent to stand trial. Many of the cases which it has brought are of benefit to psychiatry.

New York has a state-run Mental Health Information Service, and the District of Columbia provides legal services for St. Elizabeth's Hospital under the direction of an attorney who works in the hospital, Colleen Kollar-Kotelly. Many states are setting up units within their Departments or Divisions of Mental Health to investigate complaints of rights violations. Georgia's Personal Advocacy Unit, manned by nurses and social workers, investigates all complaints of violations and tries not only to redress individual wrongs but to change policies that intefere with delivery of services.

I know of several other innovative approaches designed to bring the lawyer into a useful association with the mental patient. The Mental Patient Civil Liberties Project operating in Philadelphia is a project that has elected not to work in the usual pattern, which is one-to-one problem solution with occasional test case litigation. Instead, its effort is to promote patient organization, and through this to make the hospital accountable to the consumer of its services, to achieve "consumer accountability." It has pioneered a Patients Civil Rights Manual. This project was started by David Ferleger (49). Michael Shapiro and some of his students at The School of Law of the University of Southern California succeeded in calling attention to the aversive behavior modification programs being conducted at California prisons; he has published on legislating the control of behavior therapies (50). David B. Wexler at the University of Arizona Law School, working with students, has investigated and published on many aspects of the commitment process of his state (51). At Columbia University, Jack Himmelstein is beginning a clinical program for third year law students that will involve them in the representation of psychiatric patients (52), and Jessie Goldner has a similar program at St. Louis University. Robert K. Patch is formulating a program for the legal advocacy of mentally disabled persons in the Sacramento/San Joaquin County areas of California; the staff of this program will receive advanced clinical training and experience on a part-time basis from the University of California Medical School (53). The National Institute of Mental Health has sponsored interdisciplinary teaching efforts at several universities and still maintains interest in this field; its Center for Studies in Crime and Delinquency has sponsored a monograph series in crime and delinquency topics that is an important source of information on the topic of prisoners' rights.

But my thesis is that, although legal pressures can keep psychiatrists aware of deficiencies and are needed to protect individuals, lawyers cannot implement the most effective kind of psychiatric reform. Improvement in services must be accomplished by the provider of services, which is psychiatry.

There has always been only one possible answer to the plight of the public mental hospital patient. He needs more care from better psychiatrists. To do this the terrible schism between the private practitioner and the public mental hospital psychiatrist needs to be closed. University residency programs need to be involved in the care of public patients. A dual standard for private and public care has to be eliminated. The new law cases do not accomplish any of these ends because they make public hospital work more unpleasant, less rewarding, more difficult and less respected than it has ever been. Any hope of achieving reforms from within —of interesting universities and the private sector in making public hospitals like private hospitals—has been demolished by the kind of attack that the law has made on the public mental hospital. Implicit in the new scheme is the concept that community mental health can handle the patient better than can the state hospital, but psychiatry has seen one fad after another come and go, one panacea after another hailed as the answer to its problems. Whether the paper shuffling and patient routing that goes with community mental health will bring more mental health to more people—particulary to people as disturbed as the state mental hospital patient frequently has been—remains to be seen. We are beginning to see articles in the literature describing the terrible neglect of the chronically mentally ill who have been forced out of hospitals by new restrictive admission and commitment policies. One of the recent articles has the arresting subtitle, "The Chronically Mentally Ill Shuffle to Oblivion" (54). It describes the reaction in New York to a 1968 memo from the Department of Mental Hygiene stating that it was the duty of state hospital directors to ascertain in the case of every patient and especially in the case of elderly patients whether state hospital care is the most appropriate treatment.

Word got around quickly to municipal and voluntary hospitals that the state hospital system was, by and large, only accepting the acutely mentally ill. To protect themselves from clogging acute general hospital psychiatric beds with chronic cases, the general hospitals as well began to refuse admission to the chronically ill, who were turned back to the community. Many of these patients had no families or were too disturbed for normal family living, and so the welfare system had to find places for these sick people to live.

The "new policy" has taxed to the limit already overburdened facilities in the community. Tremendous hardship has been sustained by the families of discharged patients and, where families do not exist, by the community in general. Many incidents of physical violence have occurred. In the streets, of course, the problem is more profound and widespread. Alcoholics further deteriorate; young schizophrenics are deprived of their only chance for some guidance, support and treatment; and recluses are not even thought of—because they don't bother anyone and do not ask for help. Patients are lost to follow-up, discontinue medications, and in deteriorated condition sleep in the streets or the subways. They often cannot care for their own needs and frequently pose a threat to themselves or others. The age of phenothiazines and liberalized psychiatric thinking has released patients from their straitjackets and backwards into the oblivion and slow desperation of furnished rooms, run-down hotels and subway station domiciles. (54)

The problem of the homeless mentally disabled is with us, and legal pressure continues for still further reductions in hospital populations. A paper presented at the Canadian Psychiatric Association states:

If . . . large numbers of patients discharged from mental hospitals have joined the ranks of the homeless and prison populations, the radical changes in management of severe psychiatric syndromes in western countries during the last decade may prove to have had a less satisfactory impact upon patient status than commonly supposed. (55)

There are beginning to be some second thoughts. California, which had announced plans to phase out its state mental hospitals by 1982, now plans to keep state institutions going for the "foreseeable future." (56)

Much of the present ill-will that exists between law and psychiatry, much of the present harassment of psychiatrists by lawyers, could have been prevented. Private psychiatry could have recognized its obligation to public as well as to private patients. Training programs could have sensitized psychiatric residents to the civil rights issues which they ignored in their pursuit of more "scientific" knowledge.

Peripatetic department chairmen, who have no loyalties to the communities where they work and no interest in improving community facilities, could have been replaced by a psychiatric director interested in the social welfare of people in his area. The vacuum which the law has rushed to fill should not have been allowed to develop.

Dr. Alfred Freedman, President of the American Psychiatric Association, as recently as 1973 proposed the concept of critical psychiatry (57). Critical psychiatry should have the function of reexamining psychiatric practices in the light of psychiatry's duties to society. Unless psychiatry can learn to operate as critical psychiatry, Dr. Freedman said, the preeminence of mental health professions in the decision-making process will not be reasserted, and change will be forced on psychiatry by less informed outsiders.

Some of the tasks of critical psychiatry according to Dr. Freedman are:

—exploring the equity of mental health programming in providing the finest care to all in need of care;
—examining the legitimacy of the mental health system to answer critics from within and without the system; criteria for voluntary and involuntary hospitalization, the right to treatment, and commitment procedures should be explored to answer the critics;
—defining the appropriate roles for those working in mental health to stress "connection and membership, rather than distance and superiority."

I was particularly heartened to hear Dr. Freedman stress critical psychiatry, because it followed up a thought of my own that I presented at a meeting of the American College of Legal Medicine in 1972 (58). My theme was that the old concept of forensic psychiatry as a subspecialty that would encourage lawyers and psychiatrists to find a common language or that would train psychiatrists to be more expert as expert witnesses must give way to a more far-reaching type of legal psychiatry that would emphasize in the community and in psychiatric training the legal and social framework in which patients are treated and psychiatry and medicine are practiced. I felt that legal psychiatry had begun to explore this broader role, and I suggested that, since legal psychiatry was extending its scope and moving out into the community, a broader title, such as social legal psychiatry, was needed for the subspecialty.

Some of the points which this address made were as follows.

Social legal psychiatry is a natural bridge between clinical psychotherapy and the world of social institutions, between the discipline of medicine and the behavioral sciences.

The development has been occurring on at least four fronts. *Consultative:* doctors are asked for advice from legislatures, courts, government agencies about current topics such as abortion, narcotics control, penal reform. *Clinical:* practice-oriented questions include confidentiality, commitment and control of the dangerous patient. *Interdisciplinary research:* crime and drugs are two of the areas requiring research on the part of a union of disciplines: physicians, sociologists, psychologists, social workers, lawyers. *Self-definitive:* medical and psychiatric authority has been delegated power that once was judicial and administrative, and this new role has to be defined and methods of review established.

The modern legal psychiatrist sees an enlarged role for his specialty. Recommendations by the American Medical Association's Committee on Medico-legal Problems and by authors familiar with interdisciplinary and cross-disciplinary medical and law teaching stress opportunities for legal medicine, but they do not allow for much time for social legal psychiatry at the medical school level. Social legal psychiatrists see enlarged opportunities for medical school teaching; they see modern medical students—familiar with *Catch 22* (59) and Ken Kesey (60)—as interested in the complex problems raised by the interaction of psychiatric authority and individual rights.

At more advanced levels, psychiatry residents and law students have special interests requiring or favoring familiarity with social legal psychiatry, and mixing the two kinds of students provides a new kind of learning experience.

Social legal psychiatry also has a catalytic function at a postgraduate level. It can be a focus for the interaction of professional people: lawyers, therapists, judges, penologists, police. Social legal psychiatry can be utilized as a bridge between clinical and academic psychiatry and the world of society.

Resistances and difficulties prevent the easy acceptance of social legal psychiatry—a major problem is definition of the field—but the need for a larger and better defined field is sufficiently real and sufficiently great to provide the possibility of an exciting future.

The paper on social legal psychiatry is one of the few papers which I have been unable to have published, and I think it is significant that the *American Journal of Psychiatry* did not think it significant enough to print, that it was not interested in opening up for public discussion the question of how psychiatry could better relate to courts, correction, the juvenile justice system, drug control and other interfaces between law and psychiatry so as to protect the rights of patients and to be more therapeutic. One of objections raised was that social legal psychiatry is an awkward term; so is critical psychiatry. Dr. Freedman and I are both in the market for better suggestions. The concept that we both are presenting is socially responsible and socially perceptive psychiatry.

I am still hopeful—but less hopeful than I was 2 years ago—about the ability of social legal psychiatry or critical psychiatry to make psychiatry more socially responsible. Except for a few chairs which support interdisciplinary exploration, there is little training program support for legal psychiatry. Some legal psychiatry programs support themselves through selling services such as evaluating defendants for courts or for prisons or providing therapy services for defendants, parolees and prisoners, but the more theoretical approach to legal psychiatry, in which patients' rights are emphasized, has no constituency to provide financial support.

The subjects that we are concerned with today—the Right to Treatment, competency to stand trial, commitment, the procedural rights of patients—lose out in the market place because they do not have a dollars-and-cents value. Private practice, testifying in court, even working for the correctional system have their monetary rewards. Representing patients has its rewards—although these are usually small—for lawyers. Law schools have shown a willingness to support the work of faculty members interested in exploring the field of patients' rights. But the Psychiatric Establishment, with a few exceptions, has not welcomed the critical examination of these issues into its curriculum; it has not educated psychiatric residents to be as concerned with the legal rights of their patients as they are with the clinical progress of their patients. Medical schools, which need to be concerned since the responsibility for commitment and other classifications often falls upon physicians who are non-psychiatrists, have lagged behind law schools in interesting themselves in patients' rights. They select applicants not on the basis of their interest in humanity but on their intellectual achievement. We see in interdisciplinary teaching the medical student and the psychiatric resident who do not even comprehend the civil rights issues with which the law student is so concerned.

The Medical Establishment and the Psychiatric Establishment have been dilatory. They have not actively pursued the subject of patients' rights. They have now been called to the bar of justice.

REFERENCES

1. Marohn, et al. Hospital Riot: Its Determinants and Implications for Treatment. *Am. J. Psychiatry* 130: 631, 1973.
2. *Heryford v. Parker*, 396 F.2d 393 (10th Cir. 1968).
3. Bartlett, F. L. Present-day Requirements for State Hospitals Joining the Community. *N. Engl. J. Med.* 276: 91, 1967; Address to the Annual Meeting of the Association of Medical Superintendents of Mental Hospitals, Sept. 30, 1968.
4. Ozarin and Taube. Psychiatric Inpatients: Who, Where and Future. *Am. J. Psychiatry* 131: 98, 1974.
5. Esquirol. Report to the Minister of the Interior, on his 1818 inspection of mental institutions throughout France. Quoted in *Humane Psychiatrist, MD*, 161: 163 (Feb.), 1972.
6. Solomon, H. American Psychiatric Association in Relation to American Psychiatry. *Am. J. Psychiatry* 115: 1, 1958.
7. The Lanterman-Petris-Short Act, California Welfare and Institutions Code, § 5000 et sq., 1969.
8. Georgia Code Ann. 88-502.1, 1969.
9. Georgia Code Ann. 88-502.2, 1969.
10. Georgia Code Ann. 88-502.3, 1969.
11. Robitscher, J. Controversial Crusaders. *Med. Opinion & Rev.* 4: 188, 1968.

12. Birnbaum, M. Some Remarks on the "Right to Treatment." *Ala. Law Rev.* 23: 623, 1971, n. 1.
13. Birnbaum, M. The Right to Treatment. *A.B.A.J.* 46: 499, 1960.
14. Editorial. A New Right. *A.B.A.J.* 46: 516, 1960.
15. *Rouse v. Cameron*, 373 F. 2d 451 (D.C. Cir. 1966).
16. American Psychiatric Association, Official Actions. *Am. J. Psychiatry* 123: 1458, 1967.
17. A Draft Act governing hospitalization of the mentally ill, prepared in the Federal Security Agency by the National Institute of Mental Health and Office of General Counsel. Pub. Health Publication 51, 1952.
18. *Wyatt v. Stickney*, 325 F. Supp. 781 (M.D. Ala. 1971).
19. Bartlett, F. L. Institutional Peonage: Our Exploitation of Mental Patients. *Atlantic* 214: 116, 1964.
20. *Lake v. Cameron*, 364 F.2d 657 (D.C. Cir. 1966).
21. *In re Gault*, 387 U.S. 1 (1966).
22. *Baxstrom v. Herold*, 383 U.S. 107 (1966); United States ex rel. *Schuster v. Herold*, 410 F.2d 1071 (2d Cir. 1969).
23. Steadman, H., and Keveles. The Community Adjustment and Criminal Activity of the Baxstrom Patients: 1966–1970. *Am. J. Psychiatry* 129: 304, 1972.
24. *Dixon v. Commonwealth*, 325 F. Supp. 966 (M.D. Pa. 1971).
25. *Lessard v. Schmidt*, 349 F. Supp. 1078 (E.D. Wis. 1972).
26. J. S. Mill. *On Liberty*, 1859
27. J. Rawls. *A Theory of Justice*. Cambridge: Harvard University Press, 1971.
28. *Jackson v. Indiana*, 406 U.S. 715 (1972).
29. *Souder v. Brennan*, 42 U.S.L.W. 2271 (D.D.C. Nov. 14, 1973).
30. Gillenkirk. Wyatt v. Stickney—Revolutionary Standards? *Psychiatr. News*, Dec. 19, 1973, 1.
31. *Psychiatr. Ann.*, Nov. 1973.
32. "Impending Ruling by Federal Judge Promises Hope for Neglected in Mental Institutions Around Country." *N. Y. Times*, March 26, 1972, 35.
33. Wasson. Mental Health Chief Named After Firing. *Atlanta J. & Constitution*, Oct. 1, 1972, § C, 2.
34. *Atlanta J. & Constitution*, Dec. 23, 1973, § B, 8.
35. Shils. Treatment, Not Custody: Federal Court Order Brings Big Changes in Lives of Mentally Ill and Retarded Patients in Alabama. *Wall St. J.*, Dec. 18, 1973, 42
36. Mental Retardation and the Law: A Report on Status of Current Court Cases, Office of Mental Retardation Coordination, April 1973, describes cases brought up to that time.
37. *Burnham v. Georgia*, 349 F. Supp. 1335 (N.D. Ga. 1972).
38. *Ferrici v. State*, 348 N.Y.S. 2d 236 (Sup. Ct. App. Div. 1973).
39. Kaplan, B. (ed.). *The Inner World of Mental Illness*. New York: Harper & Row, 1973.
40. 1973 Annual Meeting Proceedings, Part One, Association of American Law Schools, 1973.
41. *In re Ballay*, 482 F. 2d 648 (D.C. Cir. 1973); *Lessard v. Schmidt*, Ref. 28.
42. *Donaldson v. O'Connor*, Civil Action No. 1693 (N.D. Fla., Nov. 28, 1972), appeal filed 5th Cir., Jan. 1973.
43. Psychiatry, Pathology Demand Up. *Med. Groups News*, Dec. 1973, 5.
44. Lindman and McIntyre (eds.). *The Mentally Disabled and the Law: Report of the American Bar Foundation*, University of Chicago Press, 1961; second edition, Brakel and Rock (eds.), 1971.
45. Ennis, B., and Siegel, L. *The Rights of Mental Patients*. New York: ACLU Handbook Series, Avon Books, 1973.
46. Strand. Legal Aid for Patients in State Mental Institutions: The Cleveland Experience. *Clearinghouse Rev.* 6: 483, 1972.
47. *The V Line for Vista Volunteers*, Aug. 31, 1973, 10.
48. *Basic Rights of the Mentally Handicapped*. Mental Health Law Project, 1973, 114.

49. Ferleger, D. Mental Patient Civil Liberties Project, 3 Rough Times 7, 1973; A Patients Rights Manual, id., 12.
50. Shapiro, M. H. Legislating the Control of Behavior Control: Autonomy and the Coercive Use of Organic Therapies. *South. Calif. Law Rev.* 47: 237, 1974.
51. Wexler, D. B., and Scoville, S. E. Administration of Psychiatric Justice: Theory and Practice in Arizona. *Ariz. Law Rev.* 13: 1, 1971.
52. Himmelstein, J. Personal communication.
53. Patch, R. K. Personal communication.
54. Reich and Siegel. Psychiatry Under Siege: The Chronically Mentally Ill Shuffle to Oblivion. *Psychiatr. Ann.* 3: 35, 1973.
55. Eastwood, M. R. Risks of Premature Discharge. Quoting from address to Canadian Psychiatric Association. *Psychiatr. News*, Aug. 1, 1973, 20.
56. California Shelves Plans for Abolishing Hospitals. *Psychiatr. News*, Dec. 19, 1973, p. 1.
57. APA Head Urges Scrutiny of Psychiatry, Review of Its Priorities. *Clin. Psychiatr. News*, Nov. 1973, 3.
58. Robitscher, J. Social Legal Psychiatry. Address to Annual Meeting, American College of Legal Medicine, 1972.
59. Heller, J. *Catch 22*. New York: Simon & Schuster, 1961.
60. Kesey. K. *One Flew Over the Cuckoo's Nest*. New York: Viking Press, 1962.

chapter **10**

Massachusetts' New Mental Health Act: Process and Performance

A. LOUIS McGARRY, M.D.

Recently Stonewall Stickney has made a series of presentations around the country in which he described the behind-the-scenes processes related to the landmark *Wyatt v. Stickney* (1) constitutional right to treatment decision in Alabama. We learned, for example, that during the public clamor attending the global issues of the case, Alabama quietly, finally, racially integrated the management of their hospitalized mentally ill. In Michigan several years ago the Michigan legislature repealed that state's sexual psychopath statute, and one senior Michigan psychiatrist observed that "they did the right thing for the wrong reasons," the feeling in the legislature being that the statute was too lenient on sex offenders. It wasn't. Changes in mental health law would, therefore, at times seem to be idiosyncratic and even capricious. Some of what I write below in describing the process related to the adoption in Massachusetts of a new mental health code in 1970 will bear out the idiosyncratic-capricious theme. On the other hand, Jonas Rappeport has made the observation that, if a mental health legislative proposal is sound enough and if its supporters are tenacious enough, in Maryland at least, it will eventually pass—and it usually takes about 3 years. This, too, was our experience with the Massachusetts legislature with our new Mental Health Code. Moreover, recently in an overview of recent changes in statutory and case law in nine representative states, we found that there were discernible and consistent trends and similar social policy being articulated in mental health law throughout the country (2).

This article was supported in part by Project MH 21303-02 from the Center for Studies of Crime and Delinquency, National Institute of Mental Health.

All of this has led me to the conviction that it is valuable to try to record as accurately as possible the processes relating to major change in mental health law, no matter how idiosyncratic these processes may appear to be. There should be much that we can learn from each other in sharing accounts of the changing of mental health law.[1]

More important than process, however, is the monitoring of what the empirical impact of change in mental health law really is on the quality of people's lives and health. In what follows here, I will therefore describe the processes related to the successful passage of Massachusetts' Mental Health Reform Act and, to a limited extent, the global statistical impact which thus far has been associated with the implementation of this new law.

EARLY HISTORY

It took 7 years, from the initial research in 1964 leading to the first full draft of the new Mental Health Code submitted to the Massachusetts legislature in 1967, for the first of what turned out to be a 3-year legislative journey until enactment (after many changes and vicissitudes) on September 1, 1970 and ultimate implementation on November 1, 1971. Initially the work on this Code was sponsored by the Massachusetts Special Commission on Mental Health first created by Chapter 89 of the Massachusetts resolves of 1961. The Commission consisted of three Senators appointed by the President of the Massachusetts Senate, four Representatives appointed by the Speaker of the Massachusetts House and three citizens appointed by the Governor. Senator Leslie Cutler was appointed Chairman of the Commission, and subsequently the Commission was, and very properly so, commonly referred to as the "Cutler Commission." The fact that the work of the Commission, contrary to so many others, resulted in a new and comprehensive law is in considerable measure attributable to this indefatigable elderly lady and her extraordinary devotion to public service over almost 50 years. Senator Cutler lived to see this Code enacted, but she has since passed on.

Due largely to Senator Cutler's activism, the Massachusetts Legislature funded the early work of research which was extensive, involving con-

---

[1] The research for and the early drafts of the new Massachusetts Code were directed by William J. Curran, J.D., S.M.Hyg., who is now Frances Glessner Lee Professor of Legal Medicine at the Schools of Public Health and Medicine, Harvard University, assisted by this author and by Ernest Haddad, J.D., and Neil Chayet, J.D. This author directed the final drafting of the new Mental Health Act, assisted by Carmen Gentile, J.D., and Elton Klibanoff, J.D. Substantial procedural amendments added to the act prior to its implementation were drafted by this author in collaboration with Chief Justice Franklin N. Flaschner, J.D., of the District Courts of Massachusetts, Owen S. Walker, J.D., and Justice George N. Covett of the Brockton District Court, Brockton, Mass.

siderable in the way of empirical and field investigation. The mandate by the Commission to the research team (under the direction of Professor William J. Curran) from the beginning was that our mental health statutes were beyond amendment or rehabilitation and required a complete new codification. The ultimate product which is now law has been described as "one of the most comprehensive statutory housecleanings in modern history." (3)

The decision to mandate a complete recodification was based on the chaotic, multi-layered, anachronistic and confusing character of the old Massachusetts Mental Health Code. Reading through the old Code was an exercise in legislative paleontology, with layers of language of differing vintage and conceptual incompatability discernible. It reflected multiple tinkering attempts. Some provisions on their face were unconstitutional; others defied rational interpretation.

After intensive research activity during the summer and fall of 1964, a report was submitted to the Cutler Commission in December 1964 entitled, "A Study of the Commitment and Hospitalization Laws of the Commonwealth." This report included 67 substantive and procedural recommendations which related to abuses that the research had uncovered and which laid out the principles and procedures recommended for the new Code.

During 1965 the report was widely disseminated, and in October 1965 there was held the first of what proved to be countless subsequent public and private meetings, with one special interest group after another reaching compromise after compromise. Opinion ranged from those who thought that doctors should have the authority to involuntarily commit as a preventive to schizophrenia, to those who thought that we should abolish involuntary mental hospital commitment altogether. Thus the ultimate Code proved to be the work of many hands and the product of many compromises. At final enactment it was promptly both praised and found to be imperfect (3), and it was to be significantly amended before implementation; but more on that below.

At this point (1966) after much private and public debate, it was necessary to go back to the legislature for further funding for purposes of the actual drafting of the new Code based upon the report and subsequent input. This was accomplished with paradoxically breathtaking ease. Three minutes on my part with the Chairman of the Senate Ways and Means Committee under the wing of Senator Cutler, and the funds were provided. This is a curious phenomenon in government: change and the means of bringing about change can be staggeringly difficult and at times impossible, but they can also be amazingly simple and quick, given the right cause, presumably, the right timing and the support of the right combinations of power. During the summer and fall of 1966 a first draft of the complete Code was produced, and this went before the Massachusetts Legislature for consideration during the 1967 legislative session.

Now what was innovative about this new Code? What were we trying to attain in what Professor Curran called our "audacious" efforts? Did we attain them? Have we implemented them? And finally, if so, what has been the performance of the 2-year old statute?

This is not a law review article. Two excellent law review articles on the subject have been published by lawyers (3, 4), and a brief account of the provisions of the new Act and some early statistical data have been published by a lawyer and myself in the *Journal of the American Bar Association* (5). Those of you who wish to analyze this statute more exhaustively can consult these publications and of course the statute itself. Here I will limit its description to the principal objectives that we tried to attain.

First, following the principle that "less law rather than more law" was needed in the mental health law field (6), we attempted to shorten, simplify and clearly articulate in the statute (or so-called black letter law) the minimum that was statutorily required and to delegate (with an emphasis on protecting the civil rights of mental patients) much that had been statutory law to the regulatory power of the Department of Mental Health. In this way, much greater flexibility could be built into the administration of the statute without the delay, expense and uncertainty of the legislative process.

Second, we tried to establish, insofar as statute and regulatory authority can establish, the fullest possible exercise of civil rights and rights of self-determination by mentally ill and mentally retarded citizens.

Third, because of our conviction that the fullest exercise of the civil rights of the patients in the system requires effective legal advocacy, we provided, as an integral part of the Code, for mental health Legal Advisors (lawyers) with affirmative duties at various procedural stages and with a broad mandate to advise and assist the mentally ill and mentally retarded in legal and administrative settings.

Fourth, indefinite involuntary civil commitment was to be abolished and periodic judicial review and recommitment would be provided for the involuntarily detained. For all patients, voluntary or involuntary, periodic clinical review was required. A new and very much tighter definition of the likelihood of serious harm arising from mental illness which justified involuntary admission or commitment was developed.

Fifth, we attempted to design a statute which encouraged voluntary and conditional voluntary (3-day notice) status and discouraged involuntary admission and commitment. Thus it was established that a citizen who arrived at one of our mental hospitals accompanied by an application by a physician for a 10-day emergency involuntary admission was given an absolute, unilateral right to elect to be on 3-day notice conditional voluntary. In this status he could, if he chose, immediately signify his intention to leave the facility. In order for the facility to retain him, a petition would have to be successfully litigated by hospital authorities in the local district court.

Sixth, in an area often neglected in revisions of mental health law, that of the mentally ill offender or alleged offender, the new Code included very significant reforms. Massachusetts' program for the defective delinquent was to be abolished. This archaic program went back 50 years and had been based on the notion that there was a consistent causal connection between mental retardation and violent behavior. In the area of pre-trial mental hospital commitment, screening psychiatric examinations were to be required, a statute of limitations regarding subsequent prosecution was established based on a formula related to the seriousness of the alleged offense, and an opportunity for a trial on the merits, even for an incompetent for trial defendant, was provided. For both those defendants in criminal proceedings found either to be incompetent to stand trial or not guilty by reason of insanity, it was required that in addition they must meet and must continue to meet, on periodic clinical and judicial review, the same commitment standards applicable to the civilly committed.

Finally, with respect to the mentally retarded, involuntary civil commitment was to be abolished altogether.

With respect to the right of our patients to adequate treatment, we elected, quite frankly, to beg the issue at that time. The statute provided, in hortatory fashion, that the "highest practicable professional standards" of care and treatment be provided.

LEGISLATIVE HISTORY

Thus, with some fanfare and the full support of the Massachusetts Association for Mental Health and many others, our shortened but nevertheless substantial legislative proposal, replacing an entire chapter of our General Laws, was delivered to the legislature of Massachusetts for consideration at the beginning of the 1968 legislative session. Time went on. The usual legislative committee hearings came and went. The bill was reviewed by the Social Welfare and Judiciary Committees. Much support and little opposition was voiced. Several legislators, notably the Chairman of the Social Welfare Committee, took the time to study the complete bill, but the session wore on with no resolution, despite considerable lobbying efforts by the Massachusetts Association for Mental Health and the Massachusetts Association for Retarded Children. As the legislature approached prorogation, the resistance to the bill as drafted finally surfaced. The President of the Senate was quoted as stating that he was not going to add jobs to "the fastest growing empire in the state." By this he referred to state-supported lawyers for the indigent. At the eleventh hour we were told that if we took the provisions for Legal Advisors out of the bill, the legislative leadership would look favorably on passing the bill. We refused to compromise on this issue at that time. The bill was then described as quietly disappearing into the inner coat pocket of the Senate President. Other resistance at the same time, and we were to hear this twice more, came from Senate Counsel, who intoned that the bill was "too big, too late." All this was very discouraging. Senate Counsel at that time was called the "forty-first senator" (Massachusetts has 40 Senators). This referred to the powerful role which this gentleman had in approving or disapproving technical and legal details of legislation, and his expertise was much respected. He was relied upon to protect the Senate from passing imperfect and potentially embarrassing legislation, particularly in the case of lengthy and complex legislation such as ours. At this point, I can recall, one colleague stated that the whole enterprise, with the many weekends expended on drafting and redrafting, the many negotiations and the many compromises, had become simply "repugnant" and not worthy of his further time or energy. I recall also Elliot Richardson, then Attorney General of Massachusetts at about the same time, commenting on the failure of passage of the bill with words that have turned out to be somewhat prophetic and ironic in his own career. He said, "Why can't those people up on the hill ever trust anybody? "— meaning Beacon Hill where the Massachusetts legislature sits.

By the time the 1969 legislative session came around, however, my personal role and responsibilities had changed. I had moved from a primarily academic career to state service in the newly administratively reorganized Department of Mental Health. This latter statutory reorganization had taken place in 1966, and it was the focus of a bitter political fight between then Republican Governor Volpe and the Democratically controlled legislature. The Governor had called the legislature back into session after prorogation, as it was described at the time, "by the scruff of the neck." The Governor won that battle, but since some of the same actors of that particular scene were also involved in later attempts to get our Mental Health Code through (indeed we had collaborated throughout and taken the position that the new Department of Mental Health administrative structure should have modern commitment statutes to work with), the subsequent difficulties in the passage of the

Mental Health Code may well have been in part the angry negative political legacy of the 1966 fight. One of the principal draftsmen of the new Code had been incorrectly labeled as "Volpe's man," since he had been the principal draftsman of the 1966 administrative mental health statute.

In my new role as State Director of Legal Medicine for the Department of Mental Health, I had no choice but to keep my hand in with respect to further possible passage of the Code. By this time, four or five legislators, other than those we had primarily worked with on the Cutler Commission, had independently submitted various versions of the Code, and the Department was faced with the prospect of possibly less desirable hospitalization and commitment statutes being imposed on it.

By this time, as we had decided that there was sufficient in the way of good reforms in the Code without the Legal Advisors provisions, we elected to take the Legal Advisors out of the code and after such severance to let the Legal Advisors concept stand or fall on its own merits.[2] This meant once again, then, a redraft, in which this time I collaborated with counsel from the Department of Mental Health. As I have indicated, many of those working for and on the Code were getting tired of the enterprise. Again, despite our having resolved the major objection and resistance of the previous legislative session, the same scenario was played out. Prorogation approached, Senate Counsel intoned "too big, too late," and the bill quietly died with prorogation. I began to be convinced that the first two words of this phrase, "too big," would be the permanent epitaph for the endeavor. It appeared that the package was simply too complex to successfully grind through the legislative mill. Part of the evidence for this was the fact that (apart from the Legal Advisors provisions) the major compromises and changes made throughout the history of the various versions of the code were made in its first half, dealing primarily with civil commitment. The latter provisions, particularly those relating to the mentally ill criminal offender or alleged offender, remained relatively intact and were ultimately adopted substantially unchanged from their initial articulation. This was true despite the fact that these provisions on the criminal side, at the time, were probably the most striking departures from past practice in Massachusetts, indeed in the country.[3] It was easy to conclude that the bill was so big that those

---

[2] The Legal Advisors concept, articulated in several versions, was destined to take five annual journeys through the legislative process until a somewhat diluted measure was approved and signed into law on October 9, 1973. It has yet to be implemented (7).

[3] Subsequent to the passage of this Code, the United States Supreme Court in *Jackson v. Indiana* (1972), favorably citing this criminal part of the Massachusetts Code, established that the Constitution: *1*, required that persons committed as in-

studying it simply got exhausted before they ever got to the latter sections. In any case, at this point, this enterprise, this odyssey had taken on for me the character of a weary, unsuccessful pilgrimage, and our expectations were at their lowest.

We come now to 1970. We have a new Governor: again, characteristic of Massachusetts, a Republican with a Democratically controlled legislature. Governor Volpe and his men are out of the picture, and the legacy of the 1966 fight is thereby softened. Enter two young lawyers from the Governor's office with the fantasy that this aging horse could once again be put in harness and the journey renewed. Renewed it was: still another redraft was completed, this time destined for successful passage, but destined also for still more challenge and further redrafting before its implementation. The draft that was passed in 1970, Chapter 888, Massachusetts Acts 1970, otherwise called the Mental Health Reform Act of 1970, was substantially different from earlier drafts in certain areas. These areas consisted largely of procedurally complex civil liberties safeguards applicable to the role of the courts and judges in implementing the statute. Rather elaborate and inflexible timetables and restrictions were to be imposed on the judiciary. I had some problems with these changes, but I saw my role and expertise to be more primarily relevant to the operation of the new Code as it applied to our patients and to the staff of the Department of Mental Health. Thus the compromises that I made tended to be on the judicial and procedural legalities, and this was appropriate, since I am not a lawyer.

In the previous paragraph, out of regard for your patience, I quickly brought us to the success of all of these labors. But Chapter 888 did not pass easily. Once again the previous pattern of the approaching end of the legislative session and the intoning of "too big, too late" by Senate Counsel was repeated. But there were significant differences too. It was the eve of a gubernatorial election year. The President of the Senate clearly was going to step down and run for Governor. As indicated above, Governor Volpe and many of his associates had moved on to Washington. It was clear that Senator Cutler was about to complete her long and distinguished career, and it is likely that there was sentiment in the Senate to reward her long espousal of the Code as a gesture at her parting. The Massachusetts Mental Health Association had lobbied with particular

---

competent to stand trial must meet civil commitment standards, 2, required that, absent any progress on the part of such a person toward a state of competency, the state could retain him only for a "reasonable" period in a mental hospital awaiting trial, and 3, in dicta looked with favor on procedures designed to resolve criminal allegations against incompetent defendants short of a full trial, but on the merits of a defense. All of the findings by the Supreme Court were anticipated in the Massachusetts 1970 Mental Health Code.

vigor for the passage of the Code. On this occasion, the Democratic leadership responded, particularly the Speaker of the House. A complicating factor was the fact that landmark legislation was concurrently being hotly debated concerning "no fault" automobile insurance. Despite the importance and the heat, particularly from the threat that "no fault" posed for the legal profession, at the request of the Speaker, House Counsel spent a week with the draftsmen of the Code and with staff from the Speaker's office and the Social Welfare committee, and the Code was reviewed line by line. With relatively insignificant changes, House Counsel ultimately advised the Speaker that the Code was technically sound and acceptable for passage. Finally, I think there was another phenomenon operating here, perhaps idiosyncratic to Massachusetts, perhaps not. With the usual inefficiency and guaranteed conflict between a Republican Governor and a Democratic legislature in Massachusetts, the legislative sessions are usually long, often lasting very late in the calendar year, and they are often unproductive up to the closing days of the session. At such a late date, I think both the Governor and the legislative leadership look about for one or more matters on which they can bilaterally agree so that the given session has something worthwhile to put into the statute books, so that their own self-esteem is supported and so that it can be demonstrated to the citizens of Massachusetts that the system can work. To use a phrase Senator Cutler was fond of, in 1970 the Mental Health Code was, in the above context, "an idea whose time had come." The Mental Health Reform Act was passed with a virtually unanimous vote. Signed by the Governor in September, 1970, the new Code was to take effect on July 1, 1971 in order to give adequate time for preparing the two major systems of mental health and the judiciary for gearing up, developing new approved forms, writing new regulations and training personnel in implementing the new law.

POST-PASSAGE VICISSITUDES

The reaction of the judiciary in Massachusetts following the passage of Chapter 888 was swift. Based upon his address at the Worcester State Hospital on December 3, 1970, Chief Justice Franklin N. Flaschner of the District Courts of Massachusetts (the courts which would assume the greatest burdens in implementing the new Mental Health Code) wrote an article entitled, "The New Massachusetts Mental Health Code: A 'Magna Carta' or a Magna Maze? " (3), which appeared in the *Massachusetts Law Quarterly* in its first issue in 1971. In this article the Chief Justice generally praised the provisions of the new Code, but he was sharply critical of the procedural rigidity and complexity of the Code as it applied to proceedings in the courts.

Since there were 6 months of a new legislative session in 1971 available for possible amendments to Chapter 888 before its starting date of July 1, 1971, it was decided that the Department of Mental Health would collaborate with the Chief Justice and his associates in an attempt to amend the Code in order to clarify procedures and move toward greater feasibility and efficiency in the implementation of the Code, particularly as its provisions applied to proceedings in the courts. Assuming passage of the amendments and because of the need to design official forms and regulations conforming to the amended statute, postponement of the effective date of the new Code to November 1, 1971 was requested as part of the new amendments (8).

With the amendments safely filed, I recall one spring afternoon in 1971 when there ascended to Beacon Hill a small but determined band of officials. They included Chief Justice Flaschner, then Commissioner of Mental Health, Milton Greenblatt, Executive Assistant to the Commissioner, Thomas Monahan and myself. We had one formal appointment with the Speaker of the House, but the rest of our lobbying efforts were to be catch-as-catch-can in the corridors of the legislature for the most part and with senior staff people who disappeared onto the floor of the Senate, into offices of the Ways and Means Committee, and so on. The consistent answer came back, "No problem, no problem" with respect to the passage of the amendments. The whole process took less than 1 hour and was another example of how breathtakingly easy change can sometimes be. Chief Justice Flaschner later commented, having been newly appointed at the time, that this was his honeymoon period in office.

Despite these assurances, we were faced with a dilemma: if the slowly grinding legislative mill was unable to pass the amendments by midnight of June 30, 1971, we would be in for a major crisis. This followed from the fact that, if we proceeded to develop the necessary impedimenta (i.e. forms, regulations, etc.) for the implementation of Chapter 888 as it stood then, the passage of the new amendments would create confusion and the need for a whole new set of forms, instructions, etc.

With the assurances that we had, we elected to bet on the passage of the amendments before June 30, 1971. It was with growing anxiety that we saw the months turn to weeks and then to days as June 30 loomed. We prepared emergency forms, but it was absolutely certain that, if the Governor did not sign the amendments into law by midnight of June 30, the mental health and judicial system of the Commonwealth would have been thrown into utter chaos with respect to the implementation of the new Code.

The legislators were as good as their word, and the amendments were passed and appeared on the Governor's desk on June 30, 1971. At this point, as it was related to us afterwards, the Governor, who was reported at the time to have a distressing inner ear equilibrium problem, balked at the signing of the amendments into law. Loud angry sounds were said to have emanated from his august chambers. This is hearsay, but we were given to understand that his distress was primarily focused on the 4-month postponement of the effective date of the Act. We desperately needed this time, but the Governor apparently saw this postponement as delay and inefficiency on the part of one of his departments. One of the draftsmen of the Code, a lawyer in the Governor's office, was finally able to convince the Governor to sign the amendments into law at 4:00 p.m., with 6 hours to spare.

IMPLEMENTATION

In his "Magna Maze" article, Chief Justice Flaschner had written, "Implementation of this new mental health law by the judiciary (principally the Massachusetts District Courts), the legal and medical professions, the law enforcement officers, and most importantly, the Department of Mental Health, offers a keen challenge to the viability of interdisciplinary administrative techniques." (3) It proved to be a keen challenge, indeed.

I can recall early in all this, when my own activities were primarily academic and when we started to draft this Code, often referring to "they," meaning the Department of Mental Health. But now that the whole thing had come to pass, I had become part of the "they" and had inherited the responsibility in the Department for implementing the new statute. During the spring and summer of 1971, we had traveled about the state giving day-long training sessions in each of the seven mental health regions and in an eighth session with the judiciary. Insofar as we could, given the uncertainties of whether or not the proposed amendments would pass, and we predicated the training on the expectation that they would, we tried to train and prepare the mental health and judicial systems of the state for the implementation of the new Code with its almost totally new procedures and standards. Approximately 1300 trainees attended these sessions.

With the enactment of the amendments in June, we had 4 months to get the necessary materials together and promulgated to the appropriate mental health and retardation facilities, public and private, and to the appropriate courts. Involved was: *1*, a complete revision and expansion of the rules and regulations of the Department of Mental Health (much had been given over to regulatory authority by the Code as you will recall); *2*, designing and producing the necessary legal forms, petitions for commitment, notice forms, admission application forms and so on, which had to be legally correct (this proved to be a very difficult art form indeed); and 3, preparing a "cookbook" or indexed manual of procedures for the implementation of the new Code, a "how to" pamphlet. I will not go into detail here but rather will bring you to the final scene in this account of process.

Imagine a gymnasium in a mental health center in downtown Boston near the central office of the Department of Mental Health. Piled along one side of the basketball floor are 26 columns of forms several feet high and several feet thick, numbering in toto about 400,000 documents. Understand that these are in gross lots not broken down into hundreds or even thousands. Also to be distributed are 1000 copies of the new statute and 1000 copies of the "cookbook" of instructions. Along two other sides of the gymnasium, laid out geographically, there are places for the deposit of the various kits of forms and materials which 155 separate agencies would require in order to implement the statute. In order to understand the complexity of this "keen challenge," to use Judge Flaschner's phrase, you should realize that there was considerable variation in the needs of particular agencies. For example, a District Court having jurisdiction over a correctional agency would need particular forms in particular numbers, whereas another court having jurisdiction over a state hospital would have vastly different needs. This scene existed late in the afternoon of Tuesday, October 26, 1971. The Code was to go into effect on the following Monday, November 1, 1971.

Here I must proceed in a highly personal vein, but it is a vital final part of what happened. It had taken a considerable effort by many to arrive at the October 26 level of preparation. The forms were still coming off the press. As that scene was approaching, my wife noted that I had become increasingly preoccupied. She inquired and I shared my dilemma with her. It appeared to me at the time that I was the only person in the state who had been sufficiently immersed in the writing of the new Code and who had sufficient experience with the statistical flow of patients through the various agencies to be able to anticipate their numerical needs for the various forms, and therefore I was the only person qualified to decide the composition of the different kits. My problem was that I had long since made irrevocable time commitments for the truncated week of October 26 (Monday was a holiday) and could not possibly adequately personally supervise the collation and distribution of the necessary materials. To this my wife responded simply, "I'll do it." After 2 hours of briefing over our dining room table, my perhaps prideful conviction that I was the only person in the state who knew what needed to be done, had to be modified. Now there were at least two.

And so she did it. It took her a day and a half, using intermittent volunteer help from central office staff, mostly clerks and secretaries. I recall one scene which perhaps captures best how she did it. There are half a dozen people sitting on the floor counting out lots of 26 different forms varying in number from 15 to 500 each and piling them neatly. My wife is followed by a large dolly pushed by three men. As they proceed down the line of counted forms, she calls out, I need 500 of those, 100 of these, 35 of those, 20 of these, and so on. Having completed the run past the forms, the dolly proceeds on to deposit the appropriate kits geographically and then back again for another run past the forms. At one point with the dolly she was doing seven agencies at a clip. By Thursday afternoon, the job was complete, and the word went out to the courts and hospitals to come in and get their kits. By all manner of conveyances and through the weekend, the kits were picked up and the agencies were able to put the new Code into effect the following Monday. The last day of October, the night of Sunday, October 31, 1971 and the last day under the old Code was, of course Hallowe'en. One of my colleagues commented afterward that at midnight, October 31, "The Worcester State Hospital turned into a pumpkin."

It turned out that there was surprisingly little difficulty in the implementation of and adaptation to the new procedures, even though they were almost totally different. Commissioner Greenblatt commented later that there was a remarkable "flaklack." I cannot fully explain this, but I'm convinced that the "cookbook" or manual of procedures which was designed to be simple, concrete and clear, apparently succeeded in being so. In any case, let us get on with performance.

PERFORMANCE

How and when does one analyze the impact and performance of a new Mental Health Code? Researchers from the ENKI Research Institute recently studied California's 1969 Lanterman-Petris-Short mental health law and were of the opinion that one had to wait 2 or 3 years after enactment before valid data and a clear picture emerge (9). Ideally one would want to observe in the courtroom and assess whether, for example, a new standard for involuntary mental hospital commitment is being adequately litigated and really makes any difference, and we hope to do this in the future.

What I have to report to you are rather global statistics related to the operation of the new Massachusetts Code during its first 2 years and a comparison of these data to the last final year under the old Code. These data must be regarded as preliminary and suggestive. They nevertheless would appear to indicate that some of the goals of the draftsmen of the new Code have been impressively attained.

Total new admissions and readmissions have sharply declined in Massa-

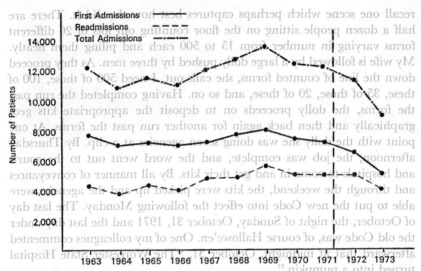

Figure 1. Admissions to Massachusetts State Mental Hospitals, fiscal years 1963 to 1973. The vertical dash line denotes the effective date of the Massachusetts Mental Health Reform Act of 1970.

chusetts during the first 2 years under the new statute (Fig. 1). (The new Act was operative during two-thirds of fiscal year (FY) 1972 and throughout FY 1973.) Decline in the total census in Massachusetts state mental hospitals has sharply accelerated during the same period (Fig. 2). Impressive also is the rise in voluntarism and the massive decline in the number of involuntary admissions and prolonged involuntary commitments. During the last full fiscal year under the old Act, 72.6% of all civil mental hospital admissions were involuntary. During the first year under the new Act, involuntary civil admission strikingly declined to only 23.3% of total admissions. Prolonged involuntary civil commitments declined from 897 in FY 1971 to 347 during the first year under the new Act. The latter is only 1.9% of total admissions.

With respect to court-ordered mental hospital admissions in Massachusetts in connection with criminal proceedings (hospital observation for determination of competency for trial and not guilty by reason of insanity) there have been equally striking declines (Fig. 3). During the last year under the old Code (FY 1971), there were 1888 pre-trial admissions for incompetency for trial work-ups. During the first year under the new Code, such admissions declined to 940. These statistics are particularly gratifying since we knew from previous research that the great majority of these admissions were unnecessary (10). Of the 1888 pre-trial

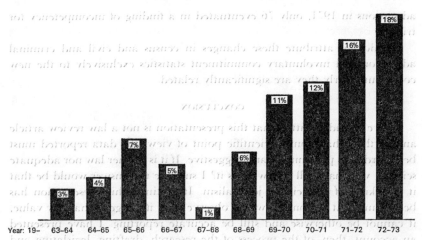

Figure 2. Annual percentage of decline in inpatient census of Massachusetts state mental hospitals. The effective date of the Massachusetts Mental Health Reform Act of 1970 was November 1, 1971. Fiscal years ending June 30. Percentages are based on the following:

$$\frac{\text{Census June 30 (year 1)} - \text{Census June 30 (year 2)}}{\text{Census June 30 (year 1)}}$$

Total census on June 30, 1964 was 16,938. This declined to a total census of 7,179 on June 30, 1973.

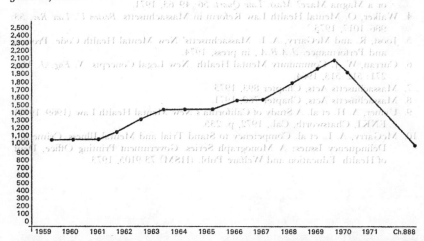

Figure 3. Incompetency for trial (observational) admissions in Massachusetts. *Ch. 888* denotes the incompetency for trial admissions during the first 12 months under the new Massachusetts Mental Health Code (Nov. 1, 1971 to October 31, 1972). The other years are fiscal.

admissions in 1971, only 76 eventuated in a finding of incompetency for trial.

We do not attribute these changes in census and civil and criminal admission and involuntary commitment statistics exclusively to the new code, but clearly they are significantly related.

CONCLUSION

I have already written that this presentation is not a law review article and further, that from a scientific point of view, the data reported must be regarded as preliminary and suggestive. If it is neither law nor adequate science, you may well ask, what is it? I suppose my answer would be that it is a kind of participant journalism. If at times this presentation has been somewhat personal, I would observe that, if the genre has any value, it cannot be otherwise and still be accurate reporting. I have presented an account, then, of the process of the research, drafting, legislating and implementing of Massachusetts' new Mental Health Code and a preliminary account of its early promising performance.

REFERENCES

1. *Wyatt v. Stickney*, 325 F. Supp. 781 (M.D. Ala. 1971).
2. McGarry, A. L., and Kaplan, H. A. Overview: Current Trends in Mental Health Law. *Am. J. Psychiat.* 130: 621–630, 1973.
3. Flaschner, F. N. The New Massachusetts Mental Health Code: A "Magna Carta" or a Magna Maze? *Mass. Law Quart.* 56: 49–63, 1971.
4. Walker, O. Mental Health Law Reform in Massachusetts. *Boston U. Law Rev.* 53: 986–1017, 1973.
5. Joost, R. and McGarry, A. L. Massachusetts' New Mental Health Code: Promise and Performance. *J.A.B.A.*, in press, 1974.
6. Curran, W. J. Community Mental Health: New Legal Concepts. *N. Eng. J. Med.* 271: 512–513, 1964.
7. Massachusetts Acts, Chapter 893, 1973.
8. Massachusetts Acts, Chapter 760, 1971.
9. Urmer, A. H. et al. A Study of California's New Mental Health Law (1969–1971). ENKI, Chatsworth, Cal., 1972, p. 235.
10. McGarry, A. L. et al. Competency to Stand Trial and Mental Illness, Crime and Delinquency Issues: A Monograph Series. Government Printing Office, Dept. of Health Education and Welfare Publ. (HSM) 73-9105, 1973.

chapter **11**

Voluntariness of Hospitalization as an Important ResearchVariable and Legal Implications of Its Omission from the Psychiatric Research Literature

MAGNUS LAKOVICS, M.D.

In *Law, Liberty, and Psychiatry*, Thomas Szasz notes that psychiatric textbooks often completely disregard the problem of commitment (1). If they do mention it, he feels that the presentation of the problem appears very slanted. Mention of commitment as a research variable is also omitted from the research literature of psychiatry. In a review of the literature from 1948 to the present, no paper could be found which was primarily concerned with studying the differences or similarities in treatment and outcome between voluntary and involuntary patients. Most papers on treatment and outcome rarely mention whether the patients chosen for their study were voluntary or involuntary. Scientific method is exhaustively used to determine the effects of all kinds of social, psychological, cultural and meteorological conditions on mental illness. Psychiatric researchers have deemed it very important to study sex and race differences in response to drug treatment in schizophrenia (2). The relationship of relative humidity, wind movement, sky cover, days of the week, moon phases and holidays to mental hospital admission rates have all been studied (3). Yet one most significant social condition of the person as mental patient has been left out of these detailed studies: i.e.

whether he is being voluntarily or involuntarily treated. One purpose of this chapter is to show that distinguishing between voluntary and involuntary patients could be a very important research variable in studying the problems of treatment and outcome of psychiatric patients.

Another purpose of this chapter is to examine some possible legal implications resulting from the omission of research of an important variable as voluntariness of hospitalization. Recently court decisions in "right to treatment" cases such as *Wyatt v. Stickney* (4) and *Rouse v. Cameron* (5) have held that involuntary hospitalization should only be for treatment purposes. The courts have also maintained that this treatment must be adequate. This chapter will discuss whether adequacy can be determined since study of this important variable has been omitted from the research literature. In addition, the little research evidence available will be discussed which supports the claim that involuntary hospitalization is for the primary purpose of "preventive detention" and not treatment.

VOLUNTARINESS OF HOSPITALIZATION AS AN IMPORTANT RESEARCH VARIABLE

Since psychiatric researchers have omitted study of the variable of voluntariness of hospitalization, one has to presume that they have assumed that voluntary and involuntary patients respond to the various treatment modalities in the same way. However, if these two types of patients respond differently to treatment, then this fact could have a profound bias upon the outcome of the treatment modality or modalities under study. This may be particularly true in studies which compare various kinds of treatment modalities such as drugs, psychotherapy and electroconvulsive therapy (ECT). Most clinicians realize the difficulty of doing psychotherapy with a poorly motivated patient, let alone one who is forced into psychotherapy. Consequently, the results of any study comparing psychotherapy to drugs and (ECT) would be incorrectly interpreted if this variable were not investigated. In addition, general statements about the comparative efficacy of these treatments certainly could not be made if this variable was not studied.

For example, in a study of the treatment of schizophrenia, Philip R. May and A. Hussain Tuma compare five treatments methods: "individual psychotherapy; drug therapy; individual psychotherapy plus drugs; electroshock therapy; and 'basic care' or 'control' " (6). The authors mention that the average patient in the study entered the hospital involuntarily. However, they do not tell us how many patients were involuntary or into which groups the involuntary patients were placed. They do say that after "selection and initial evaluation, patients were assigned by a random method" to the various treatment groups. They equated the five treatment groups "in terms of sex, age, race, education, occupation, religion and initial level of illness as gauged by the Menninger Health–Sickness Rating Scale." They do not say whether the voluntary and involuntary patients were also divided equally. Consequently, one cannot know how many patients were voluntary or involuntary in any of the treatment groups. We only know that the average patient in this study was involuntary. In summarizing the results they conclude that:

> Patients treated with drugs, with or without psychotherapy, did significantly better than the control group, in terms of nurses' ratings on the MACC and psychoanalysts' ratings on the Menninger Health–Sickness Rating Scale. On both measures, "drug" patients did better than those given E.C.T. or psychotherapy, but this was statistically significant only for the MACC. (6)

It is conceivable that, if they had chosen only voluntary patients for this study, the patients treated with psychotherapy alone might have done better than the results show. In addition, if they did not randomize for voluntariness, perhaps the psychotherapy-alone group contained more involuntary patients than did the drug group. This could explain the better results of the drug group over the psychotherapy-alone group, which then might not be attributable to the drug treatment alone. One might say that this is just a generally poor study. However, this study is only used as an example to illustrate how important it could be to take into account the distinction between voluntary and involuntary patients in both performing and reporting studies dealing with comparative treatment modalities and their outcome.

There is some research evidence in the literature which supports the contention that voluntary patients may respond differently to various treatment modalities when compared to involuntary patients. In a paper entitled "Short-Term Improvement in Schizophrenia: The Contribution of Background Factors," the authors studied 335 newly admitted patients who were assigned to one of four treatment groups: chlorpromazine, thioridazine, fluphenazine and inert placebo (7). They were treated for 6 weeks under double blind experimental conditions. The patients' backgrounds were classed into 34 predictor variables. These were then correlated to treatment outcome. Voluntariness of hospitalization was deemed one of the significant background predictor variables which was related to treatment outcome. The results indicated that voluntariness of hospitalization had the highest correlation with improvement in the placebo group compared to the other variables of sex, father's mental illness, mother's education, age at admission, age of first disturbed behavior, age of first episode and favorableness of family environment. In the drug group voluntariness appeared as the poorest correlate to improvement compared to these variables. Since the only treatment which the placebo patients received was nonsomatic therapy,[1] one could postulate from the results that voluntariness appears as a high correlate with improvement of these placebo patients because nonsomatic therapy (i.e. psychotherapy, group therapy, occupational therapy) is effective only in patients who are voluntary.

Much of the psychiatric literature supports the contention that phenothiazine therapy is more effective than nonsomatic therapy in schizophrenia (6, 8, 9). This may be a biased conclusion since the important variable of voluntariness of hospitalization was generally not taken into account as a primary research variable in these studies. Perhaps a more accurate conclusion would be to say that phenothiazine therapy may be of greater efficacy in schizophrenic patients whether they are voluntary or involuntary compared to placebo and nonsomatic therapy. What might be added to this conclusion is that the comparative efficacy of nonsomatic therapy to phenothiazine therapy in voluntary schizophrenic patients is not known based upon what was postulated here from the study on the short term improvement in schizophrenia. Again, this demonstrates how important it could be to take the variable of voluntariness of hospitalization into account.

Finally, another fact which strongly supports the importance of the variable of voluntariness of hospitalization is the difference in the length of stay of voluntary patients compared to involuntary patients. A paper written by Weinstein et al. cites statistics from New York State mental hospitals for the fiscal year which ended March 31, 1971 (10). They show that the median hospital stay of involuntary patients (this excluded patients in the following classes: criminal procedure, alcohol, narcotic, and other) was 68 days. The same figure for voluntary patients was 41 days. Many interpretations could be offered to explain why this differential length of stay pattern exists. It could be hypothesized that involuntary patients are "sicker" than voluntary ones. Thus, involuntary patients are more difficult to treat and require longer hospitalization. It could be said that treatment for involuntary patients is not as adequate as for voluntary patients. Consequently, less adequate treatment results in prolongation of hospitalization. A theory could be introduced that

---

[1] In another paper, "Phenothiazine Treatment in Acute Schizophrenia," the authors discuss more specific details of the background and methodology of the study on the short term improvement in schizophrenia. They indicate here that during "the six weeks of study treatment, patients were not permitted to receive any other drug or shock treatment but were permitted to participate in any other nonsomatic treatment that was part of the usual hospital routine, such as psychotherapy, group therapy, occupational therapy, etc." (8)

phenothiazine therapy is much less effective in involuntary patients compared to voluntary patients. This could account for the prolonged hospital stay of involuntary patients when compared to voluntary ones. It could also be postulated that involuntary hospitalization is mere social control and preventive detention. The conclusion could be drawn that social and political pressure is brought to bear upon hospital psychiatrists and administrators to keep involuntary patients away from their communities longer, which accounts for their longer hospital stay in comparison to voluntary patients. Many more hypotheses could be offered to explain the differential length of stay pattern of voluntary versus involuntary patients. However, one fact which again stands out is that the variable of voluntariness of hospitalization is important to any study which considers the comparative length of hospitalization in relation to any treatment modality.

LEGAL IMPLICATIONS

In an article entitled "Courts, State Hospitals and the Right to Treatment," Jonas Robitscher summarizes the meaning of the term and legal concept of "right to treatment" (originated by Birnbaum in 1960) as "the right of involuntarily hospitalized mental patients to receive adequate therapy as an exchange for their being deprived of their liberty." (11) Robitscher goes on to cite the legal argument surrounding this concept. Mental hospitalization on an involuntary basis is a deprivation of liberty. The Fifth Amendment protects the citizen from deprivation of liberty without due process of law. However, the benefit which involuntary patients receive from adequate treatment makes it possible for them to recover their liberty as early as possible, and this gives their hospitalization legal legitimacy. Robitscher proceeds to discuss the one case, *Wyatt v. Stickney*, which embraces Birnbaum's legal concept of right to treatment. He states also that *Wyatt v. Stickney* is the one case which clearly sets forth the concept of right to treatment "as a constitutional right and as a right for all (not merely quasi-criminal) patients." He quotes the court as finding that

> the purpose of involuntary hospitalization for treatment purposes is *treatment* and not mere custodial care or punishment. This is the only justification, from a constitutional standpoint, that allows civil commitments to mental institutions. . . . (11)

As mentioned above, if the purpose of involuntary hospitalization is treatment, then this treatment must be adequate and effective to make it possible for patients to leave the hospital as early as possible. The questions which this raises in the context of this paper are: "Who determines adequacy?" and "Can anyone say whether any involuntary patients are receiving adequate treatment?" In a discussion on implementing the right to treatment, G. H. Morris traces the historical contexts of the right to treatment in terms of the question: "Who determines adequacy?" (12) Morris believes that Chief Judge David Bazelon's decision in *Rouse v. Cameron* answered this question when he asserted that the purpose of involuntary hospitalization is treatment. He continued by saying that the hospital must fulfill its obligation to provide adequate treatment. If it does not, then the patient may secure his release from the hospital even if he is still mentally ill. Thus, Morris concludes that the answer at this stage to the question of who determines adequacy was: "The courts determine adequacy."

Morris points out that this resolution stirred up quite a bit of controversy. The American Psychiatric Association indicated that the "definition of treatment and the appraisal of its adequacy are matters for medical determination." Morris further asserts that "Judge Bazelon in *Rouse* phrased the test in terms of suitable and adequate treatment for the particular individual in the light of existing medical knowledge." Morris' discussion of *Wyatt v. Stickney* indicates that U. S. District Court Judge Frank M. Johnson even set the standards of adequate treatment in terms of square feet of floor space, furnishings in patient facilities, and patient-staff ratios.

In all these resolutions what is assumed is that the staff or experts, in this case psychiatrists, do know what adequate treatment is for involuntary patients in light of existing medical knowledge and do in fact administer this treatment. Since there are no research studies in the psychiatric literature which investigate the question of whether treatment of involuntary patients is even effective in terms other than custodial care or punishment, one wonders whether there is any reasonable justification for involuntary mental hospitalization of any patients on constitutional grounds based on the conclusions of the court in *Wyatt v. Stickney* and other right to treatment cases. One can argue that there are plenty of data researching effectiveness of treatment in mental disorders. If the hospital is using these researched treatment modalities, then certainly any court should grant that the patient has received adequate treatment in light of existing medical knowledge. As demonstrated above, this general comment does not take into account the fact that most of this research may be biased because in most studies no distinction is made between voluntary and involuntary patients. Again we can say that this variable is of no importance. But, as has been pointed out here, voluntariness of hospitalization is an important variable in determining the treatment outcome of involuntary patients as well as voluntary ones.

The little research evidence which is available on the relationship between treatment and involuntary hospitalization indicates that " 'protection' and 'dangerousness' are two major working criteria of involuntary hospitalization and need of psychiatric treatment is of secondary importance." (13) Kumasaka et al. have arrived at this conclusion by comparing structured clinical and background interviews of involuntarily hospitalized patients at Bellevue Hospital in New York City requesting court hearings to involuntarily hospitalized patients not requesting court hearings (13). They use the Psychiatric Evaluation Form (PEF) for symptomological assessment as their interview instrument and their own Structured Interview Schedule for background information. Several of their findings are pertinent here.

One finding is that the discharge rate of hearing request groups is higher than that of the nonrequest group. For example, in 1969 the discharge rate of the hearing request group was 49.3%. The same figure for the nonrequest group was 21.9%. Kumasaka et al. go on to state that "more than 80% of the cited discharges at Bellevue were made by psychiatrists who reversed their earlier recommendations of hospitalization, either prior to a hearing or during an adjournment thereof." One conclusion that can be drawn from this is that an involuntary patient requesting a hearing for discharge has more chance of being discharged than another involuntary patient who does not request a hearing. This could indicate that a most significant criterion in deciding whether further hospitalization was necessary was requesting a court hearing, and not need for treatment.

Another interesting finding is that there is no significant statistical difference in the group mean scores on the PEF between hospitalized and discharged schizophrenic patients of the nonrequest group with regard to "threat to self." There is a statistically significant difference in threat to self scores at the 0.001 level between hearing request discharged patients versus nonrequest discharged patients. The nonrequest discharged patients had higher scores on threat to self than the hearing request discharged patients. Kumasaka et al. conclude that "suicidal thought alone does not influence ultimate disposition for the nonrequest group. Once such a patient requests a hearing, however, suicidal thinking weighs heavily against his discharge." In other words, for psychiatrists "this indicates that the criteria of hospitalization change once a patient requests a hearing. . . ." Again we see that need for further treatment is not of primary importance once a patient requests a hearing. What does become important is the patient's threat to self. Yet in the nonrequest group, threat to self seems to be of minor importance in determining need for further hospitalization. As cited above, in the nonrequest group the scores on threat to self are high but not significantly different in the hospitalized and discharged patients.

Finally, of particular interest is the finding of Kumasaka et al. that schizophrenics "admitted to Bellevue following violent or suicidal episodes or threats have much less chance of being discharged than schizophrenics with other histories, even if they request a hearing." Again we see here that the need for treatment or clinical condition is not nearly as important a criterion for discharge even among the hearing request group when compared to dangerousness to self or others.

Since many patients are held for their own protection or for the protection of others against potential harm, the contention that involuntary mental hospitalization of these patients is "preventive detention" may not be far from the truth (12). The question could be posed: "What if this is the case in most involuntary mental hospitals?" The legal implications of this could be very profound. As concluded in *Wyatt v. Stickney*, the only constitutional justification for involuntary hospitalization is treatment. Yet what little scientific evidence is available indicates that treatment is only of secondary importance when compared to protection and dangerousness as working criteria of involuntary hospitalization (13). Thus, if patients are held primarily for purposes of preventive detention, then this certainly is not justified on constitutional grounds based upon court decisions in *Wyatt v. Stickney* and other right to treatment cases.

CONCLUSION

It has been noted here that the variable of voluntariness of hospitalization has been practically omitted from the research literature of psychiatry. An attempt has been made to show that voluntariness of hospitalization is an important variable in researching treatment and outcome in psychiatric patients. The legal implications have also been discussed concerning the relationship of the omission of this important variable and court decisions in right to treatment cases. What is at issue here is that the scientific problem concerning the omission of study of an important variable is intimately enmeshed with the legal problem of whether involuntary patients are receiving adequate treatment. The courts say to psychiatrists, "Show the court that you are administering adequate treatment as defined in *Wyatt v. Stickney*." Psychiatrists now can say, "We are administering adequate treatment because we provide adequate amounts of floor space, patient furnishings and high patient-staff ratios as the court requires." Yet this fact persists: what little scientific evidence is available indicates that the purpose of involuntary hospitalization is not primarily for treatment. The crucial question which remains for the courts to answer is whether floor space, patient furnishings and patient-staff ratios should be the standard which determines whether adequate treatment is being provided. This question should be answered with knowledge of the importance of omission of study of the variable of voluntariness of hospitalization, and also with knowledge of the evidence which indicates that involuntary hospitalization is not utilized primarily for treatment purposes.

Acknowledgments. I would like to thank Drs. Robert Daly and Frank Reed for their astute and critical comments in helping me to organize my ideas in a coherent form.

REFERENCES

1. Szasz, T. S. *Law, Liberty, and Psychiatry.* New York: Macmillan, 1963.
2. Goldberg, S. C., Schooler, N. R., Davidson, E. M., and Kayce, M. M. Sex and Race Differences in Response to Drug Treatment of Schizophrenics. *Psychopharmacologia* 9/1: 31–47, 1966.
3. Edelstein, E. L., Gnassi, C. P., and Mishelof, R. Weather and Admission Rates to a Mental Hospital: A Correlative Study of Temporal Sequences, Weather Conditions and Differential Admission Rates. *Compr. Psychiatr.* 7/6; 510–516, 1966.
4. *Wyatt v. Stickney*, 325 F. Supp. 781 (M.D. Ala. 1971).
5. *Rouse v. Cameron*, 373 F. 2d 451 (D.C. Cir. 1966).
6. May, P. R. A., and Tuma, A. H. Treatment of Schizophrenia. *Br. J. Psychiatry* 3: 503–510, 1965.
7. NIMH-PRB Collaborative Study Group. Short-Term Improvement in Schizophrenia: The Contribution of Background Factors. *Am. J. Psychiatry* 124: 900–909.
8. NIMH-PRB Collaborative Study Group. Phenothiazine Treatment in Acute Schizophrenia. *Arch. Gen. Psychiatry* 10: 246–261, 1964.
9. Grinspoon, L., Ewalt, J. R., and Shader, R. Psychotherapy and Pharmacotherapy in Chronic Schizophrenia. *Am. J. Psychiatry* 124/12: 1645–1652, 1968.
10. Weinstein, A. S., Dipasquale, D., and Windsor, F. Relationships Between Length of Stay In and Out of New York State Mental Hospitals. *Am. J. Psychiatry* 130: 904–909, 1973.
11. Robitscher, J. Courts, State Hospitals, and the Right to Treatment. *Am. J. Psychiatry* 129/3: 298–304, 1972.
12. Morris, G. H. Legal Problems Involved in Implementing the Right to Treatment. *Bull. Am. Acad. Psychiatry and Law* 1/1: 1–37, 1972.
13. Kumasaka, Y., Stokes, J., and Gupta, R. K. Criteria for Involuntary Hospitalization. *Arch. Gen. Psychiatry* 26: 399–404, 1972.

chapter 12

Mental Health, Criminal Justice and Social Control

PARK ELLIOTT DIETZ, M.D., Ph.D. (Candidate)

To a considerable extent, mental health systems on the one hand and criminal justice systems on the other have been viewed by both laymen and professionals as distinct and separate phenomena. This conception has not gone unchallenged, however, and the past 25 years have witnessed a burgeoning literature indicating that the distinction is by no means clear. The purpose of this essay is to consider briefly some of the dominant themes of this literature and to raise questions concerning the implications of the emergent perspective for rational policy-making.

Although there are many analogies and points of overlap between mental health and criminal justice systems, the most striking analogy in 19th century America was between insane asylums and prisons. Literary and artistic accounts of atrocities in the "dungeons and snakepits" stirred the public imagination, and the actual and potential abuse of inmates became a target for both scholarly debate and polemic. The charge that asylums were similar to prisons was viewed as a harsh indictment of the purgatorial nature of the asylum, but it did not provoke a reevaluation of the fundamental nature and purpose of these institutions. Most early critics were concerned with either prisons or asylums, but not with both. Their campaigns were directed toward the elimination of inhumane practices *within* institutions, the existence of such organizations being taken for granted. Public criticism, however, proved an ineffective tool in dealing with such autonomous, decentralized and varied institutions. While some internal reforms took place, the state hospital of the 19th century remained very much a counterpart of the prison.

Some measure of public concern has also long focused on a comparison of the processes by which individuals are incarcerated in the two types of institutions: i.e. imprisonment of criminal offenders versus commitment of the insane. Unlike convicted criminals, the mentaly ill were frequently being committed without regard for due process of law. Procedural safeguards, often cited as the cornerstone of the American criminal justice system, were nonexistent or poorly observed when it came to commitment of the mentally ill.

Among the early cases which became widely known was that of Mrs. E. P. W. Packard. In 1860 Mrs. Packard had been committed by her husband to the Illinois State Hospital, in conformity with a law which permitted husbands or guardians to have their wives or infants committed to a state hospital without the evidence of insanity which was required in other cases (1). Following her release, Mrs. Packard's reform efforts, including an exposé entitled *The Prisoners' Hidden Life; or Insane Asylums Unveiled* (2), attracted a great deal of attention and led to important statutory revisions in many states, including such formal guarantees of due process as a hearing and a jury trial for determining a person's insanity (3). Thus the courts became arbiters in the delivery of mental health care. The criminal justice and mental health systems were not simply parallel but had actually converged in the courtroom.

The issue of due process was by no means settled, however, for the majority of mental patients continued to enter state hospitals by routes other than the courtroom. Short term commitment for observation was still possible without recourse to the courts, and the predominant mode of admission became a sort of coerced voluntary commitment, with the patient's family, the police or the admitting psychiatrist encouraging potential patients to sign their own commitment papers. It was in this climate that Thomas Szasz published in 1961 *The Myth of Mental Illness* and in 1963 *Law, Liberty, and Psychiatry*. Szasz's criticism of the use of the medical model in psychiatry (4) and his concern for the constitutional rights of people with "problems in living," (5) led inevitably to the conclusion that institutional psychiatry is an agency of social control more akin to the criminal justice system than to the general practice of medicine.

By the time Szasz's work had been published, the view that the mental health system is a form of social control had been simmering for a decade in the sociological literature, and all that was needed to bring the pot to a boil was an articulate and prolific psychiatrist willing, despite his personal investment in medical training, to disinherit the medical profession of its priority claim on the mentally ill. It will be useful to backtrack a bit, in order to describe what was happening in sociology at that time.

The publication in 1951 of Lemert's *Social Pathology* (6), and the earlier work on which it was based, highlighted the development of the sociology of deviance as a field in its own right. No longer was the study of crime and delinquency to be set apart from the study of noncriminal deviance. For example, Lemert concerned himself with such varied forms of deviance as blindness, speech impairment, political radicalism, alcoholism and mental disorder, as well as crime. All were viewed as forms of social deviance amenable to sociological analysis. In particular, proponents of the Neo-Chicagoan School, as Lemert's disciples came to be known (7), shifted the focus of inquiry from the individual deviant to the social processes which serve to set him apart from individuals who have not been designated as deviant.

The very process by which people are designated as deviant became the focus of attention with the development of "labeling theory." The following quotation from Howard Becker's *Outsiders* is probably the most frequently cited passage in the sociology of deviance:

> . . . *Social groups create deviance by making the rules whose infraction constitutes deviance*, and by applying those rules to particular people and labeling them as outsiders. From this point of view, deviance is *not* a quality of the act the person commits, but rather a consequence of the application by others of rules and sanctions to an "offender." The deviant is one to whom that label has successfully been applied; deviant behavior is behavior that people so label. (8)

Thus, from the labeling perspective, "mental illness" is not a characteristic of an individual or his behavior but is rather an ascribed status. People are designated as "mental patients" by psychiatrists and other mental health professionals. And if the label is successfully applied, i.e. if the person comes to accept the designation "mental patient" as an integral part of his identity, he will embark upon a predictable sequence of activities described by Erving Goffman in his 1959 essay entitled "The Moral Career of the Mental Patient" (9).

Apart from such pioneering efforts as those of Lemert, Goffman and Kai Erikson (10), however, sociologists of the 1950s generally viewed mental illness as a more appropriate concern of medical sociology than of the sociology of deviance. It was only after the publication of Szasz's *Myth of Mental Illness* that the professional and lay literature began to swell with articles reflecting the emerging perspective that mental illness is not an illness at all but rather another variety of deviance to which the rubric "mental illness" is applied by psychiatrists and other mental health personnel functioning as agents of the community in the maintenance of social order.

This redefinition of the function of mental health services in terms of social control should not, however, be viewed as a necessarily pejorative formulation. The term "social control" is generally used in the social sciences to refer to the means by which social groups "maintain order" in the affairs of individuals. These means include the internalization of norms and values, and the legitimate, as well as the illegitimate, use of power. The family, peer groups, schools, religion, occupational organizations and so on are all agencies of social control. Thus, to say that mental health systems are agencies of social control is not to say that they are repressive, totalitarian or otherwise illegitimately coercive but merely to point out that, like other institutions, they can be.

In the political climate of the 1960s, however, when even the nuclear family was viewed by some as an instrument of repression, it was to be expected that mental health systems would be criticized as an especially undesirable form of social control. Some of us who were first developing our ideas about psychiatry during the era of Szasz, R. D. Laing (11) and the student revolution developed a stance which we called "radical psychiatry."

For me at least, radical psychiatry was founded on the premise that reality is socially constructed: that is, that the reality experienced by people in their everyday lives reflects in large part the definitions of the natural world which have been learned in the course of development within social groups (12). It follows that, in a truly pluralistic society, individuals might be free to experience their own realities, regardless of the extent to which they deviate from the shared perceptions of the dominant subculture. From this view, prisoners of psychiatry, like prisoners of correctional facilities, are individuals who have failed to conform to manmade rules dictating the permissible ways of thinking and acting (13).

I still believe this perspective to be logically and phenomenologically sound. The difficulty arises when one tries to apply it to the everyday crises of psychiatric practice. Faced with a violent patient or a suicide attempter, even the radical psychiatrist reverts to traditional tactics of control. Is this merely because he fears bodily harm or loss of his job? Or do these extreme situations serve to uncover the more general principle that social control is indeed necessary? I have come to believe that, if not necessary, it is at any rate inevitable; and we would do better, therefore, to devote our efforts not to the abolition of social control but to the improvement of the control agencies which already operate in our society.

Prison revolts in the past decade and increased rates of violent crime have left no doubt in the public mind that the present system of criminal justice is failing to control criminal behavior adequately. Yet serious attempts to make effective treatment available to prisoners have been relatively uncommon.[1] Milieu therapy, when carried out in appropriate settings, is denounced as too plush. Psychopharmacological and be-

---

[1] The terms "treatment" and "therapy" are used here with their conventional meanings for stylistic purposes.

havioral therapies, despite documented success in experimental trials (14), are viewed as unethical and unduly coercive. And individual psychotherapy is scarce to nonexistent. What usually remains, in those institutions claiming a "therapeutic" environment, is the kind of once or twice a week hybridized group therapy which was shown by Kassebaum et al. to be of no evident value in the treatment of prison inmates (15).

There would seem to be three major reasons why effective therapy has not been made available in prisons: (1) the widely held opinion that the purposes of imprisonment are punishment and the removal of the offender from society, rather than rehabilitation or behavior change, (2) the unsubstantiated belief that effective therapy would increase the cost of maintaining correctional facilities, and (3) a strong reluctance to employ recognizably manipulative techniques in changing the behavior of offenders who have been judged to be responsible for their illegal behavior.

We have already discussed the evolution of the view that the mental health and criminal justice systems provide analogous and converging forms of social control. But it is worth repeating that the debate regarding the proper use of the psychiatric-medical model contributed to the collapse of the conceptual barrier between the mental health and criminal justice systems. On the one hand, it was argued by Szasz, and more recently by Nicholas Kittrie in The Right To Be Different (3), that the disease concept was being overextended when applied to mental disorder, alcoholism, homosexuality and so on. On the other hand, Karl Menninger argued in The Crime of Punishment that even crime might profitably be viewed as a form of disease which should be treated by doctors (16). What was the public to think when it learned a few months ago that the disease of homosexuality had been voted out of existence?

It seems to me that there is a central paradox in the relationship between the criminal justice and mental health systems: those individuals who commit offenses prohibited by criminal law are subject to incarceration but not treatment, while individuals who behave in ways prohibited by the uncodified norms and values of society are subject to both incarceration and a variety of treatment modalities aimed at changing their behavior. What justification can there be for such a double standard? If it is argued that the mental patient is subjected to treatment for his own good, could not the same argument be made for criminal offenders? If it is argued that mental patients are usually treated under conditions of formal or implied consent, why do so few criminal offenders have voluntary access to treatment which, if successful, could lessen the duration of imprisonment? If cost is believed to be the major obstacle, why should a wealthy criminal be unable to purchase the best therapy available, as has long been the case with the mentally ill?

It is not my purpose to argue that effective techniques are at hand for altering the behavior of criminals (although I believe that they are or soon will be) but rather to point out that any involuntary treatments which are believed to be justified in the case of the mentally ill should be equally justified in the case of criminal offenders. Conversely, if criminals are permitted to refuse therapy, the mentally ill should be also. "The right to treatment" such as Birnbaum has advanced for the mental patient (17) should be accompanied by the right to refuse treatment.

What then is the basis of this paradox wherein the mentally ill are viewed as an appropriate target of the entire psychotherapeutic armamentarium, while criminal offenders are not? On a priori grounds, we would expect that it is the most serious offenses against society which elicit the most severe negative sanctions. Are not murder, rape, assault and so on the most serious sorts of offense? Perhaps not. Acts are strongly proscribed when they are in violation of norms based on strongly held values. Robin Williams has observed that the major value orientations in the United States include: active mastery verus passive acceptance; interest in the external world rather than in inner experience; and orderliness versus the ad hoc acceptance of transitory experience (18). It is norms reflecting such fundamental values as these that the mentally ill fail to observe. Such norms constitute an unwritten law which is far more pervasive than the formal, codified criminal law.

American culture defines humans as individually, ethically responsible for their behavior, and moreover it dictates that they be held responsible to act in certain ways. I would suggest that, in their blatant violation of these certain ways, the mentally ill threaten the validity of the premise of individual responsibility. And in order to preserve the sanctity of that premise, the societal response is to define the mentally ill as being categorically different from other humans. Thus, while "normal" criminals are considered to be responsible for their behavior, the mentally ill are not.

It is this pre-scientific view of responsibility, I believe, which accounts for the continued administrative separation of criminal justice from mental health systems, despite considerable similarity in their structure, function and probable future histories.

REFERENCES

1. Deutsch, A. *The Mentally Ill in America: A History of Their Care and Treatment from Colonial Times*, ed. 2. New York: Columbia University Press, 1949, p. 424.
2. Packard, E. P. W. *The Prisoners' Hidden Life; or Insane Asylums Unveiled.* Chicago: A. B. Case, 1868.
3. Kittrie, N. N. *The Right To Be Different: Deviance and Enforced Therapy.* Baltimore: The Johns Hopkins Press, 1971, p. 65.
4. Szasz, T. *The Myth of Mental Illness: Foundations of a Theory of Personal Conduct.* New York: Hoeber–Harper, 1961.

5. Szasz, T. *Law, Liberty, and Psychiatry: An Inquiry into the Social Uses of Mental Health Practices.* New York: Macmillan, 1963.
6. Lemert, E. M. *Social Pathology: A Systematic Approach to the Theory of Sociopathic Behavior.* New York: McGraw-Hill, 1951.
7. Matza, D. *Becoming Deviant.* Englewood Cliffs: Prentice-Hall, 1969.
8. Becker, H. S. *Outsiders: Studies in the Sociology of Deviance.* New York: The Free Press, 1963, p. 9.
9. Goffman, E. The Moral Career of the Mental Patient. *Psychiatry* 22: 123–142, 1959. Reprinted as pp. 125–169 in E. Goffman, *Asylums: Essays on the Social Situation of Mental Patients and Other Inmates.* Garden City: Doubleday, 1961.
10. Erikson, K. T. Patient Role and Social Uncertainty—A Dilemma of the Mentally Ill. *Psychiatry* 20: 263–274, 1957.
11. Laing, R. D. *The Politics of Experience.* New York: Pantheon Books, 1967.
12. Berger, P. L., and Luckmann, T. *The Social Construction of Reality: A Treatise in the Sociology of Knowledge.* Garden City: Doubleday, 1966.
13. Dietz, P. E. The Medical Model in Psychiatry: Rationale, Operations, Social Control, and the Deviant Career. Unpublished honors dissertation, Dept. of Psychology, Cornell University, 1970.
14. Lawson, R. B., Greene, R. T., Richardson, J. S., McClure, G., and Padina, R. J. Token Economy Program in a Maximum Security Correctional Hospital. *J. Nerv. Ment. Dis.* 152: 199–205, 1971.
15. Kassebaum, G., Ward, D. A., and Wilner, D. M. *Prison Treatment and Parole Survival: An Empirical Assessment.* New York: John Wiley & Sons, 1971.
16. Menninger, K. *The Crime of Punishment.* New York: Viking Press, 1969, p. 254.
17. Birnbaum, M. The Right to Treatment. *A.B.A.J.* 46: 499, 1960.
18. Williams, R. M., Jr. *American Society: A Sociological Interpretation*, ed. 2. New York: Knopf, 1960.

Index